# SCARECROW STUDIES IN YOUNG ADULT LITERATURE
## Series Editor: Patty Campbell

Scarecrow Studies in Young Adult Literature is intended to continue the body of critical writing established in Twayne's Young Adult Authors Series and to expand it beyond single-author studies to explorations of genres, multicultural writing, and controversial issues in YA reading. Many of the contributing authors of the series are among the leading scholars and critics of adolescent literature, and some are YA novelists themselves.

The series is shaped by its editor, Patty Campbell, who is a renowned authority in the field, with a thirty-year background as critic, lecturer, librarian, and teacher of young adult literature. Patty Campbell is the 2001 winner of the ALAN Award, given by the Assembly on Adolescent Literature of the National Council of Teachers of English for distinguished contribution to young adult literature. In 1989 she was the winner of the American Library Association's Grolier Award for distinguished service to young adults and reading.

1. *What's So Scary about R.L. Stine?* by Patrick Jones, 1998.
2. *Ann Rinaldi: Historian and Storyteller,* by Jeanne M. McGlinn, 2000.
3. *Norma Fox Mazer: A Writer's World,* by Arthea J.S. Reed, 2000.
4. *Exploding the Myths: The Truth about Teens and Reading,* by Marc Aronson, 2001.
5. *The Agony and the Eggplant: Daniel Pinkwater's Heroic Struggles in the Name of YA Literature,* by Walter Hogan, 2001.
6. *Caroline Cooney: Faith and Fiction,* by Pamela Sissi Carroll, 2001.
7. *Declarations of Independence: Empowered Girls in Young Adult Literature, 1990–2001,* by Joanne Brown and Nancy St. Clair, 2002.

# Declarations of Independence

## Empowered Girls in Young Adult Literature, 1990–2001

Joanne Brown
Nancy St. Clair

*Scarecrow Studies in Young Adult Literature, No. 7*

The Scarecrow Press, Inc.
Lanham, Maryland, and London
2002

SCARECROW PRESS, INC.

Published in the United States of America
by Scarecrow Press, Inc.
A Member of the Rowman & Littlefield Publishing Group
4720 Boston Way, Lanham, Maryland 20706
www.scarecrowpress.com

4 Pleydell Gardens, Folkestone
Kent CT20 2DN, England

Copyright © 2002 by Joanne Brown and Nancy St. Clair

British Library Cataloguing in Publication Information Available

**Library of Congress Cataloging-in-Publication Data**

Brown, Joanne, 1933–
   Declarations of independence : empowered girls in young adult literature, 1990–2001 /
Joanne Brown, Nancy St. Clair.
      p. cm. — (Scarecrow studies in young adult literature ; no. 7)
   Includes bibliographical references and index.
   ISBN 0-8108-4290-4 (alk. paper)
     1. Young adult fiction, American—History and criticism. 2. Girls in literature. 3. Power
(Social sciences) in literature. 4. Teenage girls in literature. 5. Girls—Books and reading.
   6. Liberty in literature. I. St. Clair, Nancy. II. Title. III. Scarecrow studies in young adult
literature ; 7.

PS374.G55 B76 2002
813'.5409352054—dc21

                                                                          2002017585

Printed in the United States of America

$\bigotimes^{\text{TM}}$ The paper used in this publication meets the minimum requirements of
American National Standard for Information Sciences—Permanence of Paper
for Printed Library Materials, ANSI/NISO Z39.48-1992.
Manufactured in the United States of America.

Lyric excerpt of "I Enjoy Being a Girl" on page 1 of *Flower Drum Song,* by Richard Rodgers
and Oscar Hammerstein II, reprinted by permission of Williamson Music. International
copyright secured.

"One, Taken to Heart" on page 25 of *Chicks Up Front* by Sara Holbrook, reprinted by permission of the Cleveland State University Poetry Center. Copyright 1998.

To our children: Linda, Jay, and Bennett; Cate and Anne.

"My mother tells me that I was a willful little girl, but I don't remember that. What I remember is later, when I wasn't willful anymore: the inner calm of knowing I was *satisfying expectations,* I was pleasing. The self isn't important in such a feeling. It was only as I began to startle and disappoint others that I was aware of myself at all—that I came to understand, slowly, that I wasn't who I had pretended to be."

*While I Was Gone*
Sue Miller

# Contents

*Preface*                                                           xi

1 That Was Then                                                      1
2 This Is Now                                                       25
3 Empowered Girls in Historical Fiction                            53
4 Empowered Girls in the Contemporary World                        81
5 Empowered Girls in Literature of the Fantastic                  127
6 Empowered Girls in Memoir                                        151
7 Conclusion                                                       177

*Selected Bibliography*                                            183
*Index*                                                            187
*About the Authors*                                                194

# Preface

We grew up separated by nearly two decades, almost a generation apart, our paths crossing only years later when we met through mutual friends. As we became better acquainted, we discovered that, despite the age gap, as children we had loved many of the same books. Like most girls, we had devoured the adventures of Nancy Drew, and we had also treasured stories about Little Maida, the sweet little girl with the little shop, the little house, and the little school. Most of all, we loved Jo March, especially the rough, tender Jo of Part I, and we had resented Professor Bhaer for stunting what we were sure would otherwise have been a promising writing career. We tried to remember other rebellious girls we had met in stories, but none came to mind. They had all been so good, so pristine. Of course they had problems (fiction, after all, requires characters with problems), but none, except Jo, had fought ferociously with siblings and none at all with parents. Nor did they seem to harbor adolescent sexual passions. Did any of these sweet girls park with boys in cars or lie with them on sandy beach blankets beneath a dark sky? Between chapters, out of range of readers' knowledge, did they skip school or cheat on final exams? Did they have bodily functions? We had no memory of any female character from our youthful reading needing the bathroom or extra-strength Midol.

Only in our adult years, first as parents of daughters and then as professors engaged academically with young adult literature, did we encounter in stories for young readers the fierce or spunky or rebellious girls—the empowered girls—who recalled our own adolescent experiences. So it was with special pleasure that we embarked on this study and discovered that they existed in even greater abundance than we had anticipated.

The very profusion of these strong, young literary heroines who began appearing with increasing frequency in the last twenty years or so, however, presented its own difficulties. Which of their stories to include? Which, then, to exclude? Which to analyze in depth and which to note only briefly in end-of-the-chapter lists of suggested readings? We had to make some arbitrary choices.

First, we have mostly limited our analyses to novels and memoirs written by Americans. Although authors of young adult literature ring the globe, the genre was first recognized and promoted in the United States, a development not suprising given our nearly obsessive attention to adolescence, with all its implications for entertainment and marketing. Nowhere is there a longer interim between childhood and adulthood than in this country; the school systems of other western nations force students to make adult career choices sooner by applying strict standards that determine who continues schooling beyond high school and the nature of that schooling, whether vocational, technical, or liberal arts. Adolescence, or course, is a cultural construct, not a biological fact like puberty, and it is decidedly more pronounced in industrial countries than developing ones, where economic pressures and ritual practices move children directly from childhood to adulthood. Given these circumstances, it seems inevitable that the United States publishes more young adult fiction than other countries.

Second, we concentrated on those novels and memoirs published in the last decade of the twentieth century and the opening year of the twenty-first, the time period when young adult literature, reflecting the postmodern directions firmly established in fiction for adults, began to adapt those trends for its own purposes. Novels written in free verse and tales of magic realism appeared. Protagonists now commonly included gay and lesbian characters as well as characters from cultures far removed from the American mainstream.

Our choices also reflect a range of how the girls in these stories become empowered and the sources of their empowerment. Some begin as spunky girls, dauntless in the face of adversity. Others begin with much less confidence, becoming empowered only in the closing chapter or pages. We have tried to provide examples of varied roads to female empowerment. Although the texts under discussion in the following pages share some common themes, we believe that each defines a particular aspect of "empowered girls."

We are indebted to those many scholars whose articles and books on representations of girls and women in literature have provided invaluable references. We're grateful for the work of our student research assistants: Patty Siffersen and Tracy Pronschinske of Drake University, and Megan Elscott of Simpson College. We would also like to thank Linda Sinclair at Simpson College for her editing suggestions, and Bev Sloan, who generously shared her resources and experiences as counselor/ teacher working with girls. Our thanks, too, to our series editor, Patty Campbell. She has been unfailingly supportive (even as she slashed pages from our manuscript!), and this project has been enlivened by our friendship with her and the laughter we have shared.

# That Was Then

When I have a brand new hairdo
With my eyelashes all in curl,
I float as the clouds on air do,
I enjoy being a girl.

I'm strictly a female female
And my future, I hope, will be
In the home of a brave and free male
Who'll enjoy being a guy
Having a girl like me.

"I Enjoy Being a Girl," from *Flower Drum Song,* 1958

*W*hen the female lead in a popular Broadway musical belted out these lyrics nearly half a century ago, audiences applauded enthusiastically, and the song became a hit.[1] Today, when eyelash curlers have all but disappeared from the cosmetic arsenal and many "female females" aspire to traditionally masculine careers such as medicine and engineering, "being a girl" is no longer defined strictly in terms of a young woman's appearance or the guy who will "have" her. Nonetheless, the persona of the song is a familiar one. She is a standard ingredient in American culture, fixated on her future with some brave male, and we have met her everywhere—in song, on stage and screen, and between the covers of books.

Until recently, she was the *sine qua non* in adolescent fiction for girls. And if she sometimes has appeared less than ebullient about being a girl, more dismayed than delighted about the hair and the guy, she has had good reason. Many of these stories have constructed her female role as

1

mandating submission, conformity, and passivity in a world that posited marriage (and, by implication, motherhood) as her fixed destination. This representation is hardly a surprise. Literature reflects the experiential world of its readers, and female protagonists mirror the expectations of women during the time in which their stories were written.

However, fiction creates as well as reflects codes of behavior. Storytellers have long been agents of socialization, playing a significant role in transmitting cultural values. Predictably, then, fiction has served to teach girls their "place," portraying them as focused on relationships with family or friends, involved with romantic or school affairs rather than pursuing adventures or ambitions. Why, asks educator and children's author Mem Fox, have girls been portrayed "as acted upon rather than active? As nurturers rather than adventurers? As sweetness and light rather than thunder and lightning?"[2] Her questions echo a chorus of critics protesting the gender bias in literature that ranges from Mother Goose to bodice rippers. Although not all of their observations apply directly to adolescent fiction, much of it is relevant, for the genealogy of the conventional heroine of young adult literature can be traced to earlier young heroines whose domestic and romantic (mis)adventures have been told over centuries.[3]

## GIRLS IN FOLK AND FAIRY TALES

One of her oldest ancestors is the maiden of the fairy and folk tales collected and published by the Brothers Grimm and their followers. The best known and therefore most influential fairy tales have at their center a passive, suffering female dependent on a male to rescue her and, by extension, validate her existence. The contrast between the heroine and hero of these stories has been frequently noted.[4] Ellen Cronan Rose puts the case succinctly:

> In fairy tales, boys are clever, resourceful, and brave. They leave home to slay giants, outwit ogres, solve riddles, find fortunes. Girls, on the other hand, stay home and sweep the hearth, are patient, enduring, self-sacrificing. They are picked on by wicked stepmothers, enchanted by evil fairies. If they go out, they get lost in the woods. They are rescued from their plights by kind woodsmen, good fairies, and handsome princes. They marry and live happily ever after.[5]

There does exist in folk/fairy tales a long tradition of clever, even defiant heroines such as Clever Gretel, who have received increasing attention from feminist scholars and writers.[6] Although the passive and active heroines of folk and fairy tales appear as polar opposites, their strategies share a common goal: to survive in a patriarchal culture by subverting, intentionally or otherwise, the powers that oppress them.

## GIRLS IN ENGLISH SENTIMENTAL NOVELS

The behavioral extremes of these young folk heroines anticipate similar complexities in the novels of sentimental romance and social satire that developed in eighteenth-century England, the products of improved technology, increased literacy, and a growing middle-class. Like the earlier folk and fairy tales, they feature heroines whose behavior ranges from defiant to docile. These novels were enormously popular; although they no longer enjoy their wide audience and are read today mostly by students and scholars, they have exerted a significant influence on the evolution of the female protagonist in young adult literature for two major reasons: first, they were primarily directed toward a young female audience with leisure for reading, and, second, they were written not only to entertain but, more importantly, to educate. Thus, they provide a fascinating map or record of cultural conflicts, embodying ideological tensions about what their readers were supposed to learn about "being a girl."

The earliest of the sentimental novels, Samuel Richardson's *Pamela* and *Clarissa*, introduced heroines who endured a multitude of troubles— isolation in British manors, mistreatment by those who held authority over them, and repeated attempts at seduction by men whose persistence prompts the contemporary reader to want to shout, "Just what part of 'no' don't you understand?" But in the world of Pamela and Clarissa, male gender signifies sexual privilege, and both heroines must fight tenaciously to preserve their chastity, and neither submits willingly. When poor Clarissa is drugged and raped, she later dies of grief and shame as a result. Pamela is more successful in preserving her virtue (the first part of *Pamela* is titled "Aggressive Chastity"), eventually reforming her would-be seducer and then setting out to marry him.

**Evelina.** In contrast to the determined (if ill-fated) resistance of Richardson's Clarissa is the protagonist of Fanny Burney's *Evelina*, a seventeen-year-old girl who is clearly intended to represent the feminine ideal of passive obedience and moral purity. A coming-of-age novel published in 1778 when Burney was only twenty-six and never out of print since, *Evelina* reveals Burney's own ambivalence about the values she seems to endorse. The text illustrates conflicting cultural values about "being a girl," the tension between the necessity for young women to be both assertive and submissive, a mixture of ideologies that continue to mark many coming-of-age novels about girls.

Abel, Hirsch, and Langland, examining the history of female protagonists in their *The Voyage In: Fictions of Female Development,* describe the tensions between these conflicting ideologies in terms of plot:

> The tensions that shape female development may lead to a disjunction between a surface plot, which affirms social conventions, and a submerged plot, which encodes rebellion; between a plot governed by age-old female story patterns such as myths and fairy tales, and a plot that reconceives these limiting possibilities; between a plot that charts development and a plot that unravels it.[7]

Their theory describes the movement of Burney's novel perfectly. Evelina, who is just entering the world, must learn about its ways without sacrificing her innocence and losing her value in the eyes of others. She at first appears so naïve that she seems almost to adhere to the facetious advice offered by the narrator of Jane Austen's *Northanger Abbey*: "A woman . . . if she should have the misfortune of knowing anything, should conceal it as well as she can."[8] However, Evelina's very innocence, her ignorance about the ways of men, makes her vulnerable to them rather than shielding her from danger. Her first foray into the social world, for example, becomes disastrous when she naively assumes that she has the right to choose her dance partner. Her rejection of one partner in favor of another earns her the scorn and contempt of the men at the ball and the pity of the women.

An essential component of Evelina's coming of age is her learning to speak out. She writes to her guardian about her frequent inability to speak at all when embarrassed, so she must become more assertive if she is to defend herself from the predatory rakes who surround her. The reader silently cheers the first time she silences an aggressive male with her wit or overcomes her social embarrassment to speak to the man she loves. Yet the ending of the novel demonstrates the mixed messages the narrative sends. The assertions of selfhood that have occurred with increasing frequency in the second half of the novel and that seem to indicate Evelina's growth cease abruptly when the man she loves proposes. Once Evelina learns that her love for the dashing Lord Orville is returned, she reverts to the conventionally passive female who puts responsibility for her happiness into the hands of others, even allowing the father who has denied her legitimacy to set her wedding date.

Burney's ending exemplifies the conflicting narratives that inform the novel. As a young girl who becomes increasingly assertive, increasingly aware of the limited options her culture allows women, Evelina charms the reader. Yet once charmed, the contemporary reader is inevitably disappointed, or—at the very least—puzzled by her passivity when her love for Lord Orville is returned. The novel ends like a fairy tale, with the expectation that Evelina and Lord Orville will live happily ever after. If Evelina has not become betrothed to an actual prince, she at least marries a prince of a man. Burney has reinforced one of the dominant cultural narratives of the eighteenth century, that marriage is "all and all to a woman."[9] Evelina has little to say after Orville proposes because, in truth, there is nothing more to say. She has acquired what a girl was expected to acquire, marriage to a good man; her story is literally over. That Burney could not imagine a happy ending for Evelina without marriage can be read to indicate the limitations of the writer's imagination, but it can also signify a coolheaded assessment of the limited options available for girls in a culture that legally labeled unmarried females as "redundant."

In succeeding works Burney created heroines of wit, intelligence, and good will—whose stories also end in marriage. Burney is hardly alone during this period in resolving all her plots with matrimony. Though Jane Austen populated her novels with assertive, intelligent, ironic and witty girls, she nevertheless marries them off in the end. Even when she mocks her young heroine in *Northanger Abbey* who too readily tries to shape her life around Gothic romance, she still provides her with a man and a marriage in the closing pages. The same is true of Charlotte Bronte and a host of other writers whose novels were read by girls. Invariably the spunky, sassy, independent heroine turns into the good wife who subordinates her wishes, indeed her very self, to the desires and needs of others. Susan Gubar and Sandra Gilbert in their ground-breaking *Madwoman in the Attic,* make clear that "Reader, I married him" provides a typical ending for novels of the eighteenth and nineteenth centuries, endings that persist to the present in literature about young women.[10]

## GOOD, GOOD GIRLS IN AMERICAN FICTION

American writers were quick to adopt the sentimental novel to their own culture, and their female protagonists fared no better than their British sisters. Leslie Fiedler's classification of young heroines in American fiction emphasizes this point. He points to the Fair Maiden who is "first (almost) raped, then rescued to be legally possessed, but *cannot save herself*,"[11] the Persecuted Maiden who becomes pregnant by her seducer, is cast out by her family and commits suicide (239), and the Good Good Girl, the "blond and asexual goddess of the nursery or orphanage" (266). Self-sacrificing and submissive, these young women fainted and wept with predictable regularity. However, like their young predecessors on the other side of the Atlantic, most of them eventually married and lived happily ever after, a reward for their innocence and reluctance to assert themselves.[12] The message they sent was clear: whatever the vicissitude, the socially appropriate response for females was helplessness, unswerving virtue, and superhuman forbearance.

The "good, good girls" became a popular staple in American fiction, heroines all; by contrast, the good good boys, such as Tom Sawyer's cousin Sid, appear as priggish fools rather than heroes. It was the fun-loving Good Bad Boys (as Fiedler has dubbed them) who played the real heroes, even though (or because) they were pranksters and rogues. While Elsie Dinsmore succeeded in defying her father's orders to play the piano on the Sabbath by crying and then fainting—a prime example of passive female resistance—Tom and Huck enjoyed hiding out at their island retreat, returning only when they could relish their own funeral. Significantly, there were no good bad girls, no female characters in American fiction to counter the mischievous Good Bad Boys like Tom Sawyer. Mary Lystad has accurately observed that while males enjoyed "amazing adventures" in stories, the girls "were usually passive and stayed at home, moving only from the subordinate role of child to parent to that of wife to husband."[13] In other words, the males had all the fun. The imagination of America, says Fiedler with some accuracy, has found "only the girl-child . . . a sufficiently spotless savior" and "boggles at the notion of a pure boy."[14]

Indicative of the gulf between the good bad boys and the good good girls of fiction were the agreeable girls of early twentieth-century series fiction: Rebecca of Sunnybrook Farm, Anne of Green Gables, and Pollyanna of the glad game. Even at their most spirited (even resistant) moments, they remained paragons of spotless virtue, and all of them succeeded in transforming the sterile adults entrusted with their care into warm and affectionate women. The unstinting love of a young girl conquered all. Boys had no such redemptive power.

When Rebecca, Anne, and Pollyanna matured in subsequent volumes, they grew up with problematic ease, sailing directly from childhood to adulthood. Rebecca, for instance, traded the promise of a remarkable career for marriage to an older man. Nor were they the only girls in literature to circumvent the stormy seas of adolescence. Most girls' fiction omitted this transitional and troublesome period until well into the twentieth century, in part because the concept of adolescence itself did not take root until the late nineteenth century as the American population shifted from the country to the city. This change in demographics required a more extended education and prolonged the financial dependence of children upon parents. The result was the interval of adolescence, but it evolved mainly for the sons of upper- and middle-class families. The idea of female adolescence lagged behind that of males, as few girls received a formal education other than domestic apprenticeship.[15]

Also, as Patricia J. Campbell has pointed out in *Sex Education for Young Adults 1892–1979,* adults in the late nineteenth century, obsessed with protecting the sexual purity of young people, perceived the period between childhood and adulthood as highly perilous to the young person's virtue, offering as it did no socially sanctioned outlets for sexual impulses. Their concern focused mainly on young men, as girls were believed to have very little sexual drive. Masturbation was a particular concern. Thus, they began to provide special instruction and guidance in sexual matters, a step that established young men in particular as an age group with its own identity and risks.[16] Young women, however, continued to be regarded as children until well into the twentieth century, defined as such until they earned the status of adulthood by entering either the world of work or matrimony. Even those heroines of sentimental and domestic novels who were in their teens confronted mostly adult problems—finding a husband, leaving home, marrying.

## EARLY JUVENILE FICTION

Not until the 1930s when publishing houses developed juvenile divisions to handle books that fell between children's and adult books did fiction begin to portray females encountering actual adolescent experiences. Although these girls lived at home and readily conformed to societal expectations, they did gain some measure of independence, often because one or both parents were either dead or preoccupied with matters outside the home. But few of these novels developed their young female characters in much depth or complexity. The emphasis was on external circumstances—a mystery or someone else's problem to be solved—rather than on the protagonist's internal workings. Problems specific to female adolescent development were ignored. Despite the many dangerous people who threaten her safety, Nancy Drew enjoys a security that many young adults today might envy: her skin seems impervious to acne, her boyfriend Ned is as dependable as her little red coupe. No breaking out, breaking up, or breaking down for Nancy.

By the decades of the 1940s and 1950s, however, many heroines in YA literature were adolescent psychologically as well as chronologically. Their stories allowed for more character development, and the narrative viewpoint was often that of the protagonist. Still, the novels, whose settings usually alternated between home and school, ignored the darker aspects of this gawky, self-critical time and the sometimes cruel circumstances that intrude on many adolescent lives: conflict between parents, cruelty of peers, teenage pregnancies. Kenneth L. Donelson perceives a "certain saccharine didacticism" in these "girls' books," and he points to all the young heroines who learned by the final pages that Mother knew best.[17] What Mother knew, of course, usually had little to do with her daughter's developing a strong, autonomous self.

Love affairs in the novels of the 1940s and '50s were without exception completely chaste, with no hint of passion or sexuality. Many plots hinged on the girls' responses to their popularity (or lack of it), which depended on their winning and keeping a boyfriend whose interests and personality determined the path of the romance. Happy endings were standard: the girl got the guy. Although some of these novels created protagonists with interests independent of the home and boyfriend—a successful artistic endeavor or a nurturing relationship with an animal, for example—the ultimate resolution brought the young woman new confidence mainly via the guy who chose to "have" her.

Not until recently have many YA novels featured girls determined to assert themselves. Jeanette Mines concluded as late as 1989 that books for young adults failed female readers in several ways. Not only were many of the recommended books "primarily masculine," such as S.E. Hinton's novels, but even in those novels that featured a female protagonist, the male characters often took the initiative while the girl stood by watching, such as in Lois Duncan's *Killing Mr. Griffith*. Or the female protagonist was cast in the role of victim, as in Richard Peck's *Are You in the House Alone?*[18] Although one can note many exceptions to Mines' conclusions—Rosa Guy's *Edith Jackson*, for example, Judy Blume's *Forever*, and Richard Peck's series about Blossom Culp—they remain exceptions, not the norm.

Critics who have examined children's books also note in them a similar gender bias. In 1971 Mary Kay Ritchie summarized the "general atmosphere" of children's books as "*boys do; girls are*," charging that the "Little Miss Muffet syndrome, which depicts females as helpless, easily frightened, and dreadfully dull, occurs over and over again in the literature [for children]."[19] More than twenty years later, Carole Kortenhaus and Jack Demarest analyzed 150 children's books published in the five decades between the 1940s and the 1980s, both Caldecott winners and non-award-winning books. They concluded that "boys were characterized far more often as instrumental and independent, while girls were made to look passive and dependent."[20]

Clearly, then, the conventional YA heroine has had plenty of company in her role as "strictly a female female," but her impact on readers is unique to her particular audience. As Robert Probst has noted, adolescents are particularly vulnerable to the stories they hear and read. The preoccupation with self that is characteristic of adolescents makes them particularly receptive to fiction. They tend to identify strongly with a story's characters, share their dilemmas, and participate in the choices that the characters make, keenly aware of the values that their actions imply.[21] And the passive girls who have dominated in young adult fiction send a distinct message.

Examining two novels written nearly a century apart, both popular and critically acclaimed in their own time—Louisa May Alcott's *Little Women* (1868) and Maureen Daly's *Seventeenth Summer* (1942)—provides a clear picture of what fiction for young adults has often told its readers about being a girl: she should practice restraint, respect and obey her elders, develop appropriate social skills, put others' needs before her own. If she behaves properly and makes herself sufficiently attractive, she will be rewarded by the attentions of a good man who chooses to "have" her. Contemporary critics, understandably finding such a message offensive, have often used these novels as examples of the unfortunate "lessons" that literature has taught young women about their "place." However, interestingly enough, each novel includes a complicating (sub)text about "being a girl" that undermines the more conventional lesson: young women can derive enormous satisfaction in achieving some measure of independence, and those who exchange their autonomy for the attentions of a prince, attractive or otherwise, may find that he is only a jailer in disguise.

Such layering in fiction about young women is no exception, as Burney's *Evelina* has demonstrated, and Peter Hollingdale, articulating a theory that parallels the ideas expressed in *The Voyage In,* points out that the ideology in children's books is present on more than one level. There is, first, the conscious, surface ideology that reflects the "explicit social, political or moral beliefs" that the writer wants to recommend to children through the story.[22] But this overtly didactic purpose is often at odds with unexamined assumptions that the writer has conveyed unintentionally, beliefs and attitudes that express his or her "essential self" and constitute what Hollingdale calls a text's "passive ideology" (31). Given these two levels of ideology, the "official" ideas of a text are often contradicted by ideas which the writer has unintentionally inserted into the story.

As even the most casual perusal of earlier novels for young readers demonstrates, most writers felt obligated to advance or reinforce conventional notions of gendered behavior, and these socially sanctioned scripts are often embedded in the text's surface ideology. However, as society has increasingly accommodated more flexible roles for its young men and women, authors seem to feel freer to explore what they see as the choices and challenges that contemporary life offers its youth and less compelled to use their work as moralizing instruments to teach their

readers how to behave as proper ladies and gentlemen. The female protagonists of many recent young adult novels provide a sharp contrast to
their literary ancestors.

Exploring the contradictions between the conflicting ideologies or
plots in *Little Women, Going on Sixteen,* and *Seventeenth Summer* is helpful
as a preface to discussing empowered girls in contemporary YA fiction.
In each novel, the attempts of the protagonist to conform to social conventions illustrate the limitations of young women in a patriarchal American culture and provide a striking contrast to the stories of many recent
female protagonists. The opposing reading, which foregrounds the strategies by which each girl seeks to become empowered, provides a context
for analyzing how young women in recent fiction develop autonomy
and demonstrates that those who imagine a future limited to the guy
who will "have" them risk emotional maturity and a firm sense of self.

## Little Women

Louisa May Alcott's *Little Women* was warmly received when it appeared
in 1868, and it has remained popular to the present. The plot, which follows the four March sisters from their teen years into adulthood, traces
their struggles to overcome personal failures and mature into unselfish,
mannerly little women. Initially, readers seemed to note only the surface
ideology that teaches girls to be docile and submissive. An early reviewer
described the novel as "one of the most successful ventures to delineate
juvenile womanhood ever attempted."[23] Another pointed to the March
family as a welcome role model for readers: "Thousands of young people will read [Alcott's] story . . . and their standard of home and happiness must in many cases be raised."[24] These reviewers, like most readers,
surely approved of Mr. March's expectations for his daughters as expressed in a letter to his wife from the front lines of the Civil War: "I
know that they will remember all I said to them, that they will be loving children to you, will do their duty faithfully, fight their bosom enemies bravely, and conquer themselves so beautifully that when I come
back to them I may be fonder and prouder than ever of my little
women."[25] Despite the severity of their father's charge—not only to be
loving, dutiful, faithful, and brave, but to practice rigorous self-repression
as well—the girls themselves never question his standards or their responsibility to meet them. Father did indeed know best, even from afar.

But on another level, the novel offers a critique of the conventional values that Marmee, Father, and the omniscient narrator put forward. The struggle to become a "little woman" is centralized in Jo, the most conflicted—and interesting—of the sisters, and her story constitutes the strongest criticism of the repressive, domestic sphere of women's lives. Jo is torn between rejecting the many conventions that constrain female lives and trying to adhere to them. She longs to be a boy, to exchange her knitting needles for the weapons of war, to become a successful writer enjoying an independent life. Yet she heeds Marmee's guidance that encourages decorum and domesticity, and, following her mother's pious example, she turns to her earthly and heavenly fathers to sustain her in her trials.

The surface ideology assumes that the implied reader will perceive Jo's headstrong, boyish spirit as a defect to be overcome. The authorial voice of the novel notes her "quick temper, sharp tongue, and restless spirit" that were "always getting her into scrapes," making her life "a series of ups and downs" (36). This is hardly neutral language, and Jo herself acknowledges the validity of the narrator's criticism: "I get so savage, I could hurt anyone and enjoy it. I'm afraid I shall do something dreadful some day, and spoil my life, and make everybody hate me" (75). Her fears seem founded in experience, for Jo's displays of temper and thoughtless comments are met with painful repercussions. Her sister Amy nearly drowns, and Aunt March denies Jo a trip to Europe; she suffers for every angry outburst and careless comment. Marmee's patient but firm counsel reinforces Jo's need to mend her ways: "[R]emember this day [when Amy has fallen through the ice], and resolve with all your soul that you will never know another like it. Jo, dear, we all have our temptations . . . and it often takes us all our lives to conquer them" (75). That is, if Jo is to live happily ever after, she must learn to curb her tongue, dress like a lady, and behave like a saint. As for Jo's dream of becoming a writer, Marmee advocates marriage over independence: "To be loved and chosen by a good man is the best and sweetest thing which can happen to a woman" (92). Over the years since the novel was published, many readers have cheered for Jo's reformation and her eventual marriage, even though it means exchanging her dream of becoming a writer for the reality of wifely responsibilities. *Little Women* is, after all, a domestic novel whose happy ending mandates that Jo and her sisters be paired off as neatly as in any Shakespearean comedy.

But it is Jo at her most incorrigible who holds the reader's attention and sympathy. As Sean O'Faolain has noted, "Without Jo March, *Little Women* would really be nothing at all. . . . Before *Little Women* there had been boys like Jo March; in her we meet for the first time a new kind of heroine, who, allowing for the changes of fashion and of morals since then, grins across the ages at many an American girl of today."[26] Viewing the novel through the lens of its passive ideology, readers can empathize with Jo's complaint that "it's bad enough to be a girl" (5) and understand her desire to change gender so that she might enjoy the privileges granted to young men—to run freely, to say what's on her mind, to gain status by earning money. Why must she learn to curb her temper when Mr. Lawrence and his grandson lose theirs with little consequence? It is small wonder that Jo longs to exchange places with the men who have gone off to fight the Civil War or that she enjoys being "man of the house" while her father is away. In the social context of *Little Women,* Jo's resistance to romance and her fear that Meg's marriage will "make a hole in the family" (188) are not unreasonable: as men become prominent in the sisters' lives, Jo's power in the family diminishes.

Jo's ambition to be a writer, signifying the potential for earning money, promises the status that her gender has denied her, and she spends many hours in her attic retreat "scribbling" sensational stories. Lissa Paul describes Jo's time thus spent as "the perfect nineteenth-century embodiment of physical, economic and linguistic entrapment. She is shut up in her attic, secretly writing romance fiction (to support the family) while her authoritarian father holds court in the main-floor study."[27] Paul's interpretation is based on the central premise of Gubar and Gilbert's *The Madwoman in the Attic,* that a disproportionate number of women in literature are physically trapped in the attic of their father or husband's home, where they succumb to madness. But Jo's attic provides her, if not a room of her own, then at least a space, and, arguably, one preferable to her father's study. In her attic, Jo derives enormous satisfaction from the act of writing itself, expressing a self that might otherwise be silenced. Her imagination takes flight while her father, on a lower level both physically and creatively, delivers only pretentious pronouncements. Jo begins to realize her ambition when her first story is published, and she is gratified by the acclaim it earns from her family, "for to be independent and earn the praise of those she loved were the dearest wishes of her heart" (145).

In New York, she succeeds in publishing more stories and might have gone on to fulfill her dream of supporting herself and her family through her writing had she not met and fallen under the influence of Professor Bhaer. When he disparages the kind of sensational fiction she writes as "trash," she feels ashamed of her work. Subsequently, she burns her remaining manuscripts, although not without a few pangs: "I almost wish I hadn't any conscience. . . . If I didn't care about doing right . . . I should get on capitally. I can't help wishing sometimes, that Father and Mother hadn't been so particular about such things" (327). Lest the reader share Jo's regrets, the narrator makes clear that Professor Bhaer, like Father, knows best: "Ah, Jo, instead of wishing that, thank God that 'Father and Mother *were* particular,' and pity from your heart those who have no such guardians to hedge them round with principles" (327).

This incident shuts down Jo's creative impulses. For a prolonged and painful interval, she abandons her "scribbling." Much later, she takes her mother's suggestion to "write something for us and never mind the rest of the world" (398), composing what she calls a "simple little story" (399). When it is published and becomes popular, Jo seems pleased, but she takes no credit for whatever is "good" in it. "It isn't mine," she says (399), a statement that distances her from her work and reveals that her writer's true passion lies in the melodramatic fiction that she has abandoned. By the time she takes her "place" as Professor Bhaer's wife, she has laid her writing aside to open a school with her husband for troubled boys. The teaching responsibilities are his; hers are to "feed and nurse and pet and scold them" (444). She says that she "may write a good book yet" (447), but that conjecture seems more wishful thinking than likely possibility, given that she must daily contend with "hard work, much anxiety, and a perpetual racket" (444). She seems to have grown not into a little woman, but a belittled one.

Jo's story provides a sharp contrast to the adventures of Dick Hunter, the protagonist of *Ragged Dick,* Horatio Alger's first novel for boys published in the same year as *Little Women.* Unlike the March sisters, Dick has no family connections; he has been deserted by his father and orphaned by his mother's death. A street urchin who lives by his wits and earns a few dollars shining shoes, he drinks, gambles, smokes, and swears. The narrator praises Dick as "frank and straightforward, manly and self-reliant,"[28] and he has an engaging, ready sense of humor—but, clearly,

Dick at the outset is not a model of ideal morality. His story, like Jo's, is a journey towards self-improvement.

Aside from this similarity, the two protagonists share little in common. Children's literature of the nineteenth century not only entertained its young readers but overtly prepared them for their adult roles in a culture that sharply differentiated between genders. Thus, the differences between Jo and Dick's journeys is inevitable. After Dick learns to read and write under the tutelage of another boy, his world of commercial opportunities expands rapidly until he ultimately gains a position that confers, if not the "riches" usually (and mistakenly) attributed to Horatio Alger heroes, at least a measure of respectability and independence. The few female characters who appear briefly in the novel make little impact on the direction of Dick's life, and religion seems to offer him not so much the opportunity for moral improvement as contacts in the commercial world. He reforms easily, directed by advice from the adult men whose paths cross his with fortuitous coincidence; once he receives instruction about one moral principle or another, he never regresses.

Jo, on the other hand, is forever suffering relapses, depending first on her parents and then on Professor Bhaer to rescue her from a slough of moral shortcomings and despair. Meg and Amy, too, profit in similar ways from parental and spousal instruction. As Patricia Meyer Spacks observes, the novel suggests that women can hope to acquire goodness only by "confining themselves within the family."[29] Thus, Jo's journey returns her to the family sphere where she began, preoccupied with children and domestic matters, her earlier hopes for autonomy replaced by financial dependence on her husband. The narrator assures readers that she is "very happy" (444), but the assertion rings hollow. Although Jo claims that "the life I wanted then [as a girl] seems selfish, lonely, and cold to me now" (447), a reader leafing through her earlier adventures will find instead a life full of promise, joy, and spirited ambition. Jo's description of herself in the final chapter as "thin as a shadow" seems sadly accurate; she is but a trace of the lively girl of Part I.

*Seventeenth Summer*

Angie Morrow is also tethered to the domestic sphere during her *Seventeenth Summer*. Author Maureen Daly began writing this novel when she herself was in her teens, and she has said that Angie "represents my life at 17."[30] Spanning the three months between Angie's graduation from high school and her departure for college, the novel is both a romance and a coming-of-age story, narrated in a first-person voice whose tone ranges from confessional to guileless. Like *Little Women,* Daly's novel received warm reviews when it appeared in 1942. Critics praised its lyrical qualities, its sensitive approach to a girl's first love, and the honesty of its ending that avoids a happily-ever-after pairing. More than fifty years after its publication, the novel is still in print and offers a historically interesting picture of what life was like for many young women in mid-twentieth century.

The surface plot or ideology encourages highly conventional behavior for young women, and Angie never questions the "good good girl" role her culture imposes on her. By contemporary standards she seems dubiously naïve for a high school graduate, so confined to her immediate environs that she can hardly imagine the world beyond her town of Fond du Lac. She assumes that everyone she knows is similarly bound: "Our family had never moved at all ever since I was born. People who live in our town stay there."[31] *Seventeenth Summer* is set in the late '30s or early '40s, but Angie makes no references to the upheavals in Europe leading to World War II. Unlike Jo, who is very much aware of the Civil War being waged, Angie seems entirely unaware of the battles developing on the other side of the Atlantic. She spends most of her days at home, doing housework under her mother's direction—dusting, ironing, washing dishes, peeling potatoes—and caring for her younger sister Kitty. She seems to have no friends or outside interests before she meets Jack. Her initial date with him is her first with anyone, and she needs parental permission to accept his invitation. She hasn't learned to drive, and sex is a complete mystery. At first, she hardly knows what to make of her own stirrings, and late in their relationship when Jack's "serious" expression conveys a measure of male desire, she doesn't know how to interpret what she sees in his face.

Jack introduces Angie to a new social milieu. The boys in his crowd smoke, and everyone drinks beer. Angie seems much more sheltered than the girls she meets through Jack, but the novel portrays her lack of experience as a virtue. The first conversation between Angie and Jack highlights their class differences when he asks her to go sailing with him. "Me and Swede Vincent have got a little boat we bought last fall" (12), he says. She doesn't comment on his ungrammatical phrasing, but her own grammar is always impeccable. Still, she seems aware of the social gap between them, and when she seeks her mother's approval, she is careful to refer not only to Dick's credentials as a star athlete but also to his family's economic status: "They're nice people. He plays basketball and his father owns the DeLuxe bakery" (14). The latter criterion is especially significant in the context of what she and her family deem important, for they are the kind of people who "always use top sheets on the bed and always eat supper in the dining room and things like that—well, she [Angie's mother] just didn't want us to go out with *anybody*" (73).

Predictably, Angie's steady relationship with Jack meets with parental resistance, particularly from her mother. Mr. Morrow is away on business most of the time, and when he appears on the weekends, he usually disappears behind the newspaper. Sometimes he does speak up, mostly to voice his disapproval of Angie's going out so much with one boy, and Angie never refutes his opinions, even when he orders her to stay home when she has a date with Jack. But more often, her father is a vague presence. As Angie says, her father's "approvals and disapprovals" usually come via her mother, who has tight control over Angie's life. It is she, not Angie, who decides what kind of formal Angie will wear to her first dance; she sets the agenda for Angie's domestic chores, and no one can touch the daily paper before she reads it. "It is an unwritten rule in our house never to ask for a piece of the paper until my mother has finished with it" (37), Angie says without resentment as she and her little sister sit patiently on the lawn one hot afternoon waiting their turn to see the evening edition.

Despite the control Mr. and Mrs. Morrow exert over their daughters, they are strangely remote from them, out of touch with their feelings. They aren't, Angie says, "the kind of family who loves each other out loud" (218). At one point, as Angie and her older sister Lorraine wait in vain for phone calls from the two men in their lives, both miserable and on edge, their mother sits sewing in the family living room, aware only of the summer storm that rumbles in the distance. "Isn't this the best night to be all home, cozy and inside?" she says (129). She also fails to understand that her adult daughters are entitled to independent lives. She disapproves when her oldest daughter, engaged to be married soon, spends her summer vacation with her fiancé and his family, and she fusses when Lorraine makes a date for July Fourth that conflicts with the family's outing: "It used to be that we could arrange things here without having to worry about individual plans" (138), she complains.

Mrs. Morrow's rigid and "habitual disapproval" helps to account for Angie's ambiguity about her budding feelings for Jack (170). Angie explains that her mother likes boys well enough as individuals, "but as dates she regards all boys with a vague, general disapproval—just in case" (72). Aware that male sexuality is suspect, she is embarrassed when Jack sees her barefooted during their first meeting in the garden, and later, even after they know each other better, she is uncomfortable eating in his presence. Any manifestation of human physicality seems to violate her intense sense of modesty. Sensual feelings, too, give rise to uneasiness. When she gets "a warm tingling" while sailing with Jack, she feels "guilty—almost as if I were doing something I shouldn't" (21). On their third date, she worries about what might happen if Jack should try to kiss her, and when Jack appears unexpectedly one afternoon as the family is finishing a picnic lunch in the back yard, Angie flees into the kitchen to feed the dog. "It didn't seem right to go outside again and sit there on the cool grass, liking Jack so well, right in front of my family" (147).

Despite her parents' restrictive attitudes, Angie values her family's judgments and wants them to think well of Jack because "it's important that a family like a boy" (32). When she invites him for Sunday dinner and he violates some standards of etiquette, Angie reacts with fierce contempt, although she has known from an earlier conversation that her family is of a higher social class than Jack's: she is going to college, he plans to work in his father's bakery. One of his grandfathers farmed and another owned a meat market. Jack has also confided that "until a couple of months ago I didn't even know what side a salad plate goes on" (19). But when he fumbles the salad servers and—even worse—clicks his spoon against his teeth while eating ice cream in front of her family, Angie is suddenly and acutely aware of their class differences and begins to "hate" him:

> I could just see his father in shirtsleeves, folding food onto his fork with his knife and never using napkins except when there was company. And probably they brought the coffee pot right in and set it on the table. My whole mind was filled with a growing disdain and loathing. His family probably didn't even own a butter knife! No girl has to stand all that. Never. (166)

Later, she regrets her anger, but she is so thoroughly socialized to accept her family's cultural standards that her response is almost predictable. In her world, people who count always do and say the right things; she herself follows social dictates with earnest compliance and expects others to do the same. Not only has she mastered such matters as table etiquette, but she has also learned the rules that govern relationships between the sexes, and she knows her "place" well: A girl must never call a boy, wear clothing as unfashionable as flat black oxfords, sit in public with a bottle of beer in front of her, accept last-minute invitations for dates, or take any initiative in a relationship with a boy. When Angie's first date with Jack comes to a close and they stand outside the door to her house saying goodnight, she reflects that a girl "can't ask a boy, 'When will I see you again?' or 'Will I *ever* see you again?'" (24).

She finds it especially important to look her best in the company of males, and she is disconcerted when Jack's friend encounters her wearing old slacks, her nose shiny. On dates she surreptitiously checks her hairdo. And she accepts the ritual of being looked over by the "checkers," the popular crowd at high school who gather every evening at the local hangout to see who's out with whom. "It is almost like a secret police system," she says without censure, adding that because the "checkers" only watch for the prettiest and most popular girls, "it is the most serious catastrophe of all not to be noticed" by them (93). There is no irony in her comment. She is completely sincere. Clearly, Angie lives in a strictly patriarchal culture where the two genders live by distinctly different codes: the young men control the social relationships and the young women strive to please them. Angie may "enjoy being a girl," but it's a role that requires constant vigilance and accommodation.

Girls who follow the rules may be lucky enough to be chosen by some desirable boy, a life-changing event: "One day you're nobody and the next day you're the girl that some fellow goes with and the other fellows look at you harder and wonder what you've got and wish that they'd been the one to take you out first. . . . Going with a boy gives you a new identity" (62). Because so much depends on that identity, the girl is responsible for seeing that the relationship progresses smoothly, and Angie assumes the fault is hers when a date with Jack goes flat. Even though Jack has behaved rudely, ignoring her to talk and dance with an old girlfriend, Angie assumes responsibility: "Anyone with a date as dull as I was would naturally want to dance with someone else," (45) she thinks. On the other hand, she is not entirely without power in the relationship. When she is abrupt with Jack on the phone, she enjoys thinking about his wondering whether she is angry with him. She isn't, but "even if you like a boy so much, it is almost fun to know he is worrying about you" (160). Although Angie is usually transparent and sincere with Jack, the disparity in their relationship leads her into devious behavior.

Girls who violate the rules, knowingly or unknowingly, come to a bad end. At best, they are ostracized for wearing the wrong clothes; at worst, they allow themselves to be used by men who discard them when something better comes along. This is the fate of Angie's sister Lorraine. Not only has she gone out many times with Martin Keefe, a new man in town, when he calls at the last minute, but the text implies that she has engaged in excessive sexual behavior—what she calls "necking"—and harbors some guilty regrets.

Although Angie never questions the values of her middle-class culture (probably because Daly wrote the novel when she herself was still an adolescent), she does develop a firmer sense of herself as her story progresses, gaining a subtle measure of independence and making choices about the kind of self she wants to be. In the course of her summer, she has the chance to observe how other girls behave around boys and rejects the models that they offer. Unlike her sister Lorraine, who assumes a role to suit her date much as she might put on a costume, Angie muses that she has "never thought of 'pretending' with a boy" (65). And although she admires Jane Rady, Jack's old girlfriend, as "smooth," the adjective takes on a negative connotation. The "smooth" people in the story are in fact shallow and affected. Jane makes a play for Jack even though he is clearly dating Angie, and Lorraine's boyfriend, Martin Keefe, proves that he is a cad. Dolly, a younger girl in Jack's crowd, drinks and giggles too much. When Jack says that the boys think Dolly is a "find," he means not a treasure but an easy prey. So although Angie thinks that it is "important to act as if you had been around" (77), she resists betraying herself by acting like someone she is not.

Margie, another girl in Jack's crowd, wonders why Angie doesn't "worry" about her relationship with Jack. "You don't think like other girls" (248), she tells Angie, and she is right. Margie cannot imagine a life that extends further than her boyfriend Fitz; their relationship has gone flat, but Margie supposes she will marry him because "a girl has to go out with somebody!" (250). In contrast, Angie recognizes that her romance with Jack, while sweet, is temporary. When he proposes marriage, she is briefly stirred, but the moment quickly passes. She knows that the summer and their relationship will end simultaneously: "Everything was so calmly and painfully clear" (269). In the closing scene, she is on the train to college, wistfully savoring the memory of her first romance but aware that other relationships await her. She is now a young woman, wiser and more mature than the earlier and childlike Angie.

Virginia Shaefer Carroll has argued that *Seventeenth Summer* is a story of personal development in the context of a romance,[32] and Angie's movement toward maturity, culminating in her departure for college, does offer a subtext affirming female independence. During the course of her summer with Jack, Angie has sensed the constraints that her middle-class home and parents impose. She feels "older" and "more important" away from her family, as if "the house were too small and the cream-colored dining-room walls were crowding in close" (126). Although Angie is no Jo March and never rebels against the constraints of home and family, she does gain some distance. For one thing, she begins to feel more comfortable with her sexuality. Earlier, she has resisted following her impulse to touch Jack when she sees "a warm, dark look" in his eyes that makes her lips tingle (176). She is unsure of what the "strange beating" in her means, and she is "afraid to know" (178). Even when Jack tells her that he and his family are moving back to Oklahoma, her response is restrained because it is "too embarrassing to be affectionate in the daytime" (218). Nor can she return Jack's profession of "love." The word is too "big." But later, she reflects that something in her has changed: "I was no longer afraid to look into his eyes or touch his hand when I talked to him. I felt much older than I had in June" (240).

Accompanying her growing sexuality is a recognition of its price. She senses with a pang of loss that the security of her childhood has slipped away, suddenly aware, rather like Jo March, that as males intrude into the family, she and her sisters "began to live [their] lives separately" (202). Her expanding world diminishes the safety of her sheltered home. "Growing up is like taking down the sides of your house and letting strangers walk in," she says (203). Her mother's illness further undermines her child's security: "I realized what an empty place our house would be if my mother weren't in it" (215). She is moving beyond her role as a child.

Her maturity, however, remains problematic. Unlike Jo, Angie has no clearly articulated ambition. Early in the novel, she says that she wants to know about everything beautiful, and much later, she expresses a wish to sense "more" of everything—the food she eats, the waves on the lake, her feelings for Jack. She seems to have developed an appetite for a life with more depth and dimension. In an impassioned speech, she tells Jack that they are different from their peers, that they could begin to work on themselves to become "great people." But she proposes to accomplish that goal by brushing her hair "every night" (238).

Carroll concedes that Angie develops only to the "threshold of maturity" without crossing it ("Romance," 18) but she may have overstated her case in maintaining that a re-reading of Daly's novel demonstrates that "Angie is autonomous and resisting" (18). Although she has moved beyond her immature self of the earlier chapters, she is still a child in many ways, and it seems most likely that her future holds little promise of true autonomy. More likely, she will follow her sister Margaret's path into the home of a pleasant fellow, where she will be a complaisant wife to the guy who chooses to have her.

That young women have so willingly subordinated their interests and sense of self for relationships with a male, viewing their own gender as inferior, is hardly limited to the pages of novels. Peggy Orenstein, author of *Schoolgirls: Young Women, Self-Esteem, and the Confidence Gap*, has this to say: "By sixth grade it is clear that both girls and boys have learned to equate maleness with opportunity and femininity with constraint."[33] Books such as Orenstein's and Mary Pipher's *Reviving Ophelia* leave little doubt that our country's culture poses a genuine risk to the well-being of its young women.

The stories of Jo and Angie might have taken a different route had they been written today. As writers and publishers have begun to recognize that stories can and should provide strong role models for girls instead of perpetuating gender stereotypes that minimize their self-confidence and opportunities, there has been an explosion of young adult novels with female protagonists whose sense of independence and assurance contrasts sharply with that of their predecessors. If storytellers do indeed play a significant role in transmitting cultural values, then such stories can provide a frame for "girls to imagine all the different ways their lives can play out."[34]

## NOTES

1. Interestingly enough, a television commercial for Visa charge cards portraying a young woman floating through the air and accompanied by the first verse of this song appeared as this chapter was being written.

2. Mem Fox, "Men Who Weep, Boys Who Dance: The Gender Agenda in Children's Literature," *Language Arts* 70 (February 1993), 84–5.

3. See, for example, *The Voyage In: Fictions of Female Development*, ed. Elizabeth Abel, Marianne Hirsch, and Elixabeth Langland (Hanover, CT: University Press of New England, 1983). Although the essays in this volume limit their discussions to novels for adults, much of what they say can be applied to adolescent literature as well.

4. See Sandra M. Gilbert and Susan Gubar, *The Madwoman in the Attic: The Woman Writer and the Nineteenth-Century Imagination* (New Haven, CT: Yale UP, 1979); Madonna Kolbenschlag, *Kiss Sleeping Beauty Goodbye: Breaking the Spell of Feminine Myths and Models* (New York: Doubleday, 1979); Olga Brouma, *Beginning with O* (New Haven: Yale UP, 1977); and Angela Carter, *The Bloody Chamber* (New York: Harper and Row, 1980).

5. Ellen Cronan Rose, "Through the Looking Glass: When Women Tell Fairy Tales," in *The Voyage In: Fictions of Female Development*, ed. Elizabeth Abel, Marianne Hirsch, and Elizabeth Langland (Hanover, CT: UP of New England, 1983), 209.

6. See Alison Lurie, *Clever Gretchen and Other Forgotten Folktales* (New York: Thomas Crowell, 1980).

7. Abel et al., *Voyage In*, 12.

8. Jane Austen, *Northanger Abbey* (1818) (NY: Modern Library, 1995), 76.

9. Fannie Burney, *Evelina, or The History of a Young Lady's Entrance into the World*, 1778 (New York: Norton, 1965).

10. Sandra M. Gilbert and Susan Gubar, *The Madwoman in the Attic: The Woman Writer and the Nineteenth-Century Literary Imagination* (New Haven: Yale UP, 1979); see Chapter 10, "A Dialogue of Self and Soul: Plain Jane's Program," 336–372.

11. Leslie Fiedler, *Love and Death in the American Novel* (Cleveland: World Publishing, 1962), 216.

12. See Patricia Ann Meyer Spacks, "The Adolescent as Heroine" in *The Female Imagination* (New York: Alfred A. Knopf, 1975) for a discussion of the ambiguities in female dependency as portrayed in fiction for adults.

13. Mary Lystad, "The Adolescent Image in American Books for Children: Then and Now," in *Young Adult Literature: Background and Criticism*, ed. Millicent Linz and Ramona M. Mahood (Chicago: American Library Association, 1980), 30.

14. Fiedler, *Love and Death*, 276.

15. See John and Virginia Demos, "Adolescence in Historical Perspective," *Journal of Marriage and the Family* 31 (November 1969), 623–33.

16. See Patricia J. Campbell, *Sex Education Books for Young Adults 1892–1979* (New York: R. R. Bowker, 1979), Chapter 1, for a full discussion of this subject.

17. Kenneth L. Donelson, "Growing Up Real: YA Literature Comes of Age," in *Young Adult Literature: Background and Criticism*, ed. Millicent Linz and Ramona M. Mahood (Chicago: American Library Association, 1980), 60.

18. "Young Adult Literature Female Heroes Do Exist," *Alan Review* 17.1 (Fall 1989), 12.

19. Mary Ritchie Key, "The Role of Male and Female in Children's Books," *Wilson Library Bulletin* 46 (October 1971), 175.

20. Carole Kortenhaus and Jack Demarest, "Gender Role Stereotyping in Children's Literature: An Update," *Sex Roles* 28 (Fall 1993), 230.

21. Robert E. Probst, *Response and Analysis: Teaching Literature in Junior and Senior High* (Upper Montclair, NJ: Boynton, 1988).

22. Peter Hollingdale, "Ideology," in *Literature for Children: Contemporary Criticism*, ed. Peter Hunt (New York: Routledge, 1992), 27.

23. *Commonwealth* 7 (April 24, 1869), 1.

24. *National Anti-Slavery Standard*, 29 (May 1, 1869), 1.

25. Louisa May Alcott, *Little Women*, 1868 (New York: New American Library, 1983), 10; hereafter cited in text.

26. Sean O'Faolain, "This Is Your Life . . . Louisa May Alcott," *Holiday* 44 (November 1968), 26.

27. Lissa Paul, "Enigma Variations," *SIGNAL* 54 (September 1987), 190.

28. Horatio Alger, *Ragged Dick* (1868) (New York: Signet, 1990), 8.

29. Spacks, *Female Imagination*, 97.

30. Lisa Ann Richardson, "Books for Adolescents: A Retrospective with Maureen Daly," *Journal of Reading* 36 (February 1993), 424.

31. Maureen Daly, *Seventeenth Summer* (1942) (New York: Scholastic, 1952), 217; hereafter cited in text.

32. "Re-Reading the Romance of *Seventeenth Summer*," *Children's Literature Association Quarterly* 21.1 (1996); hereafter cited in text as "Romance."

33. Quoted in *Once Upon a Heroine*, Alison Cooper-Mullin and Jennifer Marmaduke Coye (Lincolnwood, IL: Contemporary Books, 1998), xii.

34. Cooper-Mullin and Coye, *Heroine*, xii.

# This Is Now

A book can get lost, disappear, or simply fall to pieces, but a story plays forever once we've taken it to heart. And for the rest of what each of us will know of eternity, whenever we drag about the house in heavy shoes, wash our eyes, and search the shelf for answers, that story will survive to coax us from the empty room and back into the moonlight: A sister, teaching us to dance.

"One, Taken to Heart," from Chicks Up Front<br>by Sara Holbrook

*It* is no accident that the recent appearance of stronger female characters in young adult literature has coincided with changes in women's roles and in approaches to literary criticism. As women have moved from their mostly domestic, submissive "place" at the side of the men who would "have" them and critics began to identify the sexism in the passive, predictable characterizations of girls and women, more and more novels for young readers have portrayed assertive and confident girls. This change in young adult fiction has been inevitable, for, as Catherine Sheldrick Ross explains, "When for members of a particular cultural group the sense of reality changes, then the fictions that they tell themselves must change as well."[1] Although strong female characters have never been entirely absent in adolescent fiction, their numbers grew in what seemed like an exponential explosion in the closing decade of the twentieth century, as evidenced by anthologies published during this time with such titles as *Short Stories for Strong Girls* and critical studies that promise to *Kiss Sleeping Beauty Goodbye*. This newer fiction has been doubly welcome; the best of it has enthralled its young readers while also providing powerful role models for them.

Study after study has affirmed the significance of reading—novels in particular—on the cultural education of young adults and the processes by which they come of age.[2] As Jeanette Mines asserts, girls "deserve encouragement to read stories with female heroes who transcend their world in positive, female-oriented ways. They deserve introduction to books with strong female characters who have stories worth telling and hearing."[3] So what does it mean to speak of "strong female characters" or empowered girls in YA fiction and how does one identify the stories in which they appear? Bibliographies, of course, can provide a recommended list, but any bibliography—however comprehensive—is the product of human effort and as such, is prone to human inaccuracies. Inevitably, it will omit at least a few books, either by oversight or as a reflection of the bibliographer's biases. Also, some books will have been too recently published for inclusion, and any list becomes quickly outdated as new books roll off the presses. A definition, by contrast, gives readers guidelines to create their own lists or augment existing ones.

## DEFINING "EMPOWERED GIRLS"

Arriving at a definition, however, is complicated by the nature of the YA genre itself. Fiction for young adults almost always tells a rite-of-passage story that moves its protagonist from innocence to experience. At the heart of the genre is initiation into new knowledge, with the process of initiation divided into three stages that have marked male coming of age in so-called primitive societies: isolation, a trial through encounters with danger that require some sort of self-sacrifice or symbolic death and rebirth, and reunification with community accompanied by increased status. Because young adult fiction is essentially optimistic, the protagonist's journey usually concludes with his or her gaining some measure of maturity and independence. Steven VanderStaay says of this plot structure, "The development of autonomous thought is the principal 'rite' at the heart of YA fiction. Generally, it is followed by autonomous action, based on that thought, that enables the protagonist(s) to solve a problem thrust upon them by the adult world and achieve self-reliance."[4]

Because autonomy or self-reliance is empowering, all YA protagonists can thus be said to gain a sense of "empowerment," so any useful definition of "empowered girls" must distinguish them from their male counterparts. Abel, Hirsch, and Langland have noted in their introduction to *The Voyage In: Fictions of Female Development* that female protagonists often depend on close relations with others to realize their full potential, unlike their male counterparts, who achieve unqualified independence. Thus, empowered girls in young adult fiction may find strength by valuing positive feminine characteristics instead of striving to be as competitive, assertive, and powerful as boys, even though societal norms tend to endorse those latter qualities. The definition, therefore, should include girls whose empowerment has more to do with gaining confidence in themselves than gaining power over others. When they do gain power, ideally they should share it, using their sense of authority to empower others. Empowerment is not synonymous with entitlement, so meaningful empowerment should result from purposeful action rather than innate talent or coincidental circumstances. And because girls' stories have conventionally ended with a marriage or mating in which the female protagonist assumes a subordinate role, fiction about empowered girls must find ways to subvert that ending.

A useful definition must also be flexible enough to make allowances for differences in how girls become empowered, a point especially significant in any investigation of multicultural literature. Still, empowered girls in young adult fiction share certain attributes and experiences, as demonstrated by the analysis below of three strong female protagonists of novels published in the 1980s. Each fulfills Leslie Ashcroft's definition of "empowerment" as a "nourishing belief in capacity and competence."[5] Although their stories are told in three different genres—historical fiction, contemporary realism, and literature of the fantastic—their respective passages toward maturity illustrate that "empowered girls" in young adult fiction have much in common, and, taken together, their experiences point towards a more explicit definition of what that term embodies. Such a definition serves well to preface a discussion of the many empowered girls appearing in young adult fiction published between 1990 and 2001.

*Beyond the Divide*

Meribah Simon, the protagonist of *Beyond the Divide,* Kathryn Lasky's first young adult novel, undertakes a personal journey from dependency to empowerment when she and her father join a wagon train and travel the difficult terrain of the American West during the 1849 gold rush. Lasky resists the label of "feminist writer," saying that she dislikes being pigeon-holed,[6] but she consistently addresses feminist issues in her fiction, and virtually all of her female protagonists either have or develop a "belief in their own capacity and competence" when they encounter and resist the forces of greed, bigotry, and the corrupting effects of power.

*Beyond the Divide* begins late in Meribah's journey, then shifts to its beginning when she leaves her Amish community in Holly Springs, Pennsylvania, to accompany her father. Roberta Seelinger Trites notes that the framed tale, what she calls the "nested structure," provides "a way for women to work through problems by revisiting them at different points in time,"[7] and the structure provides exactly this opportunity for Meribah. Initially, she feels only hostility toward Holly Springs and its Amish residents, who have shunned her father for attending the funeral of a friend who did not adhere strictly to Amish ways. Forbidden to manage his farm or borrow money for seeds, her father decides to begin a new life in the West. Meribah's decision to leave her siblings and mother behind to join him, then, is an act of rebellion against conventional social structures that will lead to her empowerment, for she has felt stifled in Holly Springs, "as if the beams [of the ceiling] were pressing down from above on her, that the walls were leaning in and narrowing the living space until there was nowhere to turn, no place to think, to dream."[8] What she senses is the lack of freedom under Amish rule that, while ensuring security, severely limits individual choice: "There were the unseen walls, the unvarying measurements, the inflexible proportions that were always there" (5).

In the stories of young women, empowerment often occurs only after some overt act of rejection or rebellion against the status quo, and this is the case for Meribah. In her Amish home, she realizes, she has been defined "not by herself but others" (6). It is concern for what they might say rather than what she thinks that constrains her behavior. When she leaves her community, she feels that a deadly weight has lifted, but nonetheless she still depends on familiar ways for her identity. "We're still Amish, aren't we, Pa?" she asks along the way (23). And continuing to take her cue from what others say about her, she enjoys the glowing adjectives that other emigrants heap upon her, echoing their phrases to herself although they are far removed from her customary speech and her ways of thinking about herself: "I'm a lamb, Meribah thought absently, a charming, lovely, delicate lamb" (50).

As the wagon train moves farther and farther from her Amish home, Meribah moves further and further from her Amish upbringing. At first she tries to compromise, alternating her old ways with the more worldly ones she is learning, but, exposed to new people and experiences, her sense of self begins to change irrevocably. Her fellow emigrants are very different from the people she knew in Holly Springs, more concerned with worldly goods, more affected, more violent. She witnesses acts of greed, destruction, and cruelty that would have been unimaginable to her sheltered, earlier self. Two brothers among the wagon train emigrants murder some Apache Indians, then dangle the scalps from their belt, and they later rape her friend Serena. Meribah is distressed when the other emigrants view Serena as the guilty party—a "silly flirt," a "tart filly"—instead of the victim, and when Serena wanders off by herself one day and is killed in a mudslide, Meribah's grief and outrage overwhelm her. Then her father injures his hand repairing the wagon of another emigrant, and the wound turns gangrenous. As her father grows weaker, Meribah assumes more and more adult responsibility, taking on some of the duties conventionally ascribed to males. By the time the wagon train pushes into the precariously arid territories that border the Rockies, Meribah is torn between the Amish girl she once was and the young woman she is becoming. "She thought east and looked west. Time and distance mingled oddly, and Meribah wondered about who she had been and who she was becoming and the connection between the two persons" (118).

The person she is becoming meets each disaster with growing determination to survive. By the time the wagon train crosses the continental divide, Meribah realizes that "she could not look back, and so she turned west. There were no more choices for her" (175). With that realization, Meribah has forged a new sense of self, and the divide of the title refers not only to the geographical site that separates the waters destined for either the Pacific or Atlantic, but to a cusp in Meribah's development when, after a long and difficult struggle, she moves from childhood towards adulthood, from her constrained and sheltered Amish self towards a new and empowered young woman.

One of her father's oxen dies, and when their wagon breaks down, her father is too ill to repair it. They can go no farther without help, and the captain of the train convinces the others in the group to abandon them. Meribah asserts herself to some of the other emigrants in a manner she never would have thought possible, even leveling a gun at one man who wants to take their wheels for his own wagon. "You'll have to kill me first," she tells him (230). Stranded in the mountains alone after her father dies, she finds that she is entirely self-reliant for physical necessities, even shooting a man who tries to rape her. Yet, her world is empty without human companionship and community. In the closing chapters she finds these with a tribe of Native Americans, and living among them stills the pangs of loneliness that had gnawed at her. She becomes acculturated into the Indian way of life, emerging from the months she spends with the tribe mature and independent, spiritually attuned to the natural world.

In some ways, Meribah's strength derives from the same sources as those identified earlier in the story of Jo March. Like Jo, Meribah is sharply aware of the limitation of being female in a patriarchal world, but unlike Jo, who announces her disappointment at being a girl at the outset of the novel, Meribah only gradually becomes aware of how women's lives are constrained by gender—even in the anarchic matrix of wagon train culture. She finds herself exhausted by the end of each day on the trail, yet much of "women's work" remains to be done: muddy clothes to be washed, damp bedding dried, cows to be milked. And Meribah must help each evening to prepare a "good square meal for the menfolk" (51), as if she had not worked as hard as the males. Her friend's rape emphasizes for her the lack of control that women exert over their own lives. As she reflects on the inequalities between how society has positioned "menfolk" and "womenfolk," she grows more resistant to the obliging role constructed for her, adhering less and less (unlike Jo) to the strictures that govern female behavior. Eventually, she even cuts the skirt off her Amish dress and wears beaver leggings instead, an androgynous manifestation of the internal changes she is experiencing. She also reflects at length on how the westward movement has oppressed the Native Americans, whose lands are being seized by the white settlers. The more she becomes aware of the forces oppressing her and others, the stronger her resistance to them grows and the more empowering the resistance.

Meribah shares with Jo an expressive urge, but what she creates is more intensely private. In the early chapters, she keeps her thoughts "tight as a locked box" (24), unable to articulate her emotions freely. Then her father gives her money to buy some chalks, and she knows instinctively that they are her "kind of drawing tool . . . for representing the nuances, the shadows and smudges that suggest depth, and volume, rather than the hard, sharp edges and perimeters of things" (32). She begins to draw a map of her journey, a kind of visual diary that represents her responses to both the beauty and the traumatic cruelties she witnesses along the trail. Her map suggests "the shape of the journey rather than the direction" (41); significantly, it tells only where she has been, not where she is going. At the outset, she hardly knows her destination. As she moves from innocence to experience, her drawings change. No longer does she draw the "edgeless world and the endless wind" in an array of colors, but, needing the assurance of specific form and shape, she sketches "the close-up, finite things" (180) and uses only the gray lead of her pencil. When events stop making sense to her, her drawings cease to have recognizable shapes, and eventually she stops drawing altogether. "I guess I just started to wonder where we were moving to," she later confesses to a friend who is a professional mapmaker (241). Only towards the end of the novel, when he leads her out of the wilderness, does she begin to draw again, saying that she sometimes feels that she is reinventing the land as she moves back through it. To which her friend replies, "You are a true mapmaker. Indeed, you map more than you think, Meribah Simon" (246). Her map, of course, serves metaphorically to chart her inner as well as her literal journey, and what she has mapped is her newly constructed self as well as the land she has reinterpreted.

During her journey, Meribah develops a stronger voice, one distinctly her own. At first she uses the Amish *thee* and *thou* as terms of address, but gradually adopts the *you* of her new secular culture. As conditions along the trail grow harsher, she learns to raise her voice in defense of what she knows is right. Warned, for example, that she does not understand the impropriety of visiting her friend Serena after she has been raped, she retorts that she is "beginning to understand too much" (141). Even when she is silent, she is developing her voice by becoming more and more aware of how language constructs one's world: she observes that the rape has become "not a *crime committed* but an *incident brought on*" (148), and she carries on "furious internal dialogues in which she told everyone just what she thought" (148). As the wagon train emigrants prattle on about the "savage" Indians and their own superior "civilization"—which Serena's father defines with unconscious irony as "tea and smokes in the starlight" (78)—Meribah comes to realize that the emigrants' descriptions of the Indians contradict her own perceptions and that it is the emigrants who are the real savages. She is also quick to see through the captain's arguments when he explains why the wagon train is abandoning her and her father. She thinks, "This is supposed to sound reasonable. I keep listening for the reason but I can't find it. He says 'best.' I think 'worst.' He says 'sensible.' I hear 'insane'" (226). When he tells Meribah that it is her choice to remain, she retorts, "There is no choice for me. The choice is yours. And you know this!" (227).

Carol Gilligan, writing *In a Different Voice: Psychological Theory and Women's Development,* defines voice as a condition of being human: "To have something to say is to be a person."[9] However, Gilligan points out that too many women have believed it dangerous to articulate their honest needs and thoughts, fearing that abandonment or retaliation might result. But in silencing themselves or allowing themselves to be silenced, they risk sacrificing their essential humanity and their connections to others, for "speaking depends on listening and being heard. It is an intensely relational act" (*Voice*, xvi). Lyn Mikel Brown and Carol Gilligan conclude in *Meeting at the Crossroads: Women's Psychology and Girls' Development* that this silencing usually occurs as girls move into adolescence, when social acceptance takes precedence over revealing one's self, [10] and Jo's story demonstrates this process. Jo begins as an outspoken young woman who enjoys using "boyish" slang and saying what is on her mind, much to her sisters' distress. As she gradually takes her place as a "little woman," her voice becomes nearly indistinguishable from her sisters' more "ladylike" speech.

Meribah, on the other hand, develops an increasingly stronger voice over time. Released from the stricture of her Amish community, she becomes freer to articulate her feelings and convictions; her voice, like her map making, helps her express her growing sense of self. Roberta Seelinger Trites, writing about feminist children's authors, addresses multiple ways in which young female protagonists develop strong voices: by refusing to silence their inner voices, by using art as a metaphorical expression of voice, and by gaining awareness of the primacy of language in defining a sense of self (*Sleeping Beauty,* 48). Meribah employs all these means, and in the closing chapter her voice is strong as she explains to her friend, the map maker, why she is going no farther with him but has chosen to return to a valley through which the wagon train had passed on its way west: "It is a place that I've been to, and it is a place that I know is really my home. . . . It is a place where I can grow things, where

I can put something in the ground and make something grow out of it" (*Beyond the Divide*, 291). Asked if she can survive, she replies with ringing conviction, "I can do better than that. I can live!" (291).

Meribah also finds strength in nurture. The other emigrants become increasingly dispirited and weary, but the hardships seem to energize Meribah: "Where others' strength ebbed, Meribah's surged" (177). She takes on more and more responsibility, driving an ill friend's wagon, mending clothes, doing the wash for other families, and baking enough bread in one afternoon to last two weeks. When her father injures his hand and grows increasingly weaker, the distinctions between parent and child blur, until Meribah becomes the primary caretaker. Finally, her father's very survival depends upon her nurturing acts, and she refuses to desert him when others in the wagon train move on. Although they have offered to take her without her father, she knows that their offer carries no goodwill and replies bluntly that what they really want is "our food and our ox and a good amount of our gear" (226). As the wagon train departs without them, she shouts a challenge to their complacency: "You are not good folks. You are selfish folks, and you are murdering us" (228). In remaining at her father's side, stranded in the wilderness, she risks her life. Her willingness to do so appears to differ from the self-effacing action of Jo in abandoning her dream to write, for she can be said to respond to her deeply ingrained love for her father and her own sense of morality, not acceding to an externally constructed role. Also, filial loyalty, especially that of girls to their fathers, was deeply embedded in nineteenth-century culture, and Meribah could hardly be presented as a heroine were she to desert her father. She is caught between the proverbial rock and hard place. Thus, she chooses a model that allows her to express moral outrage while maintaining an emotional connection to a source that represents family and integrity, defying her elders while filling the culturally approved role of good daughter.

On other occasions, too, her nurturing acts involve defiance of what the emigrant society deems acceptable. Lasky has taken pains to represent the emigrants' culture as morally reprehensible, and Meribah's defiance, then, is a battle for what is right, not merely the anti-establishment rebellion of late twentieth-century adolescents. Told that it is not "proper" for her to visit her friend Serena after the "incident," she grows "stiff" with anger and says that not only does she intend to pay a visit but will invite a former suitor of Serena's to join her, a man who failed to defend the girl against the assault and has avoided her ever since. Predictably, he declines the invitation, but Meribah pays her visit without him, establishing a ritual of taking Serena each evening for a walk. Her actions evolve from a recognition of injustice and a determination to stand up to it, and her nurturing acts further empower her because they are laced with defiance of that injustice.

Because this nurturing quality has been linked primarily to females, it has sometimes been regarded as a weakness, for the nurturer risks sacrificing her sense of self. This, of course, is Jo's fate in Part II of *Little Women*, when the independent rebel is replaced by the dutiful daughter and wife. But it is not Jo's nurturing qualities that undermine her strength but a socially sanctioned gender role that requires her to relinquish her personal power to meet the expectations and needs of others.[11] In Part I she gains—not loses—strength by nursing Beth through scarlet fever and pampering Laurie when he is ill or has been unfairly castigated by his grandfather. By helping others, she gains the responsibility and stature she might otherwise lack as a young woman and also makes Laurie less of a sexual threat; the fact, too, that she calls him "my boy" underscores both the supportive dimension of her friendship for him and her attempt to wrest power from a traditionally subordinate role. Thus, nurturing, often viewed as a weak and sacrificial characteristic of the female personality, can be read in another light: it connects the nurturer to a sustaining community and in this way confers rather than diminishes power.

According to conventional theories, adolescence has conventionally been viewed as a process of separation, a struggle to establish an individual sense of self based primarily on theories of male adolescence. One can argue that the "process" is always a struggle, but there are qualitative differences in how the struggle plays itself out for boys and girls. Gilligan reframes the process of female development as a struggle to connect (*Voice*, xv), and the stories of Jo and Meribah illustrate her theory. Although Gilligan has been criticized for implying that differences between male and female development are biologically essential rather than culturally constructed, contemporary work in the field of evolutionary psychology, and, in particular, brain structure, offer support for her theories. Recently, a group of psychologists at UCLA found that in times of stress women eschew the "fight or flight" response to stress commonly noted among men and instead are more likely to "tend and befriend," nurturing their children ("tend") and turning to social networks of supportive females ("befriend"). The psychologists argue that these behaviors are less culturally learned than biologically influenced by a powerful hormone found in both sexes but amplified by estrogen, a female sex hormone.[12]

Meribah's determination to "tend and befriend" her father alienates her from her wagon train companions but leads her to a new perception of community, unlike what Jo experiences. Jo's community, of course, is comprised of her mother and sisters. In the first chapter of the novel, she proudly declares that she is "man" of the house in her father's absence. Although her declaration implies a hierarchy, with the "man" at the top, the March household is in fact more democratic than hierarchical, more matriarchal than patriarchal. Even the structure of the novel, with each successive chapter shifting its focus from sister to sister, is democratic, as Ann Douglas has pointed out.[13] Thus, the relationships among the sisters are less like a ladder than a "web," the metaphorical term used by Carol Gilligan to describe the nature of female alliances: "a network of connection, a web of relationships that is sustained by a process of communication" (*Voice,* 32). So essential is this network for Jo that maintaining it motivates much of her behavior. Her eventual resolve to conform to the behavior expected of "little women," her resistance to Meg's marriage, and her determination to stay by her dying sister's side demonstrate just how much she values the relationships within her familial community.

Unlike Jo, Meribah finds it necessary to break free of her childhood community in Holly Springs, which, she realizes, ensures security but little freedom, and as the novel explores the tensions between these two oppositions, it probes the ambiguities of "community." As Meribah explains about her former life, "It's hard to tell where one leaves off—oneself or one's family—and the community begins" (*Beyond the Divide,* 112). On the trail Meribah sometimes misses the security of the Amish community with its clearly defined "fences," but finds a "loveliness to an endless wind and an everywhere sky" (54). Still, she discovers that freedom exacts its price, and she is anguished by the human inclination to anarchy and destruction that seems to go hand in hand with freedom. Why are people behaving in such a way? To which her father responds that "there are no easy answers. There are only questions. If thou wants easy answers, they are in Holly Springs" (157). His speech implies that it is not tight control of people that keeps evil at bay. Rather, he is saying that authoritarian rule, permitting no questions, provides only rigid answers and that community that requires the sacrifice of one's self is not empowering.

But "community" takes on a more positive connotation as Meribah discovers, like Jo, the comfort that derives from human companionship. One night, after watching the emigrants dancing and singing by the campfire, "the vastness did not seem so threatening" (74). Later, at Fort Hall, she forges a bond with the Iroquois wife of the fort commander, a "silent acknowledgment of each other" that gives her a "new kind of assurance and confidence" (195). And, finally, after her father's death, as she becomes more proficient at the tasks of survival, she comes to "realize that simply to survive was not enough for her" (272). Her need for human conversation grows "as acute as hunger pangs" (272).

In the closing chapters she is sheltered by a tribe of Yana Indians, and her friendship with them, especially the woman Meli, stills the ache of loneliness that had gnawed at her. The first word that Meli and Meribah exchange is the Yana word for "woman," a recognition of their common bond. The Yana call her Saltu, meaning "other," but the term is meant kindly, a contrast to the "peculiar" label that her Amish dress earned her in Missouri when the wagon train members first gathered. Here she finds a true community, one that accepts and accommodates difference. When the winter blizzard confines the entire tribe and Meribah to the tribal lodge, she has a chance to observe their customs closely. The men and women use two distinct dialects of their common language and each perform specific tasks, but she has no sense of being constrained by gender as she did in Holly Springs or on the trail. There seems to be no hierarchy that privileges males, and Meribah finds a "pleasure" in the customs that are "not order for the sake of order but order in service to a beauty that was a part of living" (283). For Meribah, then, community implies human connection that allows freedom for the individual self.

The spring season that renews the winter-bound earth also renews Meribah. She is now able to be alone without being lonely. And in her new-found peace, she becomes reconciled with her past, with the death of her father, with her anguished, frightened days alone in the wilderness that parallel the ordeal of medieval quest literature—and is finally able to put a name to what has haunted her during her journey, that "crystalline gray, the clear early gray of the world just before dawn—

that gray she could not name. 'Mother,' she whispered" (287). Although she willingly left her mother, an act that can be read as a rejection of traditional gender roles, this reconciliation with her past is necessary. Without it, the text implies, she cannot take the final step towards empowerment.

Playwright Marsha Norman, discussing her play *'Night, Mother*, explains the interaction of past and present: "When we talk about our past casually, we can present whatever we choose. But *our* version of the past—as we feel it, as we are haunted by it, as we are held back by it, or in some way defined by it—is our own to escape or make sense of, or to triumph over, or to carry with us."[14] Empowered girls often make sense of or triumph over a troubling past.

Meribah's story adds new dimension to the meaning of "empowered girls." Because her precarious journey has posed dangers unknown to Jo or Angie, she develops a depth of courage and autonomy that her predecessors are never called upon to demonstrate. She is her own rescuer, prevailing over physical hardships and defying social codes when she perceives them as oppressive to others as well as to herself. Despite her ordeal, she never positions herself as a victim. She must become reconciled to her past before determining her future, and the power that she gains by the final page derives from a mature understanding of herself and the world about her, with its spectrum of good and evil.

## The Leaving

Because historical fiction is set during a particular period (often an eventful, even extraordinary, one), it gives the reader a human perspective on historic events through the eyes of its characters as they confront issues that transcend their personal lives. In the best of the genre, setting is not a backdrop but integral to the plot, and Meribah's story, woven tightly into the tapestry of the gold rush, depends in large part on her response not only to her individual hardships but to the destruction of the native cultures and lands of the American West. In contrast, *The Leaving*, by Lynn Hall, is set in an unspecified present in northeastern Iowa and focuses on the personal lives of its characters to the exclusion of whatever might be occurring on a larger scale. Its young protagonist, eighteen-year-old Roxanne Armstrong, has graduated from high school and now, five months later, is preparing to leave her home on the family's farm to take a job in Des Moines, Iowa's capital city. The opening episodes of the novel make clear that she harbors ambivalent feelings about her departure. She resents her taciturn mother and her insensitive father for what she sees as their failure to provide the affection and support she craves. Although she is not sorry to leave her parents, she loves the farm and the security of her community, where she had played girls' basketball for her high school team and has forged close bonds with a couple of her classmates. Nonetheless, she feels compelled to prove—perhaps more to herself than anyone else—that she can succeed in an urban world, can find and hold a job, can make new friends.

*The Leaving* departs in several ways from the formula that has dictated the plot of so many novels about young adult women. For one thing, Roxanne is not the conventionally pretty heroine. The opening page describes her as "somewhat big-nosed," her cheeks "chappy" from the cold, her lips "rough."[15] Nor does she possess any extraordinary qualities: she is a "C" student, an average basketball player, with no particular talent. She has never had a date, and her secret crushes are limited to her English teacher and basketball coach. When the reader meets her, she is feeding the hogs and cows on a raw November afternoon—hardly an auspicious introduction. What distinguishes her is her heightened sense of responsibility. Roxanne performs her chores in the "same order" each day so that she will forget nothing, and she is conscientiously frugal, salvaging the pieces of twine from the baled hay, for example, as she uses each bale for the livestock's food (2).

Over dinner of that same day, she learns that Cletus, her rough and uncommunicative father who does little work around the farm, plans to sell Buck—the horse that he had given her on her twelfth birthday. Although she protests strongly, he counters that "You ain't going to be here. You'll be off in Des Moines living in some apartment. Horse won't do you any good there" (7). Roxanne tries to argue that she will be returning for visits and hopes someday to come with her husband and children, who will ride Buck. Her father replies, "He'll [Buck] be long dead and gone by that time" (7). The inference is clear: Roxanne is unlikely to attract a man soon, if ever. Her mother Thora remains silent during this exchange, and Roxanne is outraged not only that her father would do such a thing but that her mother fails to stand up for her. She searches for an argument "so strong he wouldn't be able to fight it. But logic was no match for paternal power" (8). Implicit in her submission is the recognition that power is a male prerogative against which she has no defense.

Buck has been important to Roxanne. Earlier, he provided her with a sense of security that she so sorely lacked. Her younger school days had been haunted by fear: "Fear of being late, of coming in after the rest of the class was seated and quiet. Fear of not understanding something in the books or on the blackboard and being ridiculed because everyone else knew what it was about" (16). These anxieties were replaced in high school by other apprehensions—the continual threat of tests, the fact that no boy singled her out for attention, and the painful knowledge that while other parents came to cheer her teammates on during their basketball games, neither Cletus nor Thora was in the bleachers. So she fastened her hopes on her team's out-of-town games, where perhaps she would meet some boy who would "be valuable in his own way, as she felt sure she must be valuable in hers if she just knew what is was. Someone of her own" (20). The boy never materialized.

To compound her sense of being unloved, her parents' behavior contrasts starkly with the lavish parental affection she sees bestowed upon her best friend Norma. Thus, when her father surprised her with Buck, she interpreted the gift as "proof" that he loved her. "What a healing salve to rub into the hundreds of small hurts and neglects she had stored away against him" (11) Finally, she, like Norma, had a horse to ride, and Buck also provided her a "ticket" to the inner circle of exhibitors at the county fair.

Given this history, her rage over the impending sale of the horse is easily fathomed: she interprets it as further evidence that her parents care nothing for or about her. That evening, in a heated outpouring to her mother, her emotional needs explode. "[I]f my own parents don't love me, what in the hell are the chances that anyone else in this crumby world is ever going to?" she screams (26).

Roxanne has no way of knowing what the later chapters reveal by shifting the narrative viewpoint to her parents: that her mother loves her dearly, but, unloved herself as a child, cannot find the words or gestures to express her affection and concern, and that her father, who bought the horse as a way of earning his daughter's affection, cares enough for her to stick around until she leaves for Des Moines and sells the horse only to finance his secret escape from a marriage that has been deeply disappointing to both partners.

On the day before her departure, Roxanne puts in a fence connecting the barn to the pasture, thus allowing the calves to come up to
the barn for their hay and water and eliminating the need for someone
to haul their feed to the pasture. She has resented her father for failing
to do this work himself, but once she begins the job, "a kind of satisfaction" comes up in her. "*This* is my kind of work," she thinks. "Not
file-clerking in some office" (49). As she ponders her future in the city,
she cannot imagine a life there that will "fit around Roxanne Armstrong
and make her feel comfortable" (50). She can only think in terms of
"survival."

When she finishes her task, she decides to make it difficult for her
father to capture Buck and load him on the truck. "To heck with him,"
she decides. "If he was going to sell Buck tonight, okay, but he wasn't
going to have it easy" (51). She takes Buck for one last ride and turns
him loose at the far end of the pasture, where he can roam in almost
forty acres of rough land with dense underbrush along the river. It will
take her father at least an hour to find him. This defiance of paternal authority, coupled with anger over the way her father has neglected the
farm all these years, widens the gulf between Roxanne and her father
and heightens her sense of injustice: "He doesn't care about this place. I
do. I love it. Damn, I don't want to leave it. It isn't fair, me going and
him staying" (51). Of course, she has no way of knowing that her father
is also leaving.

Later, when her mother gives permission for Roxanne to take the
car to join her friends for a farewell outing because she "trusts" Roxanne's driving, Roxanne experiences a rush of tenderness for the woman.
Unexpectedly, she "loved her [mother] hard and suddenly, and she
wanted to cry, but she wasn't accustomed to crying, certainly not just because her mother said she trusted Roxanne's driving" (53). These strong
emotions—contempt for her father, sudden deep affection for her
mother—point to the novel's resolution without revealing it.

The next morning the two women leave for Des Moines. As they
drive, Roxanne begins to cry, thinking, "This is it. . . . The beginning of
the big adventure" (96). When her mother asks if leaving is what Roxanne really wants, Roxanne's feelings are paradoxical: "She didn't know
how to tell her mother that leaving the farm was the exact opposite of
what she *wanted*, and that was a big part of why she had to" (96). Instead,
she insists that, yes, going to Des Moines is exactly what she desires.

Her mother then asks one thing of her: don't ever compromise. "Promise me that one thing, and it's the only promise I'll ever ask of you. You study hard at finding out what you want out of this life, and then you hold out for it, and don't settle for anything less" (97). In the conversation that ensues, Roxanne learns that her mother married because it "seemed like the thing to do" (97) and that her life has been a compromise. The two have never engaged in such an intimate conversation before, and Roxanne is moved when her mother admits that hers "hasn't been a world-beater of a marriage," but adds that the union has given her the one thing that means more to her than anything else in the world: her daughter. Still, even at parting, neither uses the word "love." Roxanne manages a "Thanks," and her mother repeats her earlier message: "You figure out what you want out of your life, and don't you settle for less" (100). As seemingly terse as this scene appears, it marks a tender reconciliation between mother and daughter that allows Roxanne to understand a facet of her mother's past and make peace with her own, much as Meribah finally did.

When Thora returns home, she finds the house empty, her husband gone. His absence, however, proves a source of strength: "For the first time in thirty years, Thora Braun [significantly, this is her maiden name] felt that she belonged to herself" (104). She resists the temptation to call Roxanne to say that her father has left, deciding instead to wait for her daughter's visit at Christmas when Roxanne can assess the situation for herself. She wants her daughter home, but recognizes that the girl has her "own needs" (105). The significance of this scene to Roxanne's story lies in Thora's newfound capacity for independence. Women can get along without men, it implies.

Roxanne's experiences in Des Moines, like the earlier chapters, also subvert the formula for girls' fiction. Roxanne finds a job in a large company, but once there, she does not blossom into a beauty or develop sudden business acumen that commands notice from the company executives. However, she does enjoy a modest measure of success. Her job as file clerk is a low-level one, but she "masters" it, and her three-month review describes her as a "fine dependable worker with a better than average sense of responsibility" (115). Although a dashing young man does not appear, she attracts a suitor who is "nice enough," if somewhat disheveled. But she realizes after several dates that she was going out with him "only because it felt so good to have dates after all those years in high school without them" (110). She considers her future with him: she could "get a diamond on her left hand, and a bridal shower, and a wedding in the chapel at First Methodist, and then a little house out in some subdivision, and babies" (110). Unlike the conventional young adult heroine for whom a steady, devoted beau provides a happy ending to her story, Roxanne perceives such a future as a "dismal chain of possibilities," thinking only that it is "nice to have a chance at those things and to choose not to choose them" (110).

Despite her rejection of marriage, Roxanne is not a loner. Although she remains her quiet self, she succeeds in making friends who invite her to move from the rooming house where she has been living and share an apartment with them, another success. After living in the city for a few months, she has gained enough confidence, enough autonomy, to view her future with a clarity that she lacked earlier:

> I got a job and I learned it, and I was good at it. I made friends. I got a boyfriend, and I learned how to get to town on the buses. I did it. I was scared to death to come here, but I came anyway and proved I could do it. Now the question, is this where I really belong? (115)

Her answer is negative, as the final scene of *The Leaving* makes clear. It might well be titled "The Return," for the novel closes much as it opened. It is early spring, not fall, but Roxanne is again in the barnyard, tossing hay down to the livestock. A young sorrel quarter horse, a replacement for Buck, stands among them. As in the opening pages, she tramps into the house, where dinner waits. But there is no man at the table, only Thora and Roxanne, "comfortably smug in the knowledge that they were in for the evening" (116). The final sentence closes Roxanne's story on a note of quiet contentment: "The two women ate their meal wordlessly, but with pleasure" (116).

Roxanne's story shares several elements with Meribah's narrative. Like Meribah, Roxanne rejects the status quo to forge a new self. Although neither her circumstances nor her perception of herself change radically, she has moved not only geographically but psychologically, emerging from her journey to Des Moines more confident and mature. She knows what she wants and is able to enact her vision of what she wants for her life. Like Meribah, she needs community, in this case a comfortable community of mother and daughter made possible by an understanding and acceptance of her past. And like Meribah, she refuses to settle for less than she wants. Heeding her mother's advice, she does not compromise.

Unlike Jo and Meribah, Roxanne lacks a venue for conventional expression, concealing her deepest feelings, even from those closest to her. Yet, in her skillful execution of mundane farm chores and in her creative approach to being more efficient, as when she builds the fence to make feeding the livestock easier, she *is* expressing a significant aspect of what she deems important. And although she says little, her internal dialogue with herself reveals an intensity of emotion and sensitivity, an inner "voice" that grows increasingly expressive and more positive as she gains a sturdier sense of self. Roxanne is one of those empowered girls who must learn to accept what they cannot change, to "take the life they have been given and look it squarely in the eye."[16] She finds strength in community with her mother although it may be less than perfect. It is the connections within community that are empowering for her, not a striving for some utopian ideal. Roxanne's story, then, follows the basic initiation pattern of isolation in the early scenes when she feels betrayed by both parents, trial when she ventures out to the city and new challenges, and reunification in the final scene. Unlike Meribah, she returns home.

## The Lioness Quartet

Alanna, the protagonist of Tamora Pierce's *The Lioness Quartet,* follows a similar path to empowerment in a fantasy world. *The Lioness Quartet,* a series in four volumes, follows a young girl from early to late adolescence as she struggles with acceptance of her gender. Finally reconciled to being female and overcoming self-doubt, she is thus fully able to embrace her gifts to help those around her. *The Lioness Quartet* began in 1983 with the publication of *Alanna* and ended in 1988 with *Lioness Rampant.* Alanna also appears in a later series, *The Immortals,* but the earlier volumes are perhaps the most important because they directly challenge some of the assumptions about gender that have shaped the expectations of the main character and, by extension, those of her readers.

Not surprisingly, Alanna's story starts in unhappiness and thwarted desire, with a lonely childhood in the tradition of many folk tales: she is the daughter of a widowed father obsessed with his scholarship and interested in neither Alanna nor her twin brother, Thom. He plans to have Thom trained as a knight and to send Alanna to a convent to study magic until it is time for her to marry. These are the culturally accepted roles for noble boys and girls in the kingdom of Tortall. Though each child shuns these roles, it is Alanna who devises a plan to thwart her father: she and Thom will switch identities.

Alanna clearly possesses all talents and skills necessary to be a knight: she is strong, agile, brave, and determined. And while those characteristics are integral to her sense of self, they are not her whole self. Pierce makes very clear that an essential part of Alanna's challenge is not simply to establish that she can physically do what knights do but to come to a full acceptance of her other gifts as well. Those other gifts, magic and healing, are most often identified in her culture as female. Initially, she shuns her gifts because they frighten her, but because they constitute her venue for expression, they are a vital element of her empowerment. During the course of the four novels of *The Lioness Quartet* her gradual acceptance of these abilities parallels her acceptance of her gender as a component of her identity, but not the sole or defining one.

Alanna's challenge, then, has two dimensions, an internal and an external one. Her internal challenge is to overcome her fear of her own magical gifts and to accept her ability to be a healer. Her external challenge is to convince the world that a girl can be a knight. These challenges cannot be separated from one another, and, in fact, Alanna's old nurse tells her before she leaves for her training as a knight that denying her ability will have negative consequences:

> You see only the glory. But there's lives taken and families without fathers and sorrow. Think before you fight. Think on who you're fighting, if only because one day you must meet your match. And if you want to pay for those lives you do take, use your healing magic. . . . Heal all you can or you'll pay for it. The gods mean their gifts to be used."[17]

Alanna also resists her healing gifts because she cannot reconcile using them with her notion of how a knight should behave. At one point she tells the King, "I want to be a knight. Using my gift doesn't seem fair, somehow. It's as if I'm fighting dirty" (*Alanna,* 96).

*Alanna* covers eight years of the title character's life, the eight years required to train a knight to "defend the weak, obey your overlord, to champion the cause of right" (22). During this time she masquerades as a young man, acquiring male privilege by assuming masculine dress (much as Meribah discarded her skirts for the convenience of leggings). Her servant Coram initially is the only one who knows her sex. But gradually the circle of those who know her true identity widens to include George, the king of the thieves who in another volume becomes her lover and later her husband; George's mother, who explains the facts of life to her when she starts menstruating; Prince Jonathon, her first lover; and Myles, the older knight who functions as one of her teachers and a surrogate father. The early chapters of *Alanna* focus on Alanna's attempts to integrate herself into the group of young males who are also studying to be knights and to master the various martial arts required of a knight. She must also resolve a conflict with an older boy, Ralon, who bullies her. This conflict is her first testing ground: "She was determined to beat Ralon—it would mean she had finally earned her place among the boys. It would mean she could do anything larger and stronger males could" (68). Alanna needs to beat Ralon not only to establish her place in the group of boys but, more importantly, to silence that part of her that "was always wondering—that she was as good as any boy in the palace" (74). The plot then develops along two lines: Alanna's growing skill as a knight (and her acceptance into the group of boys training to be knights) and her gradual acceptance of her gender. These two lines may explain the great popularity of *The Lioness Quartet* among both male and female young adult readers.

Alanna's struggle to accept her gender provides much of the psychological tension in this first volume. And it is a struggle characteristic of girls facing the onset of adolescence. Peggy Orenstein has argued that sixth grade girls, Alanna's age in the first volume of the series, see their gender as a liability. Following several groups of girls this age through a year of their lives, Orenstein frequently asked them what "was lucky about being a girl?" The overwhelming answer to her question was: "Nothing really. All kinds of bad things happen to girls, like getting your period. Or getting pregnant.... There's nothing lucky about being a girl. ... 'I wish I was a boy'"[18] Alanna herself asks her brother "Why do you get all the fun?" (2), questions frequently asked by girls in novels of fantasy. Cimorene, the protagonist of Patricia Wrede's comic *Dealing with Dragons,* offers a variation on Alanna's question when she rejects "all the things a princess ought to know—dancing, embroidery, drawing, and etiquette" because they are "boring."[19]

As is appropriate for someone aspiring to a life of action, Alanna takes steps to realize her ambition, cutting off her hair to assume the identity of her fictitious brother, Alan. Her masquerade proceeds smoothly until her breasts begin to develop (even fantasy cannot ignore all the facts of life), a change that infuriates her because she associates being female with being "soft and silly" (106). Her resistance to her changing body is grounded in a refusal to accept her identity as a female, something she believes she can deny: "Maybe I was born that way but I don't have to put up with it!" (106). Interestingly, her male servant Coram ties the issue of self-acceptance to happiness while assuring her that she can be both a woman and a warrior: "'Lass, you got to accept who ye are,' he protested, 'Ye can be a woman and a warrior. . . . Alanna, child, ye'll be happy only when ye learn t' live with who ye are'" (107).

Learning to accept who she is becomes more pressing once she begins to menstruate. Pierce devotes an entire chapter ("Womanhood") to this event and its consequences. Alanna reacts with horror when she wakes up to blood on her thighs and sheets. For help she must go to her male friend George, because she lives a life without other females to guide her, the consequence of aspiring to a traditionally male role. She wakes him and reveals her sex for the first time. Because she is accustomed to his sleeping in the nude, she is surprised when he suddenly feels the need to be dressed in front of her. He takes her to his mother, who is a healer. In the space of a few pages Alanna learns that menstruation is normal, that pregnancy can be avoided, and that sex is something a woman enjoys. None of this pleases or comforts Alanna, who still views her gender as an impediment she needs to hide until she becomes a knight at eighteen. She further worries that when her male friends learn what she is, they will hate her and cast her from their circle. When George reassures her she remains disbelieving: "'But I'm a girl,' she cried. 'I'm lying. I'm doing men's things'" (139).

The loss of community is commonly feared by those who challenge conventionally endorsed behaviors, and Alanna is no exception. Perhaps a good part of what makes Alanna and the other novels a fantasy is that so few inhabitants of her world, most of whom are men, question or challenge her aspirations to be a knight and have adventures. Of course, an argument can be made that it is easy for those who occupy positions of privilege to underestimate the difficulty of resisting culturally ordained roles. Though George is marginalized by his status as a thief, he still has greater social mobility as a male than Alanna. Nevertheless, Pierce makes clear that Alanna's difficulties are more internal than external; she herself has the greatest difficulty reconciling her desires with her gender because she is unable to imagine a world in which girls are valued as much as boys and hence allowed the same options.

Orenstein argues that more often than not, girls' diminishment of self-esteem at the onset of adolescence is significantly more dramatic than that experienced by their male counterparts. Orenstein further states that self-esteem has "two sources: How a person views her performance in areas in which success is important to her . . . and how a person believes she is perceived by significant others, such as parents, teachers, and others" (*School Girls,* xvi). Clearly Alanna fits this profile: her concern that she is not, for example, a competent swordsperson motivates her to put herself through endless hours of grueling practice. Her worry that her male friends will reject her once they realize she is a girl shows the extent to which she has internalized the belief that to be female is to be inferior in every respect: "The truth was, she didn't feel worthy of being someone's squire. She was a girl and she was a liar" (*Alanna,* 172). The gap between what Alanna perceives herself to be, an unworthy girl, and what others perceive her to be is maintained until she fights a battle with Prince Jonathon. When her enemies use magic to strip off her clothing and reveal her sex, she finds that her gender has not made her weaker than they: "Alanna held up [her sword's] crystal, letting its light burn into their eyes. The crystal dimmed, and she shouted: 'I may be a girl, but I can defend—or attack as well as any boy!'" (199–200).

In the above passage Alanna's enemy has "smashed into her defenses," and while this phrase has physical implications—she experiences pain, and her clothes are stripped from her—it resonates emotionally as well. Embattled, Alanna asserts her abilities and her self-worth. This process forces her to confront her self-doubts in a way she has previously avoided and to express herself forcefully, using her newly strong voice to overcome the small voice that has taunted her from within whenever she has faced a taller, more powerful opponent. When her enemies scoff at her for being a girl, saying "she is weak, she will give way," Alanna meets their jeers by shouting, "You think so, then try this on for size!" (201).

Alanna's statement is an assertion of selfhood, and this battle functions as a key moment in her empowerment. Although Alanna's sex will not be revealed to the entire court until the next volume of the series, her ability to defeat the "Nameless Ones" (197), coupled with Jonathon's casual acceptance of her gender and her newly found awareness that she has changed internally, enables her to ask for what she has long desired, to be "picked" as Jonathon's squire. When Jonathan objects that she is a "girl," she retorts by drawing favorable comparisons between herself and other young males; interestingly enough, she refers to herself in the masculine, as a potential (swords)*man*: "Even Captain Skalr says I'll be a swordsman yet. I'm as good an archer as Alex. And he's a boy and a squire. I'm a better tracker than Raoul. And have I ever failed you?' To which Jonathan calmly replies, "I'm glad you agree with my reasons . . . I told father you'd probably accept."

An advantage of the series format is that it allows Pierce to take Alanna (and her readers) through several key developmental stages for girls and young women. Over the course of the next three volumes, Alanna and Jonathon become lovers, she is knighted, her sex is revealed to the entire court, she saves the King and Queen by overthrowing the King's wicked wizard brother Roger, she becomes a leader of a desert tribe and trains young girls to use their magic, ends her relationship with Jonathon when he presses for marriage, takes her old friend George as a lover, takes another lover, breaks with him, rescues the foreign princess who will become Jonathon's wife, and, finally, at the end of volume four agrees to marry George.

Though these events track the superficial plots of the novels, they also reveal the gradual transformation in Alanna from a young girl who sees her sex and all that goes with it as a burden to be shunned, to a woman who sees no inconsistency in shedding her armor for ball gowns and jewels. Importantly, Alanna's personal evolution is not confined to her alone but has a ripple effect, as she becomes a model for other women in the kingdom of Tortall. In *Lioness Rampant,* the last volume of *The Lioness Quartet*, Alanna undermines the stereotype of female competitiveness by assuring her friend, Thayet, that their friendship will endure even though they love the same man, King Jonathon:

> "Jonathon needs someone who will treat him like a person, not just a King. . . . I can't. I am his vassal, for all I am his friend. You were born and reared to be royalty. It doesn't frighten you. You won't let him turn into a prig. You won't let him be smug." She hesitated, then said, "I was hoping you'd like him by now."[20]

When Thayet protests that she "can't take" Alanna's man, Alanna's response is a hug and reassurance: "He isn't my man. He's yours, if you love him and he loves you. I want you both to be happy. I prefer you be happy with each other" (302).

*Lioness Rampant,* the last volume in the series, ends by foreshadowing Thayet's marriage to King Jonathon and Alanna's to George. Thus, these two young women, who have fought the king's enemies together, maintain their friendship when one of them marries the lover they have had in common.

Pierce stresses over and over again the need for girls to accept all aspects of their beings, those that have traditionally been viewed as masculine as well as traditionally feminine ones. She also stresses that the fully integrated self is necessary not only for individual happiness but also for that of society as a whole. Alanna's quest for confidence in her own self and worth is not unlike Meribah and Roxanne's experiences in the "real" world. Like them, she moves from letting her value be determined by culturally coded expectations to judging her own merit and, finally, challenging the social order because she recognizes that she cannot grow to true selfhood within its strictures. From her outsider status as a female and the daughter of an indifferent father, she constructs a meaningful place in society.

Empowered girls in young adult literature, then, travel their respective voyages on paths that are both universal and distinctly female. As the stories of Meribah, Roxanne, and Alanna demonstrate, they share with their male counterparts a need to construct a firm sense of self, but they do so by enacting behaviors usually associated with females. Some are expressive and articulate, others quietly efficient. Within a web or network that constitutes a community, they make a place for themselves through meaningful contributions to it, nurturing others without sacrificing their own selves. They come to know themselves well, both their strengths and their weaknesses, and they resist letting themselves be defined by others. When appropriate, they defy socially approved but oppressive behaviors and values, and when caught by painful circumstances not of their own making, they are able to accept what cannot be changed. They are courageous, enthusiastic, and determined.

Just as the closing years of the twentieth century witnessed a profusion of opportunities for women that could not have been imagined earlier in the century, so the representation of girls in young adult literature has also changed. However, the portrayal is hardly uniform. Genre exerts a significant influence on how the female protagonists of young adult literature travel their respective journeys from adolescence into maturity and on how they emerge as empowered young women.

# NOTES

1. "Young Adult Realism: Conventions, Narrators, and Readers," *Library Quarterly* 55.2 (1985), 179.

2. The findings of educators and critics who emphasize this point have spanned the last several decades. See G. Hanna, "Promoting Adolescent Growth through Reading," *Education* 84 (1964), 472–473; M.C. Lorang, Sr., *Burning Ice: The Moral and Emotional Effects of Reading* (New York: Scribner, 1968); L. Blau, "The Novel in High School," in *Readings about Adolescent Literature,* ed. D. Thomison (Metuchen, NJ: Scarecrow, 1970), 45–48; and, for a more recent discussion, Margaret L. Finders, *Just Girls: Hidden Literacies and Life in Junior High* (New York: Teachers College Press, 1997).

3. "Young Adult Female Heroes Do Exist," *The ALAN Review* 17 (Fall 1989), 11.

4. "Young Adult Literature: A Writer Strikes the Genre," *English Journal* (April 1992), 49.

5. "Defusing 'Empowering': The What and the Why," *Language Arts* 64.2 (February 1987), 142.

6. Kathryn Lasky, telephone interview, March 2000.

7. Roberta Seelinger Trites, *Waking Sleeping Beauty: Feminist Voices in Children's Novels* (Iowa City, IA: University of Iowa UP, 1997), 112.

8. Kathryn Lasky, *Beyond the Divide* (New York: Aladdin, 1983), 5; hereafter cited in text.

9. Carol Gilligan, *In a Different Voice: Psychological Theory and Women's Development* (Cambridge, MA: Harvard UP, 1982), xvi.

10. Lyn Mikel Brown and Carol Gilligan, *Meeting at the Crossroads: Women's Psychology and Girls' Development* (Cambridge, MA: Harvard UP, 1992), 20–21.

11. Despite Jo's ultimately conventional role and the fact that Jo is usually read as Alcott's alter ego, Alcott herself elsewhere expressed her discomfort with the nineteenth-century cult of the "true woman" that she essentially endorses in *Little Women.*

12. Shelley Taylor et al., *Female Response to Stress: Tend-and-Befriend, Not Fight-or-Flight.* Manuscript submitted for publication, 1999. Results of this study reported by Erica Goode, "Scientists Find a Particularly Female Response to Stress," *New York Times* (May 19, 2000). See also Christine Gorman, "Sizing Up the Sexes," *Time* (January 20, 1992), 44–48, 51.

13. *Little Women,* xiv.

14. Marsha Norman, *Ms.* (July 1983), 58.

15. Lynn Hall, *The Leaving* (New York: Charles Scribner's Sons, 1980), 1; hereafter cited in text.

16. Alison Cooper-Mullin and Jennifer Marmaduke, *Once Upon a Heroine* (Chicago: Contemporary Books, 1998), xiv.

17. Tamora Pierce, *Alanna* (New York: Random House 1983), 8. All other references from the four novels in this series (*Alanna, In the Hand of the Goddess, The Woman Who Rides Like a Man*, and *Lioness Rampant*) are cited parenthetically in the text.

18. Peggy Orenstein, *School Girls: Young Women, Self-Esteem, and the Confidence Gap* (New York: Doubleday, 1994), xv; hereafter cited in text.

19. Patricia Wrede, *Dealing with Dragons* (New York: Scholastic Inc., 1990), 2–5.

20. Tamora Pierce, *Lioness Rampant* (New York: Random House, 1983–88), 302.

## • 3 •

# Empowered Girls in Historical Fiction

I had often thought about what life might have been like for
children in the past when they had no power and little value.
Especially girl children.

Karen Cushman, "The Historical Novel:
At Home in Time and Place"

$\mathcal{T}$he imagined lives of girls and women in ages past has recently attracted the attention of many writers for children and young adults, a development unforeseen only a few years ago. Publishers had shied away from historical fiction, viewing it as less in demand among readers than novels of contemporary realism or nonfiction. As novelist Leon Garfield once observed, historical fiction was regarded "as being something of an embarrassment, like an elderly relative, to be tolerated out of a sense of duty and reluctantly supported in a condition of genteel poverty."[1] Teachers scrambling to find historical novels for their social studies classes had only limited choices. Then, as an emphasis on multiculturalism sharpened our sensibilities and prompted us to reexamine our perspectives on history, an outpouring of fiction appeared that addressed neglected past events or offered revised viewpoints on them. In fact, historical fiction for children and young adults has been riding such a tide of popularity that publishers are now promoting not only individual books but entire series of historical novels. Patty Campbell notes this phenomenon with ironic humor: ". . . suddenly *historical fiction* is the magic phrase on every publisher's lips, beginning to replace . . . even—saints be praised!—*horror*."[2]

The strong, active male heroes of traditional historical fiction have been joined by a significant number of strong female heroes, a predictable

53

development given the concern with feminist issues ranging from workplace harassment to abortion. Historical fiction, as Jill Paton Walsh points out, is more a reflection of the period that generated it than the time in which the story is set: "If you want to understand a period in history, don't read the contemporary literature of that time, read the historical fiction."[3] Thus, the current attention to the place of girls and women in the actual contemporary world coincides with an increasing number of historical novels exploring the place of girls and women in earlier cultures.

Most historical fiction is, by definition, set decades or centuries ago, although some novels unfold in more recent times. In an article titled "Writing Historical Fiction," literary critic and novelist Thomas Mallon cites his own experience with the genre by discussing his coming-of-age novel set in 1968,[4] the same time period as S.E. Hinton's *The Outsiders* and Paul Zindel's *The Pigman*, neither of which are classified as historical fiction. However, Mallon's novel, unlike *Outsiders* and *Pigman*, focuses on how the central characters respond to a historically significant event and their attitudes towards the time-specific circumstances of their lives. It is this focus that allows "historical fiction" to offer human perspectives on the past, and many girls in young adult historical fiction react not only to general historical circumstances but also to the constraints of "being a girl" in their respective cultures. They often resist the tyrannical dictates that constrain their behavior at the time of the story and may defy stifling social customs. They may find themselves at odds with bullying men and boys or with domineering women whose only real power lies in exercising authority over children, especially girls. They may challenge unjust systems in an attempt to right the balance of power. The novels in which they appear tend to assume a reader highly sympathetic to the protagonist's dilemma and therefore open to an increased understanding of how oppressive social practices have situated girls and women.

Although readers tend to resist didactic fiction and heavy-handed messages, they seem more accepting and less defensive of what historical fiction has to say about such sensitive issues than if a novel were directly addressing a similar subject in a contemporary setting. Novelist Erik Christian Haugaard accounts for this reaction from his perspective as a writer of historical fiction: "When you write a story that takes place in times past, you are more free. Your readers have less prejudice and will accept your tale with open minds. You and your reader have less at stake, and thus you might get nearer to the truth, possibly even to reality."[5] Readers who might otherwise reject or sneer at contemporary stories overtly arguing the harmful effects of patriarchal culture and the exploitation of females can read a historical novel making these same arguments with a clear conscience and open mind: the story offers no direct indictment of their own world or beliefs, although they may connect the fiction to the circumstances of their lives.

The female protagonists in historical fiction are almost always rendered vulnerable by both their youth and gender, and some must contend as well with tyrannical conditions brought on by race and/or class. Nonetheless, despite being victimized by greed, hatred, and persecution, they manage to achieve more control of their lives, gaining strength and status. By the final pages they have earned the accolade of "empowered" girls, their stories often following a classic quest structure of isolation, trial, and triumphant reunification. Author Ann Schlee, discussing her own historical novels, accounts for the prevalence of this pattern in historical fiction:

> In a way, almost all children's books are legends of power and weakness. One has to develop a child character who is, in a sense, a hero with power over the action of the story. Yet, in reality children don't have power over their situations. In the past children were far more exploited, but they also were much more caught up in the web of adult existence. In writing about the past, the writer has the chance to depict their extraordinary adventures and seizures of power.[6]

Although "seizures of power" aptly characterizes the plots of novels about both young men and women living in earlier times, it is particularly applicable to the stories of young women unfolding when even adult women had no legal rights and female children were perceived as having little value. Katherine Paterson has said, "The characters in history or fiction that we remember are those who kicked against the walls of their societies,"[7] and the young female protagonists in historical fiction often kick so hard that even if the walls don't come tumbling down, the foundations are at least shaken. These triumphant girls can be immensely satisfying to young readers, who have a greater need than adults to identify with the central character or characters of a story, and Jean Boreen has pointed out that their stories have produced many commendable role models for female readers.[8]

Still, this welcome profusion of strong girls in historical fiction poses its own problems. Some authors who write in the genre, including several respected for their meticulous research, have sacrificed historical credibility for the sake of creating an interestingly empowered character. For example, Karen Cushman's protagonist Birdie of *Catherine Called Birdie* records in her diary the outrages she suffers as a girl, especially because of her father's nearly successful efforts to marry her off to a repulsive nobleman. Her bawdy sense of humor and comic observations of events and people in her life combine to create a vivid, likable character. Given her feisty character, her resistance is believable, her voice engaging, and one cheers her rebellion against what are clearly oppressive practices. The novel won a Newbery Medal and garnered other critical acclaim as well, but there is merit in Roberta Seelinger Trites' objection that Birdie's literacy seems less than credible for a thirteenth-century girl.[9]

Avi's *The True Confession of Charlotte Doyle* exemplifies a similar problem. Charlotte, a young woman raised in a sheltered, upper-class family headed by a domineering patriarch, finds herself the only female crossing the Atlantic on a trading ship commanded by a Captain Jaggery. Although she initially admires him, he reveals himself during the voyage as a cruel lout, and Charlotte joins the crew in a mutiny. She emerges by the end of the novel not only sexually undefiled by any of the crew—a rough and tumble bunch apparently oblivious to the female allure of their pubescent passenger—but as their captain. This novel, like *Birdie,* reaped its share of awards, including a Newbery Honor, but it also attracted some strong criticism. While Jean Boreen notes that her female students have found Charlotte an admirable role model because of her courage and stamina, she acknowledges that "even though the book is historically well-researched, it is hard to imagine that a 'real' girl raised in the culture of early 19th century New England would have the temerity to rise up against an authority figure like Captain Jaggery" (15). Similarly, Anne Scott Macleod found the novel "a fine adventure story" but "preposterous."[10] Avi took strong exception to such objections, strenuously defending his novel as fiction and claiming that "it is a legitimate task . . . of fiction to re-invent the past, if you will, so as to better define the future. . . . Historical fiction—among other things—is about today's possibilities."[11]

This appears to be a dubious argument at best, ignoring as it does a prime criterion of credibility demanded by good historical fiction. Perhaps an author writing to "better define the future" would do well to choose other genres in which to do so, such as contemporary realism, biography, and fantasy. But to impose a current feminism on a story set 150 years ago, particularly one whose carefully researched details about ships and sea life anchors it firmly in the category of historical realism, seems less than defensible. Although the ideology of a historical novel will inevitably reflect the current sensibilities of its author, the character's actions and beliefs must be compatible with the historical framework of the story.

How, then, does a young adult historical novel portray "empowered" girls without violating its own credibility, creating a story whose protagonist is heroically compelling and also probable? Writers have developed a range of characters and plot strategies that allow for a satisfying and positive outcome while remaining true to the time period of the story. The genre is so diverse that it resists tidy classification, but, in general, the female protagonists of young adult historical fiction fall into three broad categories.

The young women in the first category become strong on a limited scale within the gender constraints of their own world. They begin in a position of extreme disadvantage, displaced in some significant way or another. Perhaps they lack family or community; they are often poor, persecuted, and despairing, resigned to cruelty and a bleak future. Their primary success often consists of conquering their own self-doubts to establish a place for themselves in the world. Along the way, they may also triumph over a specific antagonist or disrupt an unjust social structure, but these events usually rely on their growing self-confidence.

Female protagonists in the second category are more secure at the outset. Their "place" in the world as a girl or young woman may be tightly constrained by gender and the mores of their respective communities, but, restrictive as it may be, it is at least secure. They have developed a sense of self sufficiency to spark an image of a more exciting, less confined future; although they defy gender constraints, they may do so less to mount a direct challenge than to realize their aspirations, and because they initially have more to lose by violating conventions, their empowerment may exact a significant toll. Their strength comes at a price.

The young women in the third category are, like the protagonists in the second category, aware of gender constraints and other injustices, but they are openly rebellious, their resistance more a result of their wanting to escape or overturn oppressive systems than to realize personal ambition. They usually enjoy an unqualified victory made credible by some extraordinary circumstances. Granted, some novels feature female protagonists who resist fitting into any of these categories, whereas other novels develop multiple protagonists, each of whom fits different or overlapping categories. Still, this schema provides at least a framework for exploring the relationship between historical fiction and its empowered girls.

The protagonist of Karen Cushman's *The Midwife's Apprentice* exemplifies the first category as she travels an uneven path to an empowerment. Cushman writes that this novel began with its title, which she loved and carried with her for a long time. She didn't know what the story was about until she imagined "a small homeless child sleeping on a dung heap, longing for a name, a full belly, and a place in the world."[12] That child, living in medieval times when compassion for such children was rare and any social apparatus to care for them nonexistent, must develop confidence in her own competence as a prelude to any shift in her external circumstances. When the reader meets her in the opening chapter, she has burrowed into the "warm rotting" of a dung heap, where "she dreamed of nothing, for she hoped for nothing and expected nothing."[13] She has no sense of identity, no name but Brat, a reflection of the unkind epithets flung at her during her childhood. She is ignorant of her age, without family or home, and the novel's first paragraph describes her with a string of negative adjectives: "unwashed, unnourished, unloved, unlovely" (1). The village boys call her Dung Beetle, and like all the boys who have tormented the girl in the past, they are the "scrawniest or the ugliest or the dirtiest or the stupidest boys" (3) in the village, picked on by everyone else. Their taunting illustrates the village power structure that renders the girl so vulnerable: among even the boys at the bottom of the hierarchy, she is a helpless victim.

Her first step toward empowerment occurs when a village midwife discovers her in the dung heap and senses that she has found a helper willing to be exploited in exchange for food. The midwife christens her "Beetle," and although the name echoes the boys' taunts, it *is* a given name that signifies a new identity: she is now a midwife's apprentice with a "place" for herself on the floor of the woman's cottage. Her new abode may be colder than the dung heap, but it is cleaner. Still, this is hardly an auspicious beginning. The midwife, Jane Sharp, is a hard taskmaster,

quick to criticize Beetle and as free with abuse as she is miserly with rec-
ompense. Jane's greed has angered the villagers, but because they need
her, they transfer their hostility to Beetle. Nor is Beetle allowed to assist
in the births themselves, lest she observe enough to become a competi-
tor. However, accustomed to using her wits to survive, the girl is clever,
and she begins to learn the midwife's trade, discerning that "it is as much
about hard work and good sense" as magic (16).

Early in the story, Beetle acquires a pet, a stray cat who is also tormented by the village boys. Although the girl has received no nurturing
during her short life, she has nurturing instincts, sharing her meager food
allotment with the cat and providing him with a nest of baby mice that
she finds frozen in the cold. The mice are already dead, but Beetle's heart
"aches" when she thinks of the tiny bodies in the cat's strong jaws, so she
buries them deep in the dung heap for the cat to ferret. In a telling incident, the village boys tie the cat into a sack with an eel and throw both
into a pond. Horrified, Beetle drags the sack from the water, although she
is "sore afraid" of the eel, an obvious phallic symbol. However, her concern for the cat overcomes her fear, and she slits open the bag with a
sharp stone. When the eel slithers out, he looks "like the Devil himself"
(9), a parallel to her perception of the boys who have bedeviled her during her life. With the eel gone, Beetle retrieves the limp body of the cat
and lays him in the dung heap for warmth. Knowing of no prayers or
"sweet songs," she cannot speak gently to him and must settle for curs-
ing: "Damn you, cat, breathe and live, you flea-bitten sod, or I'll kill you
myself" (9). The cat does recover, to Beetle's relief, and she celebrates by
telling him what she remembers of her life. Her storytelling is empowering, for with this incident, Beetle begins to develop a voice and a sense
of self: she has lived a life worth telling about, and the cat provides the
necessary listening ear. She has taken a first step towards becoming part
of a community.

However, she suffers several setbacks. Thoroughly demeaned by the
names the midwife and villagers hurl at her—lackwit, clodpole, brain-
less—as well as the objects pitched in her direction—pots, jugs, sausages,
sticks—Beetle works twice as hard and talks half as much, afraid of being
turned out of the midwife's cottage. Her voice has been silenced. Then
fortune—or the midwife's misfortune—intervenes. Preparing to attend a
fair in a neighboring village for supplies, Jane Sharp twists her leg and,
bedridden, must send Beetle. The fair opens a new world for the girl. A

merchant, charmed by her youthful innocence, gives her a comb, a wink, and a promise that if she uses it on her long curls, she will have a lover before nightfall. Beetle, who has never owned anything except the ragged clothes on her back, now has something to call her own. The wink and the promise are also gifts that "nestled into Beetle's heart" (30), and when she sees her reflection in a horse trough, for the first time she perceives an attractive feature: curls instead of tangles in her dark hair.

Bent over the trough, she hears a man mistake her for someone named Alyce, asking her to read some marks on a piece of leather to verify his winning bet on a horse race. This is a transforming moment, and, staring once more at her face in the water, she thinks, "This face . . . could belong to someone who can read. And has curls. And could have a lover before nightfall. And this is me, Beetle" (31). Still, she reflects, Beetle is no name for such a person, and she renames herself Alyce, which sounds "clean and friendly and smart. You could love someone named Alyce" (32). Her sense of self has taken a significant leap forward.

When no one in the village accepts her new name, Alyce realizes that the "business of having a name was harder than it seemed. A name was of little use if no one would call you by it" (35). That is, one's sense of self derives from external as well as internal sources: it depends on others to validate what one perceives about oneself, and this validation comes slowly for Alyce. The first person to use the new name is one of the village bullies who, along with the other boys, has chased her to the river bank, where she clambers up a tree. The boy, drunk with ale, slips into the river and, unable to swim, flounders in the current while the other boys run off. Alyce's response is both clever and credible, for it avoids the heroic while allowing her to play the rescuer. Like the boy Will, she cannot swim, but she creeps out on a branch until its tip touches the water where Will can grab it. He praises her as "brave," but Alyce sets the record straight: "'Naw, I be not brave,' she said. 'I near pissed myself. I did it for else you'd have drowned and gone to Hell, a drunken loudmouth bully like you, and I would have helped send you there, and I could not have that, now, could I?'" (39). When Will says, "You have pluck, Beetle," the girl reminds him of her new name and he responds, "You have pluck, Alyce" (39). That night, Alyce, who had "dreamed of nothing," dreams that "the pope came to the village and called her Alyce and the king married the midwife and the cat laughed" (38). In her humbled mind, none of these events are more preposterous than what has transpired that afternoon—an acknowledgment of her newly constructed self by a former tormentor.

Still, her triumph is brief, for most of the villagers continue to ignore her, and the attention she does receive is unwelcome: the children rub chicken manure in her hair, the miller pinches her rump. Alyce cannot defy the villagers openly, so she uses subterfuge to undermine those responsible for her oppression. Living in a superstitious age, she takes advantage of the villagers' credulous nature and fear of the Devil by carving a pair of wooden hoofs and imprinting the "Devil's footprints" along a path to those who have treated her ill. When the villagers follow the footprints, they discover some dark secrets, such as the miller's theft of grain and the midwife's affair with a married baker. Alyce also uses trickery to fend off the bullies who are teasing the cat, threatening to spatter them with rat's blood (actually a vial of blackberry cordial) and to summon the Devil, who will change them into women so that they will "giggle" and "wear dresses" and "give birth" (55). Her threat, which frightens the boys so much that they worry about it until they are "quite old," signifies the rank of females in the village: it is so ignoble that the prospect of becoming female is for a male among the most terrible punishments imaginable. So Alyce is able to turn her gender, which makes her so vulnerable, against those who have taken advantage of it. Both episodes are a cross between the David-and-Goliath archetype and Brer Rabbit stories, a triumph of the powerless over the powerful and a trickster's tale with Alyce as the wily rabbit.

Trickster stories have enjoyed a renaissance lately, for powerlessness is no longer unique to women, children, and other marginalized groups. As Lissa Paul has noted, "[S]omething in [these] stories is in touch with the temper of our time. . . . And with the new consciousness of the value of the small, weak, and powerless protagonist, there is a renewed interest in a survival tactic that has long been out of favor. Deceit."[14] She adds that because deceit is not a manly virtue, it is more often the tactic of heroines than heroes, who must—after all—fight openly for their honor. Empowered girls are not above being crafty and duplicitous—but only in the service of a moral and just outcome.

Alyce's newly learned skills as a midwife empower her further. When a village boy implores her to assist his cow who is having a painfully stalled labor, she at first refuses out of fear, but stirred by the animal's mournful cries, she finally delivers twin calves, a sign of great luck in the village. When she tells the cat about the twins, she finds that her words are a rhyme and she sets them to a tune, she who earlier had known no songs. Her voice is growing strong and communicative. She now finds herself giving advice to the villagers who have learned of her abilities and seek her help. She also is on hand when the midwife abandons the bailiff's wife during a difficult labor, sure that the baby would die before it is born, and goes instead to assist in a birth at the manor house. The desperate bailiff demands that Alyce take charge, and, using what she has learned, she delivers the woman of a healthy baby girl, whom the parents name Alyce Little in her honor. This gives Alyce so much pride and satisfaction that she smiles—for the first time in her life. Her skills as a midwife have helped her to become more emotionally expressive. That night she has her second dream, this one about her mother. Although she cannot remember it in the morning, she has made a connection to her past.

A few days later she comes upon a young urchin sleeping in the cowshed, and she uses her developing empowerment to empower him, bringing him food and fending off the village bullies with threats to reveal their latest thefts or to sprinkle them with "rat's blood." The boys back off, whining that they only meant to "wag" him since Alyce is "sport no more" (64), an admission that confirms the girl's growing power. The boy says his name is Runt, but Alyce, by now cognizant of the importance of a real name, insists that the boy pick another. He decides to name himself after the king, who, Alyce discovers after making several inquiries, is called Edward. She then sends the child on to the manor house, where boys are needed to help with the threshing, and the thought of the hungry boy sated with the manor's abundant supply of food so satisfies her that it provides a protective shield against the unpleasant aspects of her own life. Her unselfish nurturing instincts have again served her well.

Then Alyce's fortunes suffer a reversal. She is called upon to deliver another baby, but the difficult birth defies her limited skills, and she must send for the midwife. After witnessing Jane's successful delivery, Alyce feels defeated, her fragile sense of self destroyed. She leaves the village, the cat following, again feeling that she is "nothing." The road takes her to an inn, where the innkeeper's wife hires her on as a helper, impressed by the girl's willingness to work hard. During her months at the inn, she comes to the attention of Magister Reese, a scholar who is spending the winter there in study, and although Alyce feels herself too "stupid" to learn anything, the man senses that the girl is clever and intelligent. Pretending to teach the cat to read while Alyce looks on from a dark corner, he introduces Alyce to basic literacy. One day, he asks her what she wants, whereupon Alyce replies after some thought, "A full belly, a contented heart, and a place in this world" (81). Then she adds that it is her "misfortune instead to be hungry, out of humor, and too stupid to be a midwife's apprentice" (81). Magister Reese slyly counters that she is not so stupid, for she can read as well as the cat. With that, Alyce smiles again. Another milestone.

Then two people from Alyce's former village stop by the inn. The first is the man whose cow Alyce had delivered of twins, and he reassures her with words that stay with the girl in the weeks to follow: "Just because you don't know everything don't mean you don't know nothing. Even Jane Midwife herself don't know everything, though she think she do" (85). Next comes that very midwife, who pretends not to see Alyce, but Alyce eavesdrops on her conversation with Magister Reese. Jane describes her former apprentice as not as "stupid" as some she has had and "better company," but adds, "She was not what I needed" (88). Alyce interprets the reason to be her earlier failure, but the midwife explains that Alyce did not meet her expectations "because she gave up" (88). Without knowing it, Alyce is learning the value of perseverance.

When spring turns to summer, she is seized by the desire to find Edward, anxious lest he be unhappy. She imagines herself bringing him back to the inn and caring for him; this, she thinks, will "make her heart content" (90), fulfilling her need to nurture. But, in fact, when Alyce sees Edward, she finds he is happy at the manor and hopes to stay. "So Alyce learned about the mighty distance between what one imagines and what is" (97), but she also feels relief that she has not failed the boy by sending him to the manor. Her relief is so great that she sighs deeply, sighs that finally turn to wracking sobs. This is the first time she has ever cried, and, like her smiles, the sobs mark a turning point in her development: she is becoming more and more in touch with her inner self and, therefore, more able to express her feelings.

Her visit to the manor contributes to her development in other ways, too. Edward persuades her to stay the night and begs for a bedtime story. Alyce's first attempt at storytelling, hardly more than an anecdote, fails to satisfy the boy, who tells her that a proper tale must have a "hero and brave deeds" (99). Alyce responds with a summary of Edward's life that could well be her own: "Well then, once there was a boy who for all he was so small and puny was brave enough to do what he must although he didn't like it and was sometimes teased" (99). Her story is an unacknowledged recognition that she, like Edward, is a "hero" capable of "brave deeds," however modest.

The next day she helps to wash the sheep before they are sheared and discovers while soaping them in the river that under all the dirt, her own skin is pink and her face, "unmarked by pox or witchcraft" (103), is indeed pretty. Although she is not interested in the attentions of men—she rejects the overtures of one by saying, "My hair may be frizzled but my wit is not. Save your sticky kisses for your wife or your cow" (91)—her confidence in her appearance helps to mend her confidence in herself, and she returns to the inn renewed. Shortly thereafter, a merchant and his wife stumble into the inn, the woman in acute pain, the man frantic because he thinks his wife, who has been barren all the years of their marriage, is being devoured by a "stomach worm." Alyce, watching from under the stairs, knows that the woman is in labor. Although the scene reminds her painfully of her earlier failure at midwifery, she is kept there by her "sympathy and compassion" (107). Finally, after an argument with herself over whether she can indeed help the woman, she steps forward and does "every single thing she had seen the midwife do and even invented some of her own" (109). When she delivers a lusty boy, the merchant falls to his knees, calling her an angel and a saint. Alyce replies with the same blunt modesty that she demonstrated when she rescued the drowning boy: "No saint, no angel. Corpus bones, I but delivered a child. Your wife never had a stomach worm" (110). Then, stepping outside, she encounters the scholar, who winks at her. In return, Alyce laughs, a "true laugh that came from deep in her gut" and that was "the true miracle" of the night (111). Alyce has traveled far: she is now self-confident, emotionally expressive, and skillful.

Suddenly, she has many offers of a "place": the merchant wants her to come to Salisbury with his family as a nursery maid, the scholar invites her to Oxford as a companion to his aged sister, and the innkeeper's wife wants her to stay on at the inn. She has moved from someone who had no place to stay to someone with a "surfeit" of place. But she rejects all these offers.

> She was a midwife's apprentice with a newborn hope of being someday
> a midwife herself. She had much still to learn, and she knew a place

where she could learn it. . . . That was her place in this world for right
now, and though her belly would likely never be full, her heart was content. (114)

That night, she has her third dream, that "she gave birth to a baby who
gave birth to a baby and so on and so on" (114). She has chosen to involve herself in a helping profession, and her dream signifies the inter-
generational connections of women down through the ages. Cushman
writes in an Author's Note at the end of the book that midwifery in medieval England was a less than honorable profession, "mostly because it
was practiced by and on women" (119). But Alyce is oblivious to its relative status. She knows where her future lies, and only one leg of her
journey remains. She returns to the midwife's cottage.

At first, the midwife will not have her, although Alyce declares that
she now knows about "babies and birthing, singing songs and cooking
chickens, crying and laughing and reading" (115). Rejected, she turns
again from the village, but this time, the cat refuses to follow. And Alyce,
now understanding the meaning of the midwife's "need," shouts through
the closed door to the midwife, "I can do what you tell me and take what
you give me, and I know how to try and risk and fail and try again and
not give up. I will not go away" (116–17). In the novel's closing scene,
the door opens, admitting Alyce. "And the cat went with her" (118).

The protagonist of *The Midwife's Apprentice* is, like Birdie of Cushman's earlier novel, an engaging character, but unlike Birdie, she is not
privileged by class. She must develop the spunk and skills that lead to her
empowerment, and her gradual progress is plausible. In overcoming ab-
ject poverty and unbridled persecution, she is indeed the "hero" that Edward has demanded of a story. Although her "brave deeds" are not those
of high adventure, they nevertheless demand courage and grit. But
Alyce's triumph is distinctly female, depending as it does on her becoming emotionally expressive and nurturing, on her need to empower others as she herself becomes empowered, and on a strong desire to find a
secure place within a community. And although at certain junctures she
depends on the kindness of strangers, she ultimately takes responsibility
for her own empowerment. This characterization is deliberate on Cushman's part. She writes:

As children are what they eat and hear and experience, so too they are
what they read. And this is why I write what I do, about strong young

women who in one way or another take responsibility for their own lives; about tolerance, thoughtfulness, and caring; about choosing what is life-affirming and generous; about the wonderful ways that people are the same and the ways they are different and how rich that makes us all. ("Historical Novel," 29)

## OUT OF THE DUST

In many ways this description of "strong young women" also fits Billie Jo Kelby, the protagonist of Karen Hesse's *Out of the Dust*. However, Billie Jo's story falls into the second category of a protagonist who begins with some degree of confidence, whose circumstances early on engender an ambition that drives the story, and who overcomes gender constraints and other obstacles to realize it—but at a cost. Unlike Alyce, Billie Jo enjoys a "place" in the world, secure as the only child of a hard-working Oklahoma farm family during the Dust Bowl years of the early 1930s. And if she lacks a "full belly" in this time of drought, she is at least served the requisite meals by her mother, even though the portions are scanty and heavily laced with dust. What she lacks is a contented heart, for she has a "hunger" for playing "fierce piano," an ambition sparked by lessons from her musically talented mother and fueled by her own innate ability.[15] At the outset, it seems likely that she will satisfy her hunger. The local music teacher asks her to play a solo at the Palace Theatre and then at a party in honor of President Roosevelt's birthday. Billie Jo exults in her performances, feeling "the best" she's ever felt while "playing hot piano," "sizzling" as her classmate Mad Dog sings along. She feels a sense of community, and the camaraderie lifts her spirits out of the dust.

Hesse tells Billie Jo's story in the girl's voice, her narration cast as a series of poems in free verse, each with its own title. The novel spans an entire year, with eight sections divided by seasons, beginning with Winter 1934 and closing with Autumn 1935. A significant plot development in each section moves the story along at an even pace. Billie Jo's voice is strong, and her vivid imagery conveys the grit and desolation of the dust's ceaseless invasion. Yet, despite the arid landscape and the difficulty of her family's struggles, the novel opens on an emotionally warm note. Billie Jo's mother is pregnant again, hopeful that she will deliver a full-term baby after several miscarriages, Billie Jo feels confident that her "place in the world is at the piano" (49), and her father trusts that the next spring will bring rain and a bumper wheat crop. There is a real sense of caring among the people in Billie Jo's community; they look out for each other, sharing the little they have with those in greater need, and they enjoy the simple pleasures of small-town living—the country dances, the local talent contests, the small but satisfying triumphs of daily life.

Like Alyce, Billie Jo has "found a way of gaining what [she] wants" by playing the sly trickster —in this case, permission from her mother to perform at the Palace. "I can ask her something in such a way/ I annoy her just enough to get an answer,/ but not so much I get a no . . . by catching Ma off guard," she confides. "Right out asking her is no good" (12). Although her communication with her parents is inhibited by their own needs—her father had hoped for a boy instead of a "long-legged girl/ with a wide mouth/ and cheekbones like bicycle handles" (3), and her mother is withdrawn, distracted by the coming birth and the dust— Billie Jo nonetheless has developed an expressive self, her narration and musical ability articulating deeply felt emotions. She is a strong student, scoring at the top of her grade on a recent test and so proud of her achievement that she longs for praise from her taciturn mother instead of the perfunctory "I knew you could" that Ma offers (30). Billie Jo complains that "she makes me feel like she's just/ taking me in like I was/ so much flannel dry on the line." Yet she loves her Ma, who can coax soft glances from Billie Jo's exhausted father "with her fine tunes" and "fancy fingerwork" at the piano (25). Later, when Billie Jo accidentally catches a glimpse of Ma, by now heavy with child and streaked with dust, showering in a light spring rain, her description is tender: "My dazzling ma, round and ripe and striped/ like a melon" (56).

Then irrevocable disaster strikes. Billie Jo's father has carelessly left a pail of kerosene next to the wood-burning stove in the kitchen, and her mother, thinking it water, pours it to make breakfast coffee. The pail full of kerosene bursts into flames, sending Ma running out of the house. Billie Jo, mindful of the "bone-dry kitchen," grabs the burning pail and throws its contents out the door, not knowing Ma is running back in. The flames splash on her mother's apron, turning her into a "column of fire" (61). Frantic, Billie Jo tries to beat the flames out with her bare hands, burning them severely, but her efforts are in vain. Her injured mother dies days later giving birth to a son, who lives only briefly, leaving Billie Jo scarred both physically and emotionally. She has almost no use of her hands, and, having overheard the neighbors explain the accident by saying "Billie Jo threw the pail" (71), she is overwhelmed by a sense of guilt. She also harbors a searing resentment of her father, who took the emergency money Ma had put away—mostly a few dimes that Billie Jo earned playing piano—and, while his wife lay in her death throes, had gone to town and drunk himself into a stupor.

Billie Jo, then, is faced with the monumental task of adjusting to life without her mother and the expected baby and of forgiving her father, who has withdrawn into a silent, brooding man, grieving for his wife and his wheat crop lost to dust and grasshoppers. He ignores the cancerous spots that have appeared on his face, although he knows what they are; his father "had those spots too" (154). Billie Jo fears that she will lose her father as well as her mother. Nor, with her hands so crippled, can she find solace in playing her beloved piano.

Her emotional and physical recovery is both slow and torturous. Hesse has said that "every relationship in the book—not only the relationships between the people but also the relationships between the people and the land—is about forgiveness" (*Dust*, n.p.), and Billie Jo must learn to forgive her father, just as the land must heal from years of abuse. Her teacher, Miss Freeland, has explained the causes of the Dust Bowl, the history of the destructive farming practices that brought short-term profit at great cost to the future. "Such a sorrow doesn't come suddenly,/ there are a thousand steps to take/ before you get there," Miss Freeland says (84), and the land must take another "thousand steps" towards recovery. Although it rains in the early sections, these rains are either too scant to soak the ground or so hard and fast that they do little more than muddy the surface.

Billie Jo, too, must take her "thousand steps" before she can put the past behind her. At times she tries to find relief from her sorrow, but like the land, her heart remains arid. Her attempts to play the piano again either create intolerable pain or paralyze her at the keyboard, and the hands that swing uselessly at her sides are "only lumps of flesh/ that once were . . . long enough to span octaves" (73). Her father is a "stranger," obsessed with digging an enormous hole to hold pond water "to feed off the windmill" (77). Billie Jo's mother had argued in vain for such a pond, unable to convince her husband of its merit, but now, as if to atone for his carelessness, her father digs and digs. Nonetheless, although she can "almost" forgive him for taking Ma's money and getting drunk, she can't forgive him "that pail of kerosene" left by the stove. She feels as if there is no escape. Had she been the boy her father wished for, she could have joined the CCC, but her gender—like the other circumstances that bind her—has closed off that option.

Billie Jo finds her mother's absence as painful as her burnt hands. When her school class tops all of Oklahoma again on the state tests, she longs to share the triumph with her mother. This time, her mother's "I knew you could" would be "enough" (99). Yet, there are hints that healing has begun, for both the land and Billie Jo. A January rain revives the frail wheat stalks, although its aftermath is nothing but a coat of mud on everything, and at the President's Birthday Ball, Billie Jo dances with her father to the music of the Black Mesa Boys. "Most of the night I think I smiled," she says. "And twice my father laughed./ Imagine" (116). A migrant family, the mother "pretty far along" with child, moves into Billie Jo's school, and the children make a big pot of soup each day to share with them. Billie Jo brings a few things intended for Franklin, her dead brother, and when the baby is born, a "perfect" little girl, she is dressed in a feed-sack nightgown that was Franklin's. All is not death and dust. Billie Jo even gathers up the courage to enter a local talent contest and manages to win third prize for her piano playing. Momentarily, she feels "part of something grand," even though her hands hurt so much that she can't hold her ribbon or prize dollar (133).

Still, such moments of gratification cannot begin to balance her pain; she is too "filled with bitterness,/ it comes from the dust, it comes/ from the silence of my father, it comes/ from the absence of Ma" (195). Finally, Billie Jo wants only to be "out of the dust," and in the middle of one August night in 1935, she surreptitiously leaves her father's house, knowing, as she says, "that I'll die if I stay,/ that I'm slowly, surely/ smothering" (197). She hops a boxcar on a train headed west, and this journey, which is both inward and outward, marks a turning point in her rite of passage.

After two days on the train, she is joined by another person fleeing west, a man who has left behind a wife and three children. Billie Jo gives him two of the biscuits she has taken from her home, although she knows she'll be hungry that night, and he tells her his story, a variation on her own: the dust, his hungry children, the feelings of failure. She tells him about her Ma dying, about Ma's piano, about her father. The man, Billie Jo decides, is "like tumbleweed," whereas her father is "more like the sod./ Steady, silent, and deep." In the comparison lies an epiphany: "My father/ stayed rooted, even with my tests and my temper,/ even with the double sorrow of/ his grief and my own, he had kept a home/ until I broke it" (202). When the train reaches Flagstaff, Arizona, Billie Jo gets off, and a government worker helps her arrange a return trip home.

Once back, she begins to reconcile with her father, calling him "Daddy" for the first time since her mother's death. She also realizes that the dust, which she so longed to escape, is "inside" her. Her words to her father constitute a recognition that she cannot run away from who and what she is: "I tell him he is like the sod,/ and I am like the wheat, and I can't grow everywhere,/ but I can grow here, with a little rain, with a little care,/ with a little luck" (205). The closing lines of this section signal her willingness to make peace with her past: "I am forgiving him, step by step,/ for the pail of kerosene./ As we walk together,/ side by side/ in the sole-deep dust,/ I am forgiving myself/ for all the rest" (206).

She is healing physically, too. She and her father pay a visit to the doctor, who—hoping that the cancer has not spread—cuts the malignant spots from her father's face and gives Billie Jo some ointment for her hands along with the advice to "quit picking at them" and use them, assuring her that they will "heal up fine" if she does (210).

Billie Jo's final steps to moving on with her life involve a woman named Louise, who has stayed with her father the days she was gone. Without intending to, Billie Jo "likes" her, although with reservations: "I didn't know/ if there was room for her/ in me, [but] I could see there was room for her in Daddy" (213). Slowly, Louise wins the girl's affection, listening without comment as Billie Jo confides her feelings about the accident, her hands, her love for her mother's dust-covered piano, "And I know she's heard everything I said,/ and some things I didn't say" (218).

The novel ends on an upbeat note. The pond stays filled, nourishing Ma's garden and apple trees, the wheat crop is promising, and there is "the smell of green,/ of damp earth,/ of hope returning to our farm. . . . And the certainty of home, the one I live in,/ and the one/ that lives in me" (220–21) Billie Jo has learned that all that time she was trying to get out of the dust, what she is is "because of the dust" (222), and what she is, she says, "is good enough./ Even for me" (222). Predictably at this point, Daddy declares his intentions to marry Louise, telling Billie Jo of his plans at her mother's grave. "Ma's bones didn't object./ Neither did mine" (224), Billie Jo says with some satisfaction, and in the closing lines of her story, she is seated at the piano, which Louise has cleaned, stretching her fingers over the keys, and she plays.

The price that Billie Jo has paid for her hard-won maturity is high: she has lost her mother and brother, has suffered alienation from her father and her own self, and endured the pain of guilt as well as physical injury. But she emerges strong and at peace. As Jean Feiwel says in an afterword to the Teacher's Edition of the novel, *Out of the Dust* is a "stirring example of a girl facing the worst in herself to get to the best" (n.p.). Readers of Billie Jo's story will learn the history of the Dust Bowl and its ramifications for those who lived through it, but the politics and economics of that difficult time serve mainly to provide a backdrop to what is, finally, a story of personal victory.

## TRUE NORTH

By contrast, the complex moral and political issues that lurk submerged in Billie Jo's tale drive the narrative thrust of Kathryn Lasky's *True North*. This novel is set in the United States in the years preceding the Civil War and alternates between the stories of two very different young women: Afrika, a runaway slave, and Lucy Bradford, the youngest member of a distinguished Boston family. Afrika has escaped from her plantation and is making her way to freedom alone, guided only by the North Star and aided along the way by "conductors" on the Underground Railroad. Her journey ends in the study of Lucy's grandfather, an abolitionist. However, he has died, and it is Lucy who discovers Afrika hiding in a clock during a dramatic scene that brings the two strands of the story together. The girls' story culminates several chapters later when they reach the Canadian border, a triumph in which they have made no concession to any constraints of gender. Nor does it ultimately extract any sacrifice. Both go on to enjoy a fruitful life, Afrika in Canada, Lucy back in Boston. They have gained everything, lost nothing. Like all girls in the third category, they can claim an unqualified victory.

*True North* uses a structure more complex than *Midwife's Apprentice* or *Out of the Dust*. Rather than being narrated entirely from a single viewpoint cast in the first person, it alternates between the third-person perspectives of Lucy and Afrika. In addition, the novel also uses a more complicated nested arrangement, beginning with an Epilogue and closing with a Prologue set decades after the central events of the novel, but within the nested narrative are several flashbacks to Afrika's life as a slave, presented as dreams and formatted in italics—narratives within narratives within narratives. The framed structure in this case operates less to give the characters a chance to "work through problems by revisiting them at different points in time," as Seelinger posits, than to hook the reader's interest in the first chapter and to tie up loose ends in the final pages, with the dream sequences serving mainly to underscore for the reader the brutality of slavery and to strengthen Afrika's resolve to escape. Although both Lucy and Afrika are caught up in the slavery issue, neither has to "work through" an approach to it, unlike Billie Jo's complex feelings about the Dust Bowl. Both fiercely oppose the institution, Afrika for obvious reasons, Lucy because her grandfather's ideology has strongly influenced her thinking. *True North* is more an adventure story than a psychological study, a coming-of-age novel with plenty of suspense and a mystery revealed only in the final pages.

Afrika's strand of the narrative dramatizes the almost insurmountable obstacles that confronted runaway slaves, and the dream sequences convey her brutal experiences prior to her escape: separated from her mother as a tiny child, auctioned at a slave market, she has been beaten and raped repeatedly by the plantation overseer. Like much of young adult historical fiction, *True North* probes the injustices inflicted on a marginalized culture. It could be categorized as "multicultural literature" as well as historical fiction.[16]

Afrika has sustained her soul by "finding and loving the smallest and most fleeting thing"—the scent of a flower, the glimpse of a star.[17] She flees her plantation in a group led by Harriet Tubman but becomes separated from the other fugitives when she gives premature birth to a daughter conceived by rape. The infant, three months early, cannot survive, and in a scene that establishes her internal fortitude, Afrika refuses to move on until the baby dies, determined to give her "a good sending" (2). Oppression has made her strong. A young girl with "flint in her eyes" (2), Afrika demonstrates throughout the novel that she also has flint in her soul, an obdurate element that sparks flames of stubborn endurance. She knows that "[d]ying is easy—being alive was the hard part" (6), and she is determined not only to live but to live free. At her first stop on the Underground Railroad, she is provided with a disguise, and she becomes Joe Bell—going as a boy, practicing to move as a male, hunching her shoulders forward and "punching ahead like a man walking down the road" (33). When female characters dress as boys, they often do so to appropriate the privilege and power of males. However, because she is black, she can exercise no power. Her disguise serves only to conceal her true identity.

Afrika, of course, is illiterate, for slaves were forbidden to learn to read and write. She remembers that those who disobeyed were severely punished: overseers not only whipped them until the blood ran but cut off their fingers and toes. The severe punishment indicates the empowering nature of literacy and the plantation owners' tacit admission that a literate slave is an oxymoron. As Afrika makes her way north, she is taught to recognize the letters in the name of the cargo ship that will carry her to the Boston harbor, and she treasures those symbols. Not only do they represent her transportation to freedom but her initiation into becoming an educated—and thus empowered—person.

Her journey is harrowing. She must avoid capture by dogs and slave catchers. She must forge a river, slog through swamps, wade through a Boston sewer. She hides in a barrel beneath layers of oysters, in a coffin beneath a corpse. But she never thinks of giving up. Her trip on the Underground Railroad ends when she and Lucy meet, but the danger is not yet over: drugged and caught by slave catchers, they must find a way to outwit them and escape.

Although Lucy has led a sheltered life, she is hardly daunted by the danger of aiding a fugitive slave. In fact, it is just the kind of excitement that she has yearned for. In the early chapters, she is restless and bored, impatient with her role as a proper young lady. The energies of her socially established family are entirely channeled on planning for their oldest daughter's wedding, and Lucy, who views all the ado through skeptical eyes, is expected to participate in good spirits. Lucy, however, prefers escapades to etiquette and would welcome a hurricane with winds that "blistered the varnish off wood" (8). She longs to go west like her cousin Francis Parkman, where she could see "rattlesnakes thick as a man's arm, the herds of elk with antlers clattering . . . a buffalo hunt" (27)—an ambition that might horrify other well-bred girls. But instead of chasing after rattlesnakes and buffaloes, she must sit patiently and embroider dozens of linens for her sister's trousseau, which she calls a "cruel custom that yoked every female relative and every female servant in the bridal household to an embroidery hoop" (9–10).

While this burden pales in comparison with Afrika's struggle to survive, Lucy's strand of the story points up the constraints of being female in mid-nineteenth-century New England, when young ladies were expected to defer to gentlemen and wear flounced dresses selected by their mothers. Lucy refuses to do either, noting that some girls would "settle" for anything to attract a man's attention, and she complains bitterly that flounces make girls look "silly" and "dumb." To compensate, she goes sailing with her grandfather because on board "it didn't seem to matter that she had been born a girl" (61), and from him she learns to maneuver his sloop and navigate by the stars.

Lucy's resistance to decorum often puts her at odds with her sisters and mother, whose characterizations are almost a parody of how women were expected to behave. When Lucy reflects that her sisters are "like compasses with no northing" (187), she is not far from the mark. All are snobs, and one is such a fool, so eager to marry well, that she cannot see that her suitor is a slave catcher and a crook; she knows only that he is handsome and "beautifully mannered" and that his business "representing Southern interests" (i.e. catching fugitive slaves) earns a healthy profit. Lucy's mother, originally from the South, remains fixated on social matters while debates about slavery rage around her.

Lucy knows she is different from the other women in her family. Even her name is different. Her sisters are all named after flowers, whereas she is named after a ship, her name meaning "light" or "lucent." And she speaks her mind, oblivious to social niceties. Like Jo March, she likes "good strong words" that mean something. Her forceful voice, blunt and straightforward, speaks of her honest and straightforward character. When she describes the color of a detested gown as "bile," her mother tells her not to use such an "awful" word. Lucy tries to explain: "It's not an awful word. It's a brownish-yellow liquid secreted by the liver" (67), she says, but the scientific clarification only elicits horrified shrieks of "Freakish!" from her mother. Her sisters are equally upset by Lucy's language. She has always called her grandfather "Pap." They insist she refrain from using the term, for it is what "little pickaninnies call the Negro men down on the plantations in the South" (72). Again, Lucy responds sensibly if stubbornly: "I'm not a little pickaninny, and this isn't a plantation in the South. Pap is what I've called him ever since I can remember" (72). As this speech indicates, she is aware of both the denotative and connotative value of language, and in the wake of her grandfather's death and an argument with her sisters, she resolves, "I shall always call him Pap" (189).

Her resolve is understandable, for it is only with her grandfather's support that she learns to see herself as a person with merit, not a "freak." Although she is initially shocked to learn that her beloved Pap is breaking a law by aiding escaping slaves, she is encouraged by the example he sets when he tells her that it is better to break an immoral law than to abide by it. The parallel between Pap's behavior and her own resistance to foolish social conventions is clear. When she becomes secretly involved in the abolitionist movement, her rebellious streak has found a justifiable outlet. She has also found the excitement and challenge that she has craved. After her grandfather dies, she is smart enough to decipher his code that indicates the Boston stations of the Underground Railroad, and when she and Afrika are caught by the man who has been posing as a suitor to one of her sisters, she musters the cleverness and courage to outwit him, using her sailing abilities to send him to his watery grave. The two girls then fake their own deaths and finally make their way to the Canadian border, where they part company, with Afrika headed into the new country to begin a new life and Lucy returning to her family in Boston. As in *The Midwife's Apprentice,* the story of Lucy and Afrika is largely a tale of the powerless winning out over the powerful by cunning and subterfuge—a pair of Brer Rabbits outfoxing a host of adversaries.

When Lucy and Afrika are reunited years later in an epilogue, Lucy has been married and widowed, but the text makes clear that these experiences have not dampened her unorthodox thinking. She eloped instead of having a proper wedding, kept an independent bank account during her marriage, and set up a trust for special causes, which she has managed herself. Her husband surely was unusual for his time; he "supported his wife in all her endeavors" (254). Afrika, too, has led a fulfilling life. Once in Canada, she enrolled in a school and quickly became well-educated, and she and Lucy have corresponded regularly. She has also married, her husband a fugitive slave like herself, ten years her senior.

In earlier fiction, Lucy and Afrika might have been created as males instead of females. The adventurous roles the two girls play are more commonly undertaken by boys in a traditional heroic quest. Lucy is separated from her community, first by her secret abolitionist activities and then by her flight to Canada, returning as a more mature individual who enjoys enhanced status. Afrika undergoes a severe trial on her way north, transcending her years as a slave to emerge at last as a respected—and free—member of her community, first a teacher of children and then a "teacher of teachers." Henry Seidel Canby's statement that historical fiction is "more likely to register an exact truth about the writer's present than the exact truth of the past"[18] is a fitting epigraph for *True North*. The novel was published in 1996, when women were already filling roles once reserved only for men—as astronauts and Supreme Court justices, as university presidents and state governors. There is no reason why girls should not be heroes in literature, and many recent novels of historical fiction portray them as undertaking dangerous adventures, where (to borrow a phrase from William Faulkner) they—like Lucy and Afrika—not only survive, but prevail.

As the stories of Meribah and Alanna have already demonstrated, empowered girls are courageous, and in historical fiction they often perform brave acts in the service of justice. Their courage is not of the foolhardy, risk-taking variety, but the kind one calls upon to confront danger when it is necessary to battle evil and help others, courage fueled by a sense of moral agency and integrity. Such courage often requires physical stamina and keen intelligence. Afrika and Lucy can claim both attributes. Lucy is not only well read but smart about matters frequently considered the domain of males: astronomy and navigation, which she learned from her grandfather. Afrika initially lacks Lucy's schooling, but she possesses a native intelligence. Both survive the harsh autumn weather of the far north.

So perhaps Avi was not so far off the mark when he spoke of historical fiction as being about "today's possibilities." If the genre does not necessarily "reinvent the past," it at least populates it with characters who could successfully meet the challenges of the present. Today's young women enjoy many freedoms that girls in earlier centuries could hardly imagine, but those very freedoms have exacted their own costs. In fiction as in life, all girls who traverse the difficult territory between childhood and adulthood have much in common with each other. The female protagonists of both historical fiction and contemporary realism rely upon many of the same strengths, but, as the next chapter demonstrates, the girls living in fictional worlds of the late twentieth century respond to the specific dilemmas of their own—and very different—time period, and their respective paths to empowerment are largely determined by the historical moment in which they enact those journeys.

## SUGGESTIONS FOR FURTHER READING

Armstrong, Jennifer. *The Dreams of Mairhe Mehan*. New York: Knopf, 1996. Mairhe comes to New York from Ireland, hoping for a better life, but she must cope with her brother's determination to join the Union Army in the Civil War.

——. *Mary Mehan Awake*. New York: Knopf, 1997. Mairhe, now Mary, moves to upstate New York to find the peace and spiritual tranquillity that has eluded her during the Civil War. Taking a job as a maid, she finds serenity and even romance.

Avi. *The True Confessions of Charlotte Doyle*. New York: Orchard Books, 1990. When Charlotte Doyle is thirteen, she boards a ship sailing from England to America with plans to rejoin her family. During her voyage, she discovers that the Captain whom she had trusted is a corrupt and evil man, and before landing in the United States, she joins the crew in a mutiny that involves murder.

——. *The Secret School*. New York: Harcourt Brace, 2001. Fourteen-year-old Ida Bidson is determined to finish eighth grade in 1925 Colorado, even after the school board decides to end the school year prematurely. Ida takes over, swearing the students to secrecy, and she sees her students though to final exams.

Cushman, Karen. *The Ballad of Lucy Whipple*. New York: Houghton Mifflin, 1996. When her widowed mother catches gold dust fever, Lucy Whipple finds herself transported from her comfortable life in Massachusetts to Lucky Diggins, California, and learns, in a series of comic episodes, that home is not a geographic location but the place that claims one's heart.

——. *Catherine Called Birdie*. New York: Clarion, 1995. Catherine—or Birdie—is the daughter of a nobleman. Her family is determined to marry her off to an old, disgusting man whose property makes him a valuable asset to Catherine's family. Catherine's spunk and humor come through clearly in this novel, written as a diary, although some of her discomforts—fleas, an exasperating mother, the prospect of an unsuitable marriage—might well be more disturbing than amusing.

Dowell, Frances O'Roark. *Dovey Coe*. New York: Atheneum, 2000. Spunky Dovey Coe is at odds with the nasty son of the town's richest man, who is determined to marry Dovey's sister. Suddenly, she finds herself accused of his murder and, assigned an inexperienced lawyer, has to solve the mystery herself.

Garden, Nancy. *Dove and Sword*. New York: Scholastic, 1995. The young Gabrielle, fictional friend of the historic Joan of Arc, accompanies the Maid into battle disguised as a page. Her adventure leads her to examine her views on the righteousness of war, the nature of justice, and her own faith.

Hesse, Karen. *Letters from Rifka*. New York: Henry Holt, 1992. Rifka's journey from the Ukraine to America is fraught with dangerous obstacles, but her cleverness and strength see her through to her planned destination.

Ho, Minfong. *Rice Without Rain*. New York: Lothrop, Lee & Shepard, 1990. Jinda's village in rural Thailand is threatened by drought. She must cope with the prospect of starvation and a changing world when two foreigners enter her life, first earning and then abusing her trust.

Holland, Isabelle. *Behind the Lines*. New York: Scholastic, 1994. Katie O'Farrell finds herself caught up in the tensions of the pre-Civil War debates as the Irish slum where she lives erupts into violence.

Karr, Kathleen. *Oh, Those Harper Girls*. New York: Farrar, Straus and Giroux, 1992. In the closing years of the nineteenth century, the six Harper girls set out to save their daddy's Texas ranch. In their daring adventures, they defy rules of etiquette and the law, but the final pages of this comic novel conclude with happy marriages.

Matas, Carol. *After the War*. New York: Simon and Schuster, 1996. A Holocaust survivor, Ruth Mendenberg joins an underground organization that smuggles immigrants out of Europe. Leading a group of children to Palestine, she skirts disaster and capture, and her experiences help heal the wounds inflicted by what she experienced as a prisoner at Buchenwald.

Matcheck, Diane. *The Sacrifice*. New York: Farrar Straus Giroux, 1998. A young Apsaalooka Indian girl, an outcast among her tribe, flees to the west and is captured by a group of Pawnee Indians. Treated well, she at first believes herself fortunate until she learns that she is being prepared as a sacrificial victim.

Meyer, Carolyn. *White Lilacs*. New York: Harcourt Brace, 1993. Rose Lee Jefferson's comfortable life in her all-black town of Freedom is threatened in 1921 when the surrounding white community decides to raze the town and move its residents.

Osborne, Mary Pope. *Adaline Falling Star*. New York: Scholastic, 2000. Adaline Falling Star is the mixed-blood daughter of Kit Carson and Singing Wind, an Arapaho Indian woman. When Singing Wind dies and the girl is sent to live with Kit's cousins in St. Louis, she is treated like a slave and eventually runs away, embarking on a journey to find her Arapaho people and her father.

Paterson, Katherine. *Lyddie*. New York: Dutton/Lodestar, 1992. When her family's farm goes into debt, Lyddie tries her hand in the textile mills of Massachusetts. She eventually becomes involved in the labor movement and finds both a community of friends and empowerment.

Porter, Tracey. *Treasures in the Dust*. New York: HarperCollins, 1999. Annie remains behind in the Oklahoma Dust Bowl when her friend Violet leaves with her family for California, but their friendship survives the separation through the frequent exchange of letters that convey the details of their now separate lives.

Rinaldi, Ann. *In My Father's House*. New York: Scholastic, 1993. Oscie Mason has no use for her stepfather, and the battle that rages between them is matched by the bloody battles of the Civil War.

———. *Wolf by the Ears.* New York: Scholastic, 1991. Harriet Hemings, daughter of Thomas Jefferson's slave Sally Hemings, is rumored to be Jefferson's daughter. When she has a chance to leave his plantation, she must decide whether to remain at Monticello as a slave or pass for white in the outside world.

Schwartz, Virginia Frances. *Send One Angel Down.* New York: Holiday House, 2000. The mulatto slave Eliza, fair-skinned and blue-eyed, is put on the auction block to satisfy her owner's daughter, who is jealous of the beautiful Eliza. Bought and freed by a northern abolitionist, Eliza must make her way in a new world.

Sinclair, April. *Coffee Will Make You Black.* New York: Hyperion, 1995. Stevie is a young African American girl growing up in the 1950s. As the title indicates, she injects her story with humor as she moves from adolescence to young adulthood.

White, Ellen Emerson. *The Road Home.* New York: Scholastic, 1995. When Rebecca Phillips returns from her stint as a nurse in Vietnam, she is haunted by the horrors she has witnessed. A journey across the country helps heal her wounded spirits.

Yolen, Jane. *Briar Rose.* New York: Tom Doherty Associates, 1992. Yolen subtly alludes to the folk tale of Sleeping Beauty as Genna tells the story of her Holocaust experiences to her granddaughters.

## NOTES

1. Leon Garfield, "Historical Fiction for Our Global Times," *The Horn Book Magazine* (November/December 1988), 737.

2. Patty Campbell, *The Horn Book Magazine* (September/October 1996), 636.

3. Quoted by Katherine Paterson, "Connecting Past and Present to Ourselves," *SIGNAL* 23.2 (Summer 1999), 13.

4. Thomas Mallon, "Writing Historical Fiction," *The American Scholar* (Autumn 1992).

5. Interview with Erik Christian Haugaard (and Ann Schlee), "Only a Lampholder: On Writing Historical Fiction," in *Innocence and Experience,* ed. Barbara Harrison and Gregory Maguire (New York: Lothrop, Lee & Shepard), 270.

6. Interview with Haugaard and Schlee, "Only a Lampholder," 265.

7. Quoted in "In Their Own Words: Authors' Views on Issues in Historical Fiction," Lawrence R. Sipe, *The New Advocate,* 10.3 (Summer 1997), 6.

8. Jean Boreen, "Images of Women in Historical Fiction: Seeking Role Models," *ALAN Review* (Winter 1999), 14–21.

9. Roberta Trites, *Waking Sleeping Beauty: Feminist Voices in Children's Novels* (University of Iowa Press, 1997), 144.

10. Anne Scott Macleod, "Writing Backward," *The Horn Book* (January/February 1998).

11. Avi, "Writing Backwards but Looking Forward." *SIGNAL* 23.2 (Summer 1999), 21.

12. Karen Cushman, "The Historical Novel: At Home in Time and Place," *SIGNAL* 23.2 (Summer 1999), 25.

13. Karen Cushman, *The Midwife's Apprentice* (New York: HarperTrophy, 1995), 2; hereafter cited in text.

14. "Enigma Variations: What Feminist Theory Knows About Children's Literature," *Signal* 54 (September 1987), 189; hereafter cited in text.

15. Karen Hesse, *Out of the Dust* (New York: Scholastic, 1997; teacher's edition), 3; hereafter cited in text.

16. For a more complete exploration of multicultural literature, see Chapter 4 on young female protagonists in contemporary settings. Whereas multicultural historical novels tend to emphasize the circumstances of the historical setting, multicultural novels unfolding in the contemporary world tend to foreground the multicultural milieu itself. However, the difference is more a matter of degree than kind.

17. Kathryn Lasky, *True North* (New York: Blue Sky Press, 1996), 49; hereafter cited in text.

18. As quoted by Kenneth I. Donelson and Alleen Pace Nilsen, *Literature for Today's Young Adults,* 3rd ed. (Glenview, IL: Scott, Foresman, 1989), 169.

# Empowered Girls
# in the Contemporary World

I wake to sleep and take my waking slow,
I learn by going where I have to go.

"The Waking," Theodore Roethke

$\mathcal{T}$he above lines might have been spoken by many of the young female protagonists who define themselves by going where they "have to go" in the contemporary world. Like their male counterparts, they become empowered by encountering and coping with challenging, unexpected events, but their coming-of-age experiences are often marked by the specifically female characteristics that also shape fiction about girls in other genres. Although the novels discussed in this chapter are all set in the here and now, they vary widely in mode, ranging from social realism that reflects serious concerns of girls in the experiential world to romance and adventure stories that offer an escape from it.

## SOCIAL REALISM

In the fiction of social realism, sometimes categorized as "problem novels," the protagonist may find strength by confronting current issues such as sexual harassment, racism, or AIDS; she may become empowered by coping with teen pregnancy or by engaging in political causes. She may emerge stronger by turning from cultural standards of female beauty and accepting her own body, however imperfect, or by resolving conflicts with family and friends. Her journey towards maturity may take place in a comfortable suburban home, in a harsh urban environment where she lives on the social and economic margins of American society, or in a country far removed from the industrialized western world. It is hardly coincidental that many novels of social realism involve young women of color, and the frequency with which such characters appear demonstrates the degree to which the difficulties of growing up female are compounded by issues of race and culture.

*Make Lemonade*

Virginia Euwer Wolff's *Make Lemonade* serves well as an example of how novels of contemporary realism represent empowered girls. LaVaughn and Jolly, *Lemonade*'s two young protagonists, must confront and overcome the multiple challenges of poverty, ethnicity, sexual harassment, and single motherhood, and their story unfolds against the gritty background of an unnamed inner city.[1] Children themselves, they take on adult responsibilities and, sometimes skirting close encounters with defeat, emerge victorious. Fourteen-year-old LaVaughn has taken a job babysitting for Jolly's children to earn money for college, her ticket out of poverty. Although Jolly, only three years older than LaVaughn, has never finished school, she is already the mother of two small children—baby Jilly and three-year-old Jeremy—each by different fathers.

LaVaughn narrates the story in lyrical free verse that adroitly captures the voice of an inner-city child. She is expressive in the best sense, her speech abounding with precise images that convey her emotions in colorful language. For example, when her mother introduces the idea of college, LaVaughn says, "This word college is in my house, and you have to walk around it in the rooms like furniture."[2] Later, when she and Jolly's baby daughter Jilly rush to praise Jeremy for using the toilet instead of wetting his diaper, she describes the two of them as "a committee of congratuations" (31). Through her expressive abilities, she is ultimately able to convince Jolly to return to school and turn her life around for the better.

LaVaughn is also nurturing. She especially loves Jilly and Jeremy, and she worries about how Jolly will survive. As discussed earlier, this nurturing quality, linked primarily to females rather than males, has sometimes been regarded as a weakness, for the nurturer risks sacrificing her sense of self. However, LaVaughn's sense of nurture has boundaries, and she refuses to subordinate her dreams to the needs of others. When Jolly rejects her boss's sexual overtures and loses her job, she wants LaVaughn to lend back the money that she has paid the younger girl for baby sitting. LaVaughn declines, even though she's aware of Jolly's acute need. She reasons, "That's my exit money . . . / I need it for some kind of college. / . . . I got more right to that money than she does. / But she's got more burdens than I do. I look at her and say, 'That won't help.' / She think I mean there's not enough. I don't change my eyes / to help her misunderstanding. What I mean is / that money is not going to help her because it's saved to help me / not end up like her" (63).

LaVaughn does, however, find other ways to help Jolly, and, like many strong girls in young adult fiction, LaVaughn finds that empowering others empowers her. As she steers Jolly towards more autonomy, she herself becomes more independent and self-assured. A teacher commends her for her "leadership" skills, saying that "I have high hopes for you" (118). By the novel's end, LaVaughn plans on going to college to be a teacher, and Jolly has enrolled in a Moms Up class for young mothers, working to earn her GED.

*Make Lemonade* is notable for the relationship it portrays between mother and daughter. LaVaughn's father has been killed in a random shooting incident, and her mother, resolved that LaVaughn's life be better than her own, keeps track of her daughter's every move. "My Mom has an attention span that goes on for years," LaVaughn says (12). Her mom instills a sense of purpose in LaVaughn, insisting that she take responsibility for her own life. Mom's motto is, "Bootstraps go in two directions, / either up or down. / You choose / and you remember you chose . . . / in taking care of ourselves we don't mess around / waiting for somebody to do it" (92). LaVaughn's mom clearly disapproves of Jolly, but she is there when LaVaughn and Jolly need her. Not all empowered girls have supportive mothers, but their appearance is a plus in young adult fiction, which often treats mothers as blocking, negative figures.

However, LaVaughn sometimes chafes at her mother's fierce concern, and on occasion she secretly goes against her mother's wishes. In doing so, she demonstrates the defiant streak that empowers some of the other female protagonists discussed earlier. LaVaughn's defiance grows initially from her empathetic determination to help Jolly despite her mother's opposition. Early in the novel, LaVaughn withholds certain information from her mother about her new job, knowing that such details would preclude permission to take it. She justifies this deviousness by saying, "It's too complicated. My Mom would have opinions" (15), and she shrewdly presses Mom into giving consent by representing Jolly's situation as urgent: "You can corner even a big Mom like mine sometimes / when you have to have an answer in a hurry" (19).

Her growing awareness of the dangers implicit in being young and female reinforces her defiant resolve. When she learns about Jolly's losing her job because Jolly rebutted her boss's sexual advances, LaVaughn becomes angry, and her anger further motivates her to find a way out for Jolly and her children. She feels especially protective of Jilly. As she readies the baby for bed, "changing and washing her and powdering all her folds," she says, "I tell her her folds are private, that part is hers, / it's precious / and she don't let nobody, not anybody, / ever go near her privacy till she knows he loves her to stay with her her whole life" (59). Jolly, whose pregnancies seem to have been the result of sexual abuse, provides a powerful example of just how vulnerable young women can be. Telling LaVaughn about what happened with the man she calls "Mr. Fingers Boss," Jolly shouts, "Do I hafta wear a SIGN / says NO MORE MEN CLIMBIN' ALL OVER ME, / LOOK WHAT YOU DONE ALREADY?" (57). LaVaughn's rebellion, then, transcends mere chafing at social constraints. As she comprehends the dangers inherent in being female, she also begins to understand the power that male predators like Jolly's boss hold over their victims. She also realizes that many young women—especially those marginalized by poverty—have little recourse. By the end of the novel, LaVaughn is fighting against such injustice by trying to ensure a better life for Jolly. She is not as openly defiant as Lucy Bradford, more a subversive guerrilla than a public rebel, but she is every bit as determined to change an outrageous status quo. Her defiance confers freedom to act.[3]

Life is a serious business for LaVaughn and Jolly, but both girls have a sense of humor that relieves the dreariness. Jolly is particularly witty, and her clever comments on what would otherwise be cause for despair evoke admiration in LaVaughn as well as the reader. One evening while the two girls are watching Jolly's TV, which has no vertical hold, they turn off the sound and ad lib their own commentary. Jolly announces the weather news in language that parallels her own circumstances: "The whole world is rollin' up into the sky / and there is increased speed of everything / disappeared [*sic*] into space" (43). Later, Jolly writes a letter requesting help from a billionaire known to donate money to worthy causes. When he writes back that he will reward her "tenacity" when she can verify that she has earned her GED, Jolly swallows her disappointment and turns the setback into comedy, making a "billionaire speech" while holding her toothbrush up for a mustache: "We ain't gonna reward / your little eensy one-a-city, two-a-city, / we're gonna save it all up / and reward your ten-a-city when you get it" (180). As LaVaughn says in admiration, "She's the one makes it [misfortune] funny" (166). Jolly's sense of humor lightens circumstances that otherwise might overwhelm her with gloom and allows her to move on. Like LaVaughn's defiance, it is empowering.

At the outset of the novel, neither girl can claim a complete family. Jolly has no "folks" other than her children, and LaVaughn's father has been killed in a random shooting. As the story progresses, they fill the vacancies in each other's lives. Even though LaVaughn grows sometimes impatient with Jolly's careless ways, she can appreciate the tremendous struggle that is Jolly's life, able to discern and encourage progress that might escape a less empathetic eye, and she provides the emotional support that Jolly has sorely needed. Although Jolly sometimes resents LaVaughn's advantages—her caring mother and academic self-confidence—without LaVaughn's support, she and her children would be doomed to a cycle of poverty; they in turn become the extended network of relatives missing in LaVaughn's life. Together, the four of them create an ironic family "from the continent [as LaVaughn says] of I don't know what" (91). The two young women also realize that the common experience of menstruation links them to a larger network, the family of women, and they marvel at the connection: "Where does it all go? / A whole ocean of blood. / All those thousands of years / all the ladies and girls been bleeding. / Where would it all be? / In the ground someplace" (152). Then Jolly laughingly concludes, "like she's making a report to the class, / 'That's why they call her Mother Earth'" (152).

However, despite the close relationship that has developed between them, ultimately they must go their separate ways. They are very different people with different visions of what life holds for them. LaVaughn says, "I like things all the way done. / All the way is my ticket out of here" (130), whereas Jolly settles for "part way." She leaves her homework "part way" done; her floors are sticky with accumulated food, and the children's clothes, not completely dried, lie moldering in drawers. Finally, LaVaughn, tactfully quiet about such carelessness until now, loses patience: "That the way you did the birth control too? / Part way is good enough? (131)." She immediately regrets her outburst, but her refusal to be silenced any longer nudges Jolly along the path to independence. Although the girls reconcile at the end of this scene, it foreshadows their eventual parting.[4] As LaVaughn says regretfully, "I been broken off, / like part of her bad past. / I was the one that knew the saddest parts of Jolly" (198).

In a less realistic novel, the girls might remain friends forever, but *Make Lemonade* says as much about the nature of friendship as it does about poverty and single-parenthood. Friendships are always dynamic, not static, and when they are destined to falter, empowered girls are ultimately able to move on while retaining the best of what they have gained from even a temporary connection. LaVaughn has lost Jolly's friendship and the children she has come to love, but she clings to a warm memory that began as a nightmare: when Jilly choked on a toy, Jolly saved her baby daughter's life using the CPR skills she learned in her Mom's Up class, with little Jeremy remembering his numbers and dialing the first digit of 911. In the aftermath of that ordeal, LaVaughn has taken Jeremy home for the night. She remembers the scene—her own Mom lifting the boy into the air and swinging him around: "Here he is / a cheerful child / a boy in the air / ready for his dinner, / in his forgetful joy he's laughing down at my Mom / who's looking up there to him, her mouth wide open and full of praise" (200). She has learned to let go of the "bad past" without bitterness, treasuring its best moments. Out of life's lemons, both young women have made lemonade.

## MULTICULTURAL REALISM

As *Make Lemonade* demonstrates, empowerment is a psychological process occurring within a cultural context that shapes both how it progresses and the forms it takes. LaVaughn's sense of empowerment is constrained by her ethnicity and class, and a middle-class girl growing up in suburban America might find that it fails to meet her own expectations. What appears as empowerment to a girl in one culture may seem repressive to girls elsewhere.

This point is especially significant in any investigation of multicultural literature. In her groundbreaking feminist study *The Second Sex,* Simone de Beauvoir argues that sexism reduces all females to the status of the "other" in relationship to the dominant culture, valuing masculine practices as normative and demeaning traits associated with the female. However, such factors as race, ethnicity, class, and sexual orientation can further magnify a girl's outsider status, increasing her distance from the norm and complicating the process by which she becomes empowered, simply because she has more obstacles to overcome. And the fact remains that some cultures repress females more than others. Although no girl is free from the restrictions imposed by gender, the cultural restrictions of some girls are much more exacting and burdensome than others. Obviously, this impacts a girl's sense of life's options as well as how she and her culture define empowerment. Thus, a white, middle-class American girl and a Pakistani girl may both be considered empowered within their respective cultures, yet what appears as empowerment to a girl in one culture may seem repressive to a girl in another.

For many years, young adult literature assumed that all girls experienced "girlhood" similarly, that it was a universal, generic state of being. "Difference" was narrowly defined, reduced to matters of class or—more rarely—race. In most instances, the resolution involved girls erasing difference by adapting their behavior to the dominant culture; they earned money, for example, to buy clothes that conformed to what peers deemed appropriate or they eschewed clothing and customs distinctively ethnic. The relatively few stories about girls who weren't white and middle-class lacked depth and understanding; the literature ignored lesbians completely. By the 1960s, young female protagonists had become more diverse, but the stories tended to locate the conflicts of "difference" in external circumstances such as integration as a barrier to be overcome, a problem to be solved. In contrast, much current literature approaches "difference" of all kinds—race, class, sexual orientation, ethnicity—as a subject to be explored, with considerable attention to the internal or psychological tensions of the character.

## *Haveli*

Suzanne Fisher Staples' two novels, *Shabanu* and *Haveli,* for example, depict practices that for western readers constitute child abuse. Over the course of the first novel, Shabanu, the main character, is beaten by her father and betrothed at eleven to Rahim, a man old enough to be her grandfather who has three other wives.

While this plot outline may elicit both horror and sanctimonious self–righteousness from western readers, Staples is trying to accomplish something infinitely more complex than simply indicting Islamic culture. She does a certain amount of that: it is clear that Shabanu is sacrificed on one level to cultural and religious forces that allow her little say in determining her destiny. But what ultimately emerges is a moving and ultimately hopeful story of an intelligent and strong-willed girl trying to negotiate a life for herself that allows her to keep the aspects of her culture she loves while rejecting and subverting those she finds damaging.

The first novel establishes Shabanu as a spirited young girl, the second daughter in a family of camel herders. Her parents have no son, and it remains for them to arrange financially advantageous marriages for their daughters. After considerable resistance, Shabanu accepts her parents' plans for her marriage out of fear for her life and the filial sense of duty common to her culture, although to acquiesce means sacrificing her own dreams and the unusual independence she has enjoyed. The questions that Staples implicitly raises are these: in a culture where girls are commodities of exchange, where they live their lives "according to the wishes of their fathers and their princes,"[5] what possibilities for selfhood exist and what forms of resistance are there that are not, ultimately, suicidal? The external circumstances of this novel's ending are not, on the surface, either happy or empowering for Shabanu. She has attempted to escape from her planned marriage but is caught and beaten by her father. Yet she is consoled by her cousin Sharma's advice to "recall the beauty of things in [her] world" and, she says, "like a bride admiring her dowry, I take them out and, one by one, then fold them away again deep into my heart. . . . Rahim-sahib [her husband-to-be] will reach out to me for the rest of his life and never unlock the secret of my heart" (240). Internally she has experienced a change, has had an epiphany of sorts that allows her to believe she will be able to exert some control over Rahim, and thus, be hopeful about her future with him.

When the second novel opens, Shabanu is eighteen, married to Rahim-sahib and mother to a six-year old daughter, Mumtaz, whom she loves dearly. That she has only one child is deliberate. Before she married, she worried about her ability to hold Rahim's attention once she started to have children, afraid that childbearing and mothering would so age her that her husband would "start looking for another woman younger than I to fall in love with."[6] Sharma, however, gives her a twig that functions as a contraceptive, thus allowing Shabanu to exert some control over her body.

And she has carved out both peace and space for herself in Rahim's household. She is his favorite wife, the one of his four to whom he gives his free time, and she feels a genuine affection for him. Although the other wives are jealous and contemptuous of her desert ways, her lower class, and her lack of education, she copes by moving herself and her daughter to a room by the stables and by refusing to acknowledge their petty acts of malice. When she is forced, for example, to mend all their clothes, she does so without complaint. Still, she asserts herself covertly by gradually taking in all their seams until nothing seems to fit and the women are forced to diet. She becomes the trickster who exerts power by undermining an existing power structure.

The plot of *Haveli* has three components: first, Shabanu must plan how to care for herself and her daughter once Rahim, now in his sixties, dies. She knows that without his protection the other wives will try to enslave her and Mumtaz. Second, she must somehow save her best friend, Zabo, from the marriage that has been arranged for her with Rahim's retarded son. Finally, she must somehow deal with the love she feels for Omar, her husband's nephew, who has returned from six years study in the United States to marry one of Rahim's daughters. All of these dilemmas are further complicated by the machinations of Nazir, Rahim's younger brother and Zabo's father.

Shabanu is marginalised on several levels. As a female she shares the second-class status of all females in her culture. She is further marginalised by her class, which is considered lower than that of Rahim's other wives, by her illiteracy (which is a function of both her class and her gender), and by her youth and beauty. Though she chooses to live in a room off the stables, suggesting an alliance with Rhahim's servants, these mostly treat her with the contempt their mistresses feel. In these circumstances she works with the tools she has: her cunning, Rahim's love for her, and the support she gets from her cousin, Sharma, as well as from Rahim's older sister, a strong-willed, well-educated, childless widow.

She finds subversive ways to empower herself and her friend Zabo. She convinces Rahim to take her to the capital with him during a legislative session, and, once there, arranges for her daughter to be taught to read and write, sitting in on the lessons so that she herself will learn. She and Zabo devise a plan that will allow Zabo to escape her husband soon after they are married, and she teaches Zabo about birth control. Often, she must cope with difficult or even terrifying situations. When she meets and falls in love with Omar, she must decide between love and duty. She sees her husband assassinated, and she is kidnapped by Zabo's father, Nazir, who threatens to marry her.

In each of the above situations Shabanu is torn between following her own inclinations and fulfilling her culturally assigned role. She explains to Omar, her husband's nephew, " My whole life has been a struggle to appear to do what's expected of me while I continue to think what I please" (163). When he tells her never to stop thinking independently because it is one of her "greatest charms," Shabanu feels "a surge of joy at the simple freedom of being able to speak openly with him" (163). Omar represents, briefly at least, a world of possibility Shabanu has never imagined. He tells her that after living in the United States, " I will never again regard women in the same way "(162), convincing her that he is "different from Rahim and his father" (163).

When Omar and Shabanu fall in love and he asks her to meet him alone, she knows she is starting on a "dangerous and uncharted journey" (169) because " the sin of desiring another man is punishable by death at the hands of her husband" (169). In spite of this risk, Shabanu secretly prepares a long unused summer pavilion on the roof of her sister-in-law's townhouse or *haveli* as a trysting place. Ultimately this summer pavilion becomes Shabanu's retreat, the "room of one's own" that Virginia Woolf argues all women need if they are to create. Here, Shabanu reads, writes, and hides the money that will fund Zabo's escape and her own life after Rahim's death.

However, the pavilion never does become a place for Omar and Shabanu to meet. Faced with choosing between her heart and her duty to her husband and daughter, she chooses the latter despite the love she feels for Omar, telling him that she has "learned to live with what is possible" (193). When Omar refuses to believe her because she is a girl "who never could obey," Shabanu replies, "In America do men respect the wishes of women? . . . Then take the best of what you have learned of duty in Pakistan and respect in America, and leave me in peace" (193).

Omar leaves as she has requested. Ironically, it is clearly implied that though he loves Shabanu, Omar would never break off his engagement with Rahim's daughter or in any way violate his own sense of family obligation. Shabanu later reflects on " how like Rahim he had become, how committed to duty and the family" (227).

Both *Shabanu* and *Haveli* end problematically. Rahim is dead, Shabanu's plan to help Zabo escape fails, and Zabo dies. Mumtaz is in the desert with her mother's family and Shabanu, presumed dead by Nazir, is hidden in the summer pavilion, protected by Rahim's widowed sister. She knows that as long as she is thought dead, her family is safe and so she contemplates "how to live her life as a ghost " (304). But bleak as this ending may seem, it still hints at the possibility of a better life: Shabanu now knows how to read and write, something neither her sister nor other female relatives have ever learned. She has not been prematurely aged by repeated childbearing and rearing. She had successfully separated herself from Rahim's jealous other wives and prevented those wives from making Mumtaz into a servant. She has money enough to support herself and her daughter for ten years, and both Sharma and her sister-in-law offer her homes. Although she still longs for Omar, she has come to understand that there are "worse things than longing," and recognizes that "she could never stand against his commitment to the family" (319). Though she was not able to bring Zabo to safety, she has learned that she is not "one of those helpless women who wrung their hands and walked about moaning, 'What to do, What to do'" (242). In spite of all she has endured, Shabanu lives "with hope. One day Mumtaz would be with her at the *haveli*, and she would go to school, and become a part of the larger world" (320). And so, though the novel ends with Shabanu on one level imprisoned by the need to hide from Nazir, it still holds out the possibility of change and of Shabanu's carving out a satisfactory life for herself.

## Habibi

Shabanu's spirit and appetite for freedom make acceptance of her culture's gender roles difficult. These same factors, coupled with her experience of other ways of living, also make life difficult for Liyana, protagonist of Naomi Shihab Nye's *Habibi*. Liyana's father is an Arab doctor married to an American woman. The family has lived in America all of Liyana's life, but at the start of the novel her parents announce that the time has come for the family to move to her father's birthplace, Jerusalem. Liyana's father is motivated by his desire to have his children "know both sides of their history, become the fully rounded human beings they were destined to be" and to give them "doubled lives."[7] Liyana's parents have discussed this move for years, but her father's announcement comes at a moment of change in her life: she is about to start high school and has received her first kiss. Both of these events make her reluctant to move. Even more importantly, she realizes that the move will force her to assume the status of immigrant, one that she has known only indirectly and intellectually from her father and from her social studies books. But now "Liyana started thinking of the word 'immigrant' in a different way at that moment and her skin prickled. Now she would be the immigrant" (5).

Her new status forces Liyana to ask new questions about herself and her place in the world. As they land in Israel, her father says "There it is, there's my country." In response, Liyana silently asks herself, "Well, where was hers?" (12). Adapting to a new country requires that Liyana reestablish herself, that she start from "scratch" in a place where "no one really knew her here, no one knew what she liked or who her friends were or how funny she could be" (53). As an important part of reestablishing herself, she must adapt to different cultural expectations for being a girl. Specifically, she has to learn and accept that female behavior is more circumscribed in the Middle East than in the United States. As she packs, her father tells her to leave her shorts behind because "No one wears shorts over there" (19). Liyana disagrees, saying she has seen pictures of people wearing shorts in Jerusalem. Her father remains firm, adding, "We're going to spend time in older places where shorts won't be appropriate. Believe me, Arab women don't wear shorts" (19). He has moved subtly from the broad "No one" to the more specific "Arab women." Nonetheless, Liyana at first resists her father's restrictions and then begins negotiating with him to achieve at least some control over her wardrobe. The next time he refers to Arab women, she yells, "I am not a woman, or a full Arab either" (20), then runs to her bedroom, slamming the door behind her. When her father comes to her room to placate her, she reminds him of her multi-faceted identity: "I'm just a half—half, woman—girl, Arab—American, a mixed breed . . ." (20). Later, she apologizes and asks, "What if I don't take my very short shorts? What if I only take the baggy checkered, old-man shorts that come down to my knees?" Her father agrees.

Liyana's conflict over the shorts is representative of something much larger: how will Liyana accommodate her experiences of being an American girl with her new culture's expectations? This question becomes even more complicated when she learns that the process of adjustment and assimilation will involve more than simply accepting different cultural attitudes toward females. She must also cope, for the first time, with her ethnicity as a potential problem. Though she was identified as half Arab in the United States, that identity had little affect on her daily life. She was able to put it on and take it off at will, as she did the red velvet ethnic dress her Arab relatives sent her. In Jerusalem, however, she must assume, whether she wants it or not, membership in a group that represents conflict and threat. Both gender and ethnicity, then, complicate Liyana's search for empowerment.

In an essay Liyana writes for her American social studies teacher, she tries to recap the conflict in Jerusalem between the Arabs and the Jews. She does this in response to his questions: "Why do you think people have had so much trouble acting civilized over there?" (27). In trying to answer this question she draws on her father's experience as an Arab boy who grew up playing harmoniously with his Jewish friends until "the pot on the stove boiled over" (29). She describes how her father's family lost their home in Jerusalem and how he saw many friends killed in the conflicts between the Jews and the Palestinians. She writes that when her father came to the United States, he was saddened by stories of Native Americans because "he knew how they felt" (31). Liyana ends her essay optimistically, describing the peace talks and noting that "Palestinians had public voices again" (31), a clear recognition on her part that to speak is to be empowered.

But just as Liyana is forced by her parent's move to close the gap between an intellectual understanding of immigrant status and the actual experiencing of that status, so is she forced to learn the difference between saying Palestinians are able to assert their voices and using her own voice as a newly-minted Palestinian girl.

Almost as soon as Liyana's family arrives in Jerusalem, they learn that life there is still difficult, even dangerous for Arabs. Their passage through customs takes longer than it does for non-Arabs. Her father's family is late to greet them because they are stopped at several points by Israeli guards. Liyana's mother says: "I thought things were supposed to be so much better now?" to which her father replies: "That's not what they [his friends and family] are telling me. They say the rules change every two days and they almost never come into the city anymore" (44).

In this new environment Liyana tries to follow her mother's advice and look for the "silver lining" (52), but she is isolated by her lack of Arabic. Missing her friends, she resists identifying her new culture as hers. She decides not to decorate the walls of her new room, instead "trying to live with blank walls for a month or two" (66). She repeatedly rejects her Arabic grandmother's requests that Liyana visit her village on weekends so she can "teach her [Liyana] things" (67). Liyana describes herself at this stage as "floundering and lonesome" (69).

Her acceptance of her new status begins when she is enrolled in an Armenian school, one where the students speak Arabic, English, and Armenian. During an admissions interview she is asked what she knows about the Armenians. She tells the priest who is interviewing her that she knows they have had "a long and troubled history, like everyone else over here" (77). When she adds that she loves the stories of William Saroyan and that she feels "very close to what I know of Armenian culture through Saroyan's stories" (78), the "air in the room changed" and the priest decides to admit her even though she has no Armenian blood. By drawing on her reading, Liyana starts to forge a connection between what she knows intellectually and the application of that knowledge to her new life.

Not long after this incident Liyana feels "as if a compass had swung around inside her" (85) and she agrees to spend a weekend at her grandmother's village (85). During this first visit she begins to learn to make bread. More importantly, she learns that her dependency on a translator [her grandmother, Sitti, speaks no English] has lessened and that she no longer feels like an exotic animal in the village. Rather, she is able to feel as "invisible and happy" (87) as she used to feel at home riding her bike. It is only after Liyana begins to feel at home in her new country, once she no longer feels so much the outsider, that she is able to engage with her culture in an active way.

She feels anger when she witnesses acts of bigotry and then wonders what to do with that anger: should she hold it in or express it? Significantly, she asks herself what Sitti would do. She answers her own question: "Sitti might have howled like a coyote" (95). She writes: "What good is a mouth if it won't open when you need it to?" (93). Her instinctive turning toward Sitti as a source of knowledge and her rhetorical question suggest that she has come to see speaking out, or using her voice, as a moral imperative.

Liyana's need to speak out gradually increases. She initially speaks out only when self-interest is involved, but slowly learns to use her voice to address and ameliorate injustice and bigotry. She begins to use it to assert herself, first when she is attracted to a Jewish boy and then later when she tries to help her father when he is arrested after a shooting in a Palestinian refugee camp. Finally, she directly addresses her own family's discomfort with Jews when she invites Omer, her Jewish boyfriend, to her grandmother's village.

Liyana met Omer at a ceramics shop she has visited with her father. He is a close friend of the owners. When he asks her to attend a concert with him she knows she has "rounded the bend where conversations with her parents were no longer going to be as easy as they once were" (160). Nonetheless, she convinces her mother to take her to the city without revealing the details of her plans. Like LaVaughn, she resorts to concealing information when necessary. When her mother learns that Liyana intends to meet a boy, she panics and immediately worries about her husband's response: "Do you know what your father would say? . . . This is his country. It is a very conservative country. . . . Remember the shorts? Remember his story about someone getting into trouble in the village simply because he talked to a woman in the street? People have supposedly been killed! For little indiscretions!" (160).

During her first date Liyana learns that Omer is Jewish. She responds by launching into a recitation of how badly the Jews have treated Arabs. Omer calmly replies, "It's a bad history without a doubt. . . . What are we going to do about it?" (166). His response assumes something can be done, and Liyana assents to his optimism. Later, when her father hears that she has not only been with a boy but a Jewish one at that, he is left almost speechless, able only to mutter, "What? Who? Where?" (171). But Liyana throws his own history back at him as well as the need to put his own theories of ethnic harmony into practice: "This isn't a book report you know. . . . Remember when you told us you had Jewish neighbors when you were growing up here? Remember how we had plenty of Jewish friends back in the United States?" (171). Her father, Poppy, responds, "Never, never, never," yet Liyana persists, arguing that a commitment to peace is only an abstraction if not accompanied by a change in how one lives: "What good is it to believe in peace and talk about peace if you only want to live in the same old way?" (240). By the end of the novel her father has consented to take Omer to his mother's village for a visit. There Sitti greets him warmly, seeing in him the spirit of a Jewish man she had loved as a young woman and admonishes him to "[r]emember us when you join your army" (258).

Liyana's willingness to confront her father with what she sees as his hypocrisy prepares her to speak out in the service of others. When a shooting occurs in a refugee camp for Arab refugees and Poppy tries to help a victim, Israeli soldiers arrest him. Liyana learns this and rushes to the jail to find him. When she asks to see her father, a soldier tells her, "It is not possible" (227). Hearing this, "Something shifted inside her. . . . She stomped her foot at the soldiers. 'Of course it's possible!' she said loudly. 'He is my father! I need to see him NOW! PLEASE! It is necessary. I must go in this minute!'" (227) Liyana is allowed to see her father, and upon leaving, she speaks out one more time to the soldiers. She speaks because "she cannot stop herself. . . . You did not have to be so mean! You could be nicer! My father is a doctor! My friend who you shot is a gentle person! YOU DO NOT HAVE TO BE THIS WAY!" (232)

Liyana's assertion signifies her willingness to see herself as a moral agent, an agent of change. From this point on she seldom wonders about her friends in America, about whether they miss her or what her identity is in a land where few know her or her history. Rather, she is occupied with philosophical questions on the nature of violence, anger, and hate as a way of helping her understand her new country and its problems. Her shift in focus does not mean that she is no longer interested in issues of identity, only that she has placed those issues in a particular cultural context.

*Habibi* charts the gradual empowerment of a girl finding herself through her interaction with and gradual acceptance of another culture, one that is part of her heritage. Over the course of the novel, Liyana moves from being an outsider looking in to someone who claims membership in her new country. Once she does this, she is persistent in her efforts to enact peace and not just talk about doing so.

Ultimately, *Habibi* ends on a hopeful note. Liyana and Omer hold fast in their determination to maintain a relationship, despite cultural opposition to do so. Nye ends the novel with a verbal version of "A Peaceable Kingdom," with American, Arab, and Jew all sitting down breaking bread together. Liyana says, "We want to write a new story" (240). Nye seems to suggest that Liyana's willingness to speak out, to put theory into practice, will make a new story possible.

### Rain Is Not My Indian Name

Rain, the narrator and protagonist of Cynthia Leitich Smith's *Rain Is Not My Indian Name*, is, like Liyana of *Habibi*, a mixed-race child like her parents, both who are of white and Native American heritage. Understandably, Rain refers to herself as a "mixed blood girl."[8] Though Rain is, on the surface, comfortable with her Indian identity, when pushed, she acknowledges the difficulty of reconciling her own sense of self with that of the larger world: "I'm used to being me. Dealing with the rest of the world and its ideas, now that makes me a little crazy sometimes" (115). The specific aspects of the "rest of the world" that make her crazy are the stereotypical representations of Native Americans dominating popular culture that she finds demeaning: "I'd seen so many tacky looking dream-catchers over the years, the kind with fakelore gift tags and flamingo feathers" (73). She instinctively compares white society's depiction of Indian culture[9]—"construction paper feathers, a plastic paint pony, and Malibu Pocahontas"—(51) with the authentic tear dress her dead mother had made and the antique bead necklace her friend Galen gives her, angered by the dissonance between her experience and the representation of that experience by mainstream culture.

Rain's strategy for coping with this dissonance is to silence herself in public and confine her frustrations to her journal. Though proud of her culture and well aware that she is one of only "nine Indians living in town" (50), Rain is unwilling to publicly align herself with the small community of Native Americans in her area. This is made clear at the beginning of the novel when she refuses to join the summer Indian Camp her aunt Georgia is starting for Native American children.

Her reluctance to publicly embrace Native American identity is partially a reflection of her father and brother's ambivalence about their heritage. Though Rain's mother had embraced Native American culture before she died, claiming tribal status, her father and brother are more ambivalent about doing so. Her father sees no need to educate his children about their heritage, and her brother Fynn sends his younger sister mixed messages. Though he signs Rain up for Indian Camp and is disappointed when she refuses to attend, he has not always been willing to identify himself as Native-American. Rain notes in her journal that when he registered himself for college, "he changed the marks in all the boxes from 'Native American/American Indian to White'" (94). Smith implies that both Rain's father and brother's ambivalence about their race stems from their awareness of the marginal position white culture has assigned Native Americans. Rain's reluctance to align herself with the teenagers identified as Native American is not only a consequence of the mixed messages she receives from her father and brother but also a result of her own experience as a minority in the public school system. She notes that "I'd always been the only Indian near my age who'd attended Hannesburg middle-school, prayed at the first Baptist Church, and gobbled fries at the local McDonald's" (51). Her minority status is further reinforced by an academic curriculum that pays only token attention to Native Americans:

> At school the subject of Native Americans pretty much comes up around Turkey Day, like those cardboard cutouts of the Pilgrims and the pumpkins and the squash taped to the windows of McDonald's. And the so-called Indians always look like Bogeymen on the prairies or windblown cover boys selling paperback romances, or baby-faced refugees from the world of Precious Moments. I usually get through it by reading sci-fi fanzines behind my textbooks until we move on to Kwanza. (13)

Rain's desire to keep her Native American identity separate from white culture's understanding of that identity is a reflection and acceptance of the position to which the dominant culture has relegated her. Her marginalization is further reinforced in the opening chapters of the novel by her intense grief over the accidental death of her best friend, Galen. After he is hit and killed by a car, Rain deliberately isolates herself from her established sources of support. "My choir and soccer buddies, my school counselor and the youth pastor. . . . I fell out of my regular circles" (16–17), she says, confining herself to her house, where she spends her time cleaning, reading sci-fi fanzines, and surfing the Internet. The challenge then for Rain is to reconcile herself to the loss of Galen, reconnect with her community, and to find the courage to voice her dissatisfaction with mainstream culture's representation of Native American experience. She needs to find the courage to give public expression to the honest, witty, and slightly acerbic voice that characterizes her journal writings.

The process by which she fulfills these needs is initially slow. Six months after Galen's death she begins to tire of her self-imposed isolation, realizing that "hiding out had become boring" (25). More importantly, she remembers the promise she and Galen made to each other, always to remember the other's birthday. As his birthday approaches, she searches for a fitting tribute for him, feeling the need to honor the commitment she has made. The task of publicly claiming her identity as an Indian begins when she is hired by the local newspaper to take photographs of the camp she has refused to attend. Rain's role as a paid photographer, in effect, allows her to straddle two cultures. As an employee of the newspaper she is expected to maintain a certain amount of distance from the camp, i.e. to try to maintain objectivity. Her editor tells her that she will be fired if she joins the camp or any of its activities. Yet as a photographer she has the power, through the images she creates, to influence how white culture views Native Americans, to offer a counter narrative to the images promulgated by the mass media. But while Rain's photos allow her to shape cultural perceptions of Native Americans, she is also acutely aware that she also uses her camera to create a "wall" (126) between herself and others.

Inevitably, as a photographer she becomes acquainted with the various campers and increasingly empathetic to their responses to their minority status. When two campers resist talking to a reporter about their lives as Native Americans, Rain is sympathetic: "Maybe they felt like they shouldn't have to explain themselves. Like they didn't particularly care if Hannesburg got a glimpse into their lives" (66). The campers' response, or lack of one, echoes Rain's earlier feelings when she had argued, "My heritage was not something to be talked about in the local news" (36). Rain's growing sense of connection to the campers crystallizes when Mrs. Owen, Galen's mother, writes a letter to the local newspaper protesting the use of city funds to support the Indian Camp and insists that the city council vote on this expenditure. Rain initially dismisses this issue as "not that big a deal" (84). But when another camper reminds her that "It's about *us*. You're here for the paper, not Indian Camp" (82), Rain is forced to decide where her loyalties lie and whether she is content to be a mere recorder of her culture. She decides to align herself with the Indian Campers and agrees to try to persuade Mrs. Owen to drop her objection to camp funding. She does this knowing full well that her editor will interpret her actions as a conflict of interest and fire her.

Rain's decision to join Indian Camp produces mixed results. She *is* dismissed from covering the Indian Camp, and her efforts to dissuade Mrs. Owen to stop funding for it fail. When she identifies herself as a member of the camp during the city council meeting, her Uncle Ed, a member of the council, refrains from voting on the issue, and funding for the camp is defeated by a single vote. But in terms of Rain's personal growth, the consequences are wholly positive. She becomes more creative, improving her photography and now is able to create a memorial for Galen. Thus, in speaking out, she frees a part of herself that has been repressed. Further, she no longer feels she is the "only Indian" her age. Instead she has gained membership in a community whose members offer each other support and encouragement. Rain's world is no longer confined to the four walls of her room. Rather, her sense of the world and of her place in it has expanded. When a local gossip asks Rain about her plans she announces that she is going to "run like night creatures and howl at the moon" (131). Her response reveals her newly won self-perception of herself as a girl who moves freely and speaks loudly.

## Saying Goodbye

Marie G. Lee's *Saying Goodbye* also depicts a girl coming to grips with her ethnic identity who, in doing so, finds her voice. Like Rain, she forges connections with a community she previously rejected. In the process she learns that the nature of racism is complex, that following her own sense of ethics often has painful consequences, and that she must chart her own course in life. *Saying Goodbye* continues the story of Ellen Sung, the daughter of Korean immigrants, first introduced to readers in Lee's *Finding My Voice*. In this sequel Ellen has been admitted to Harvard, something her parents told her "meant I'd be set for life."[10] Ellen herself is not so certain. As she arrives on campus, she is tempted to tell the cabby "to take me back to the airport so I can return to Mom and Father and all my friends in Arkin [Minnesota]" (2). Her anxieties at this point are those of any first-year college student leaving home for the first time, and they are assuaged when she meets her roommate, Leecia, an African American who genuinely seems to like her.

It is Leecia who introduces the theme of ethnic identity when she comments to Ellen, "They put an Asian-American woman and an African-American woman at the same address. . . . You'd think they'd want to spice up the diversity of some of the other housing units. . . . Even Harvard wants to make sure that white students learn a little about exotic cultures while they are here. Multiculturalism is big right now" (8-9). Ellen's own experience with multiculturalism is limited: her family is the only Asian one in her small town; her parents stress assimilation, and she herself admits, " I have also never personally known a black person" (9). When Leecia, who is taking several African-American courses, suggests that Ellen might want to take a course in Asian-American literature, Ellen is genuinely puzzled. Leecia tells her "You're Asian, doesn't it make sense to study those works?" (22). Because her favored authors are Mark Twain and Flannery O'Connor and because she "was never into The Joy Luck Club" (21), Ellen wonders if "that make[s] me some kind of weirdo—being Asian but not especially interested in reading Asian authors?" (22).

Ellen's lack of interest in Asian-American writers is an extension of her lack of community or connection with the other Asian and Asian-American students on campus, something she herself is surprised by: "So now I'm here with people who look like me, and it's a big . . . disappointingly big, so-what. Somehow I thought I'd feel magically connected, more confident, whatever" (27). However, Ellen does begin to feel connected to other Koreans when she joins the Harvard Tae Kwon Club and starts to develop friendships with other Asian-American students, in particular Jae Chun, a boy to whom she is attracted. Through him she is introduced to another group, the Korean-American Students of Harvard (KASH) and through this group, to the politics of ethnic identity.

Ellen's story, for much of *Saying Goodbye,* is one of blossoming as she says goodbye to her high school world and enters into one with greater choices and, correspondingly, greater responsibilities. She makes the decision to take a class in short story writing, something she loves, even though it is not a recommended part of her pre-med major. She gets a short story accepted for publication in the teen magazine *Sassy.* As her friendships with Leecia and with Jae deepen, Ellen interacts comfortably with both African-American and Korean-American students. But when the African-American Students Alliance decides to bring a rapper, Professor T, to campus for a performance, Ellen is forced to choose between conflicting loyalties. Her Korean-American friends, many of whom have families whose businesses were destroyed in the Los Angeles riots, are deeply offended by Professor T's song, "Get Down, Nuke Koreatown," and plan to protest his visit. Her roommate and friend, Leecia, counters Ellen's concerns by arguing that "'Get Down, Nuke Koreatown' is one of the few outlets we [African Americans] have to express the rage that comes from all the injustices we have to suffer everyday" (167). Leecia also argues that any dissension about Professor T's visit is "censorship, plain and simple" (167). Inclined to agree with Leecia, Ellen nevertheless tells herself, "I should listen to the lyrics myself before I make any judgment" (167).

Hearing the lyrics, Ellen tries to remember what Leecia has told her about " rap being art, creative expression" (179), but all she can see as she listens is "Jae and his mother and father, standing amid a pile of smoking ashes" (179).[11] When the song ends she is "suddenly sure exactly which side I am standing on" (179). Ellen's willingness to align herself with KASH is a rejection of political passivity and movement into political activism. When a KASH leader asks if she has any ideas about how to get attention for their cause during Professor T's visit, she suggests replacing the African-American Students Alliance's welcoming banner with another that denounces Professor T's racism. She is able to do this because Leecia, assuming that Ellen shares her views about the rapper, has confided to her about where the banner will be stored. Although Ellen has mixed feelings about her decision to sabotage her roommate's banner, feeling "fleetingly like Benedict Arnold" (179), she also believes that if she does nothing, "We'd get nowhere." Ellen also believes, naively, that Leecia will "understand why I need to do this" (181).

However, Ellen's actions not only disrupt the welcoming rally but destroy her friendship with Leecia. Both girls are caught on national TV as Ellen tells Leecia, "You're not protecting free speech, you're protecting Professor T's right to sling cheap hate and that makes you as much a racist!" (190) Though Ellen almost immediately regrets her words and tries to apologize, Lucia refuses to accept either Ellen's apology or her explanation that racism directed at Koreans is as offensive to her as racism directed toward African-Americans is to Leecia. Ellen regrets her words and mourns the loss of Leecia's friendship. Her identification with other Korean-Americans as well as her willingness to oppose Leecia on racial issues reveals a newfound confidence in her own voice. Through much of the novel she has kept her disagreements with Leecia to herself. But the Ellen at the end of the novel is very different from the insecure first-year student who opens it. More outspoken, more willing to defend her beliefs, she also has a greater understanding of the world's complexity and the difficulty of achieving happy endings. As she considers the end of her relationship with Leccia, she acknowledges this: "If I could figure out exactly what went wrong and then fix it, I would. But I think I am coming to realize that life in all its complexity doesn't work like that. I could spend the rest of my life trying to figure out what went wrong and I still wouldn't know" (212). Ellen's acceptance of the world's complexity coupled with her acceptance that her actions will not always bring her happy conclusions is not the happy ending many readers would wish for. Ellen's friendship with Leecia is over and she accepts it. But her increased understanding of the world and her role in it hints at a happier future.

Lee, Staples and Nye all end their novels on cautiously optimistic notes. Ellen, Shabanu, and Liyana have each effected changes that benefit not only them but also those around them. But their accomplishments are, at least partially, a function of favorable material circumstances, specifically their respective social classes and the position of those classes within the larger culture. All three hold membership in large and stable family units that function as safety nets. Shabanu, for example, though she comes from a poor family, is married into wealth and so is able to secret funds that will ultimately make possible a better life for her and her daughter. And though, in the novel's sequel, her husband's other wives scorn her family's occupation as camel herders, her family is, nevertheless, stable and respected by others. Likewise, Liyana, the daughter of a doctor, never has to worry about her next meal and therfore has more time to worry about issues of identity. Though she struggles with her identity as an Arab, she, too, is sustained and nurtured by a stable and extensive family. Ellen's father also is a physician. All the girls' achievements are not simply the products of individual will but of the external circumstances that shape that will and allow it to flourish.

## Under the Feet of Jesus

What is empowerment for a girl who has neither wealth nor a stable family to draw on and whose ethnicity places her on the margins of mainstream culture? What possibilities are available to her for finding her voice and using it to enhance the lives of others? Helena Maria Viramontes explores these questions in *Under the Feet of Jesus*, the story of

Estrella, a thirteen-year-old migrant farm worker and the oldest of five children abandoned by their father years ago. When the novel begins, her mother, Petra, is pregnant by another man, Perfecto, a carpenter in his seventies. Neither Estrella nor Perfecto is aware of this.

As migrant workers, Estrella and her family's lives are shaped by factors over which they have little control: "It was always a question of work, and work depended on the harvest, and the car running, their health, the conditions of the road, how long their money held out, and the weather, which meant they could depend on nothing."[12] Over the course of the novel these factors either falter or fail completely. Estrella's family life is further complicated by its Hispanic status in a predominately Anglo culture, one that is dependent on their labor but seldom rewards them with the fruits of those labors. Petra tries to teach her children how to claim a place in a culture that is theirs by birth but which views them with suspicion. She hides her children's birth certificates under a statue of Jesus she carries with her as they move from work site to work site and reminds Estrella never to forget the location of these important documents:

> Don't run scared. You stay there and look them [immigration officials] in the eye. Don't let them make you feel like you did a crime for picking the vegetables they'll be eating for dinner. If they stop you, if they try to pull you into the green vans, you tell them the birth certificates are under the feet of Jesus, just tell them. (63)

Despite her status as a birthright citizen, Estrella is the "other" by virtue of her looks and class. Clearly not the stereotypical blond and blue-eyed American girl, she is sharply aware that many of her teachers focus more on her hygiene than her desire to learn:

> Estrella hated when things were kept from her. . . . The teachers in the school never [gave] her the information she wanted. Estrella would ask over and over, So what is this, and point to the diagonal lines written in chalk on the blackboard. . . . But some of the teachers were more concerned with the dirt under her fingernails. They inspected her head for lice, parting her long hair with ice cream sticks. They scrubbed her fingers with a toothbrush until they were so sore she couldn't hold a pencil properly. (25)

Living a life shaped by poverty and bigotry, Estrella has few opportunities to assert herself. Unlike her friend Alejo, who tries to follow his grandmother's advice to "seize the chance and make something of yourself in this great and true country" (54), Estrella is more cynical about the possibilities of Hispanics grabbing the American dream. She wonders as she helps pull down an old barn if her life won't be like the barn's, where "people just use you until you are all used up, then rip you into pieces when they're finished using you" (75). Her resistance to powerlessness initially takes the form of small acts of generosity, such as giving a piece of fruit to a much older and exhausted co-worker. Her sense of connection to others comes from sustaining them in whatever ways she is able and is inherited from her mother, who maintains, "We have to look out for our own" (97).

The turning point in Estrella's seemingly hopeless existence comes when her family takes the critically ill Alejo to a heath clinic. At the clinic the nurse's barely suppressed irritation with the migrant workers convinces Estrella that "God was mean and did not care and she was alone to fend for herself" (139). When the nurse tells her that Alejo must be taken to a hospital, the family is thrown into a crisis: the ten dollars they have paid the nurse leaves them no money for the gas they need to get to the hospital. Angered by the nurse's refusal even to acknowledge their plight, much less help them, Estrella chooses to "do something to get the money for gas for the hospital for Alejo" (148). She takes a crowbar and threatens to smash the windows of the clinic if the nurse does not return the money they have paid her. After keeping her thoughts to herself, she suddenly gives voice to them: "Give us back our money!" she demands of the nurse (149). The violence of her actions frightens Perfecto and Estrella's mother. More important is Estrella's own surprise at her action. Having, in effect, given birth to a new self, she "felt like two Estrellas. One was a silent phantom who obediently marked a circle with a stick around the bungalow as the mother had requested, while the other held the crowbar and the money" (150).

Estrella's actions do not immediately affect the larger, external circumstances of her life or her family's lives. It is not even clear that Alejo will survive once he is admitted to the hospital, and Perfecto fears the nurse will press charges against Estrella, forcing them to move on again. Nevertheless, Estrella's actions impress her younger siblings, who now believe "that their big sister had the magic in her hands to split glass in two" (*Jesus*, 156). Estrella herself believes her response is the only one possible in a social structure where "[y]ou talk and talk and talk to them and they ignore you" (151). The change, then, that has occurred is primarily an internal one, similar to Shabanu's. Nevertheless, it allows Estrella to re-assess herself and the possibilities for her life. At the end of the novel she climbs to the top of the barn she has been helping to tear down and looks out at the sky and "believed her heart powerful enough to summon home all those who strayed" (176).

## When Kambia Elaine Flew in from Neptune

Like Estrella, Shayla, the twelve-year-old narrator of *When Kambia Elaine Flew in from Neptune*, comes from a family marginalized by race and class. Shayla, her Mama, and fifteen-year-old sister Tia live on the outskirts of Houston in an area known as the Bottoms, a name that literally designates Shayla's family's social position. Poor and African-American, they scrape by on what their mother can make at her job as a convenience store clerk and the help their grandmother Augustine can spare. Though Shayla's mother and grandmother provide constant love, she is nevertheless surrounded by and drawn into conflicts she is only beginning to understand, all of them sexual. These conflicts involve her sister, her mother, and, most importantly, her new neighbor and friend, Kambia.

The novel opens with a fight between Mama and Tia, one that begins when Mama finds condoms in Tia's bureau drawer: "You just better keep your dress down and your drawers up! Don't you be bringing home no babies for me to feed," Mama says.[13] Mama's anger with Tia stems from her fear that her daughter will repeat her own history: "Mama had done the same thing at her age . . . had gotten pregnant with Tia when she was only fifteen" (3). When Tia breaks into tears, Shayla wants "to tell her it was alright [*sic*], but I couldn't. I was a reader and a writer but, not much of a talker, at least when it came to feelings and stuff" (3). Ironically, though she cannot speak out, Shayla's voice as a writer is strong and lyrical and reveals a luminous understanding of feelings. After the fight between her mother and sister, she writes in her journal, "Everything's a mess. . . . Anger is covering our house like pitch on a rooftop" (3). One of her challenges then, is to make her spoken voice as strong as her written, to move from her position of silent witness to that of someone who plays an active role in resolving the conflicts that surround her.

The conflict between Tia and Mama is over Tia's involvement with a twenty-three-year-old man nicknamed Doo-witty, someone Shayla characterizes as a "slow, drop-jawed, long-headed dope" (7). Shayla is herself befuddled by her sister's attraction to this man, saying "Tia with Doo-witty, it wasn't possible. Tia was fine, and she made great grades in school, like me she could choose" (7). Shayla's belief that the power of choice carries with it the possibility for a life greater than what the Bottoms offers is sorely tested when Mama catches Tia in a compromising position with Doo-witty:

> There can't be but one woman in my house. I won't have no woman-child. If you feel like your wings done sprouted and you ready to fly, take off—but the only woman in my house is me. You can make up your mind, Miss Tia. You can either be a girl or a woman, but I only got room for girls under my roof. (51)

Tia makes her choice and disappears without a clue. Convinced that Tia has run off with Doo-witty, Mama makes no effort to try to find her, maintaining, "She went out of here on her own. Let her come back the same way" (74). Nevertheless, Tia's disappearance throws Shayla, her mother, and her grandmother, Augustine, into a depression, one that makes Mama particularly susceptible to the attentions of Shayla's father, Mr. Anderson Fox, when he turns up in the town. Shayla herself is deeply suspicious of Mr. Anderson Fox, a man she refers to as "my sometime father" and about whom she has "no idea of how I am supposed to feel. Should I feel glad or angry? I'm only sure that I don't like playing daughter every time he feels the need to hear at least one of his kids calling him Daddy" (73). While Shayla tries to sort out her feelings for her father, Mama puts out extra effort to make him feel welcome, motivated by the desire for any child support he might offer as well as by lingering attraction. Angered by her father's dismissal of her interest in her reading and writing and by her mother's flirtatious behavior, Shayla turns to her grandmother, asserting she "didn't want anything from him" (80). Her grandmother's response reminds Shayla of the material needs that drive much of the behavior in her community: "I know you didn't, baby, but your mama did. I'm not proud to say this, Shayla, but sometimes you have to go down the wrong path to get to the right place . . . it don't make you feel good but it won't kill you either" (80).

Shayla's confusion over her father, mother, and sister's disappearance is intensified by her developing friendship with her new neighbor, a girl her age named Kambia Elaine. Kambia Elaine is Shayla's physical opposite, small and thin, whereas Shayla is heavy-set. Nevertheless, the two share important similarities. Both suffer from poverty, though Kambia's is the greater, and both are avid readers and storytellers. But whereas Shayla writes in her journal and creates stories to record and understand her difficulties, Kambia tells stories that allow her to distance herself from an abusive home life.

Significantly, the stories Kambia tells contain the elements of fairy tales, magic and transformation. When Shayla first meets her, Kambia is trying to retrieve a bracelet she has lost in a storm sewer. After she retrieves it, Shayla characterizes it as "just an old plastic bracelet. You can buy 'em for nothing downtown" (5). Kambia rejects Shayla's assessment, arguing, "When I hold it up in the moonlight, I become so tiny that only the ants can see me. When the wind blows real hard, I blow away like the dust until I find a wonderful, beautiful place to land" (5). Kambia's need to become "tiny," to "blow away like dust," is a response to the abuse she experiences daily. Her mother, a prostitute who works out of their home, allows her customers to sexually abuse Kambia. Kambia's stories are an attempt to shield her from the poverty and abuse she experiences daily by creating a parallel universe that allows for beauty. When asked by her teacher how babies are made, Kambia says "they dropped out of the violet, dew-drenched flowers early in the morning when everyone was asleep and crawled to the homes of their new mothers" (13). Hearing this, her teacher makes her leave the classroom. Like her teacher, Shayla is initially put off by Kambia's stories until she recognizes that they serve the same function as her own journal and fiction writing. She comes to this realization after Kambia defends to an adult Shayla 's right to express herself in her own voice, one that uses "street rhyme . . . plenty of slang" (30). After Kambia has come to Shayla's defense, Shayla decides that "next time [Kambia] told one of her tales I would listen. Maybe it would help me figure her out" (41).

The crisis in Shayla's relationship with Kambia comes one morning when they are walking to school and Kambia begins to hemorrhage from the sexual abuse she has suffered that morning from one of her mother's clients. Though she is ignorant of the cause of Kambia's injuries, Shayla knows she needs to get her help. Doing so, however, means breaking trust with Kambia, who has made her promise never to tell about the "wallpaper wolves" (59) in her home, creatures that "reach out and grab you with their claws" (60). Once Kambia is hospitalized, Shayla is pressured by her grandmother and the police to reveal what she knows about her friend's life. She wonders, "Was it okay to break a bond or promise if it was going to do something good for someone?" (211). Before she reveals what she knows, Shayla tells Kambia what she is going to do. When Kambia says "You're not my friend," Shayla, though pained, is able to respond, "Yes, I am, I'm your best friend" (211). Shayla's intervention literally saves Kambia's life and helps her into a new home with loving parents. Shayla herself is left with a more complicated, more sophisticated understanding of the ethics of friendship and loyalty, one that enhances her understanding of the adults around her and their reasons for behaving as they do. Additionally, Shayla's newfound ability to speak out helps her reunite her family. She finds Tia and convinces her to communicate with Mama. Tia comes home, and though her homecoming is "rocky," she and her mother achieve a new level of understanding and respect. Finally, Mr. Anderson Fox, who has moved into Shayla's home, moves out. Though he leaves Mama for another woman, Shayla exchanges her hatred of him for pity, aware that the new life he is starting won't "be any better than the life he had," and she resolves "not to hurt him like he had hurt me and Mama" (245). Shayla's decision is an attempt to gain control over her own life, to "get peace for myself" (245) and, as such, reveals her newfound determination to speak out for what she needs.

The internal transformation these protagonists experience has the effect of opening their imaginations to lives of wider possibilities. Prior to this shift, they all seem stuck and hard-pressed to imagine satisfying lives for themselves. For example, before her confrontation with the nurse, Estrella cannot imagine her life holding anything more than back-breaking farm labor done for the benefit of others. After the confrontation she is able to envision herself as powerful. Shayla, though still poor, has brought her mother and sister together again and in the final scene of the novel she is scattering dried rose petals onto her front porch, so that "goodness was sprinkling down on the porch like powdered sugar . . . to make sure it was only good things that got tracked in the house" (246).

## *The Year They Burned the Books*

Nancy Garden has explored this same transformation in four novels, all dealing with girls coming to grips with their identities as lesbians. Like the other protagonists discussed in this chapter, these girls must learn to accept an "otherness" that goes beyond simply being female. However, unlike the protagonists discussed earlier, their otherness is not initially apparent to those around them or even to themselves. Starting with *Annie on My Mind* and moving on to *Lark in the Morning, Good Moon Rising,* and *The Year They Burned the Books*, Garden has depicted protagonists (with the exception of *Lark in the Morning*) whose struggles for self-acceptance must be resolved before they can address other goals. In all four of these novels, she depicts girls whose conceptions of self are incomplete until they recognize and are reconciled to their lesbianism. Their coming out to themselves is accompanied by an involuntary public coming out as well, one that is the result of their culture's homophobia. The protagonists' conflicts, then, are both internal and external as they struggle to accept and assert themselves in a culture that is often hostile to their very existence. Ironically, in the most recent of these four novels, *The Year They Burned the Books,* Garden focuses on a girl whose public persona and voice is well established: Jamie Crawford, a high school senior, who is editor of her high school newspaper. Although adept at manipulating the language of her chosen career, Jamie has neither listened to or expressed her inner voice. At the start of the novel Jamie is unsure of her sexual orientation. Over the course of the book, Jamie recognizes her identity and struggles to acknowledge it publicly.

In *The Year They Burned the Books*, Jamie initially identifies herself as a "Maybe," someone who may or may not be homosexual.[14] She knows she is different and is frightened because of the response of others to her difference: "Jamie had always felt different in some undefined way, but eventually she began to understand why, and the more she understood, the more the name calling hurt and frightened her" (11). Over the course of a year she gradually makes the transition from being a "Maybe" to a "Probably." This process is facilitated by two external events: her growing attraction to a new girl in her school and the efforts of a local conservative group to remove from the curriculum any books they deem immoral. This group, Families for Traditional Values, targets books dealing with premarital sex, birth control, and homosexuality. Jamie uses her position as editor of the school newspaper to oppose this group and in doing so becomes increasingly self-confident. At the beginning of the book, closeted, she identifies herself as a "coward" (86). By the end she has come out to her friends and family and has organized successful community resistance to the reelection of its most conservative member to the school committee.

Jamie's process of coming out and redefining herself as someone willing to publicly take on difficult issues is facilitated by her skills as a writer. Over the course of the novel Jamie uses these skills in three very different venues. First, she edits the school newspaper, the *Wilson High Telegraph*. In her capacity as editor she learns to negotiate and balance her sense of truth with that of others. When the *Telegraph* is severely censored by the school committee, Jamie and her friends respond by putting out an alternative newspaper, the *Renegade*, a vehicle for free expression. While writing for both these papers, Jamie also keeps a journal in which she writes about her emerging sexuality as well as her anxieties over her public role as school newspaper editor. Jamie's changing attitude toward her journal parallels her growing comfort with her sense of self: at the beginning of the novel she keeps it hidden from her family. By the novel's end, she is comfortable enough to leave it out on her desk.

## Hard Love

Writing as a mode of discovery and affirmation also figures prominently in Ellen Wittlinger's *Hard Love*. The novel is narrated by an alienated sixteen-year-old boy who gradually emerges from his shell and his self-absorption through his friendship with Marisol, who describes herself as a "Puerto Rican Cuban Yankee Lesbian." John, the narrator, first becomes acquainted with Marisol by reading her 'zine, "Escape Velocity." An aspiring 'zine writer himself, he is drawn to Marisol's work because he admires how she "just lays her life out for people to see, like she loves the weird way she is, and if you had any sense you would too."[15] While most of the novels discussed in this chapter depict girls working toward empowerment, *Hard Love* focuses on a girl who already is empowered and shows the powerful effect she has on those around her.

Determined to meet Marisol, John contrives to be at Tower Records in Boston when she is there to distribute the newest edition of "Escape Velocity." His description of his first meeting with her emphasizes the sense of power she conveys. She is, he says, "tiny . . . though her voice was big" (21). When she speaks, her voice is not just big but "like her haircut, sharp and dangerous. . . . Kind of scary. . . . She reminded me of a little bitty Clint Eastwood" (21–22). As they become first acquaintances and then friends, John learns that Marisol's power comes not just from her intimidating presence but from her strong sense of integrity and self-worth. When John refers to his own 'zine as "Not a big deal" (26), Marisol is indignant over his seeming lack of seriousness: "So why bother then if it's just some half-assed way to waste your time? If you're not committed to having people read what you've written? What have we been talking about all morning? . . . I really hate that, people who don't take things seriously" (26–27).

John has to process Marisol's contempt for people who don't take things "seriously." Hurt by his parents' divorce, his mother's refusal to have any physical contact with him, and his father's bachelor lifestyle, John has a heavy emotional investment in maintaining a façade of cynical nonchalance. Yet Marisol reveals his façade for what it is, a lie that he must give up if he wants a friendship with her: "It's a lie, you know, to pretend that nothing is important to you. It's hiding. Believe me, I know, because I hid for a long time. But now I won't do it anymore. I don't lie and I don't waste time on people who do" (27).

Marisol goes on to expand the definition of "coming out" so that it encompasses heterosexual as well as homosexual experience. She also makes clear to John that there are other closets than those occupied by homosexuals: "Do you know what 'coming out' really means? It means you stop lying. You tell the truth even if it's painful, especially if it's painful. To everybody, your parents included" (27). When John protests that he is not gay, Marisol counters, "There are other closets" (27).

All of this occurs during John's first conversation with Marisol, and it establishes the issues he will confront over the course of the novel. John began his relationship with Marisol with a lie when he introduced himself as Giovanni or Gio rather than John because the Italian version of his name seems more interesting. Soon, however, a bigger lie emerges, one with greater consequences: John lies to himself about his growing attraction to Marisol and his acceptance of her lesbianism. Marisol agrees to have coffee with him at their first meeting only if he is not "some crazy person who thinks he could turn me straight" (24). John assures her he is not. But it becomes increasingly clear to her and to the reader, if not to him, that on some level he cherishes such a hope.

By the end of the novel John and Marisol separate, both because of his difficulty in accepting her for what she has always professed herself to be and her desire to be with other lesbians. Though John is clearly pained by these events, he has become a stronger person. When Marisol leaves for New York to live with other women, he is able to thank her for "touching me" (223).

What are the consequences for John of having been touched by Marisol's strength? For one, he no longer lies about the pain his parents' treatment of him has caused, and he is able to share his feelings with them. Though this affects no dramatic change of attitude on their part, the closing pages hint that a transformation is occurring in the parent-child relationship. More importantly, he is able to drop his mask of cynicism and honestly acknowledge a whole range of emotions. Watching Marisol depart, he says, "In a funny way, it was wonderful" (223), and as he contemplates rejoining his family, he is "very anxious, more than a little scared, susceptible to anything that might happen" (224).

Novels such as the ones discussed above, then, addressing issues that lie outside mainstream culture, contribute to our understanding of the many ways in which girls come of age, and any definition of "empowered girl" must take into account the context in which the protagonist develops her sense of competence and autonomy, while allowing for cultural differences.

## ROMANCE AND ADVENTURE

What Donelson and Nilsen categorize as the "adventure/accomplishment romance" provides an additional venue for young female empowerment in contemporary settings. In contrast to the sometimes harsh circumstances and problematic endings of the more realistic novels, these stories close on an upbeat note not compromised by the ambiguities of the real world. Like the heroines in problem novels, the girls in adventure and romance stories endure a difficult journey that may be internal or external, but they finish on a note of triumph, their ultimate victory heightened by the severity of the events that have preceded it. Donelson and Nilsen point out that the structure of these novels includes the three stages of initiation into the adult world as practiced by many cultures:

> First, the young person is separated both physically and spiritually from the nurturing love of most or all friends and family. This is one of the reasons

that so many accomplishment stories include a trip. Another reason for the trip is that the new environment provides new challenges and learning experiences. During the separation, the hero, who embodies noble qualities, undergoes a test of courage and stamina that may be mental, psychological or physical. In the final stage, the young person is reunited with former friends and family in a new role of increased status. (147)

Despite the structural similarities, the nature of the "accomplishment" story varies from novel to novel, from youthful flirtations to heart-stopping escapades. For decades girls in fiction have been discovering where they have to go by falling in (or out of) love, and they continue to do so, but in their pursuit of romance, they are more independent than their predecessors. Unlike Angie Morrow, they do not depend entirely on the boy to set the tone of the relationship. Now the girls themselves sometimes make the first move and are often equal partners in establishing its direction.

Girls have also invaded fictional territory that was once the almost exclusive domain of boys—the adventure story. Like their male counterparts, they are climbing mountains and exploring deserts, navigating rivers and crossing oceans, sometimes in the company of a male friend but, not uncommonly, alone or with other young women. Although these adventure stories appeal to male and female readers, romance fiction remains (with a few notable exceptions) mostly gender specific—novels for girls featuring female protagonists and told from a female point of view.[16]

## Rules of the Road

Joan Bauer's *Rules of the Road* fits the structure of the accomplishment novel perfectly. Although it combines elements of the problem novel and romance, it is mostly an adventure story that sets Jenna Boller, the protagonist, off on a road trip in the best tradition of those American novels such as *Huckleberry Finn* and *Lolita,* whose characters also undertake a literal voyage. Still, Jenna's story is uniquely hers. She is no Huck floating surreptitiously down the river with an escaping slave: rather, she leaves with her mother's full if reluctant permission. She is escaping not from slavery but from a lifelong bondage to guilt over her father's alcoholism, and at the end, she returns home instead of lighting out for the territory. Nor, at sixteen and nearly six feet tall, does she resemble Nabokov's nubile nymphet. The photo on her driver's license reveals a flat nose, a face that is (she claims), as round as a globe, and auburn hair that hangs "frizzed and heavy" on her shoulders "like so much fur."[17] And she is hardly the captive of a sexually obsessed middle-aged man: she has agreed (with some trepidation) to serve as a driver for the dignified Mrs. Madeline Gladstone, seventy-two years old and the executive director of Gladstone's Shoes (176 outlets in 37 states), accompanying her from Chicago to Dallas, the site of Gladstone's flagship store. Still, during her journey she skirts disasters and outwits villains corrupt and ill-intentioned enough to rival any of the nemeses that threaten Huck and Lolita and who provide the challenges demanded by the genre.

At the novel's opening, Jenna is already a competent salesperson at Gladstone's Shoes. This job, her one unqualified success, has eased the pain of the previous year when she suffered a disastrous Sophomore Slump. She had gained seventeen and a half pounds, gone from center forward to second-string guard on the girls' basketball team because she couldn't jump, received a C- in History because the teacher didn't like her final paper ("Our Shoes, Ourselves—Footwear Through the Ages"), and endured the taunts of Billy Mundy, who called her Ms. Moose until she shoved him against a wall and threatened to rip out his left kidney. She considers herself a "social zero" and rebukes her mother's encouragement to develop social skills by taking ballroom dancing: "The boys come up to my armpits," she says (20). To complicate things further, her alcoholic father, whom her mother divorced several years ago, reappears after a two-year absence, no more sober than when he left. Small wonder Jenna wonders why God invented adolescence.

Despite Jenna's genuine problems, the tone of the novel is distinctly comic. Jenna narrates her story in a voice that shifts from self-mockery to genuine concern to anger, but whatever her emotion, she expresses it with an overlay of humor that captures the absurdity—however painful—of the misfortunes colliding in her life. When she comments that her younger sister Faith "got the beauty in the family" while all she got was "the personality" (8), there is no bitterness in the remark. Instead, she adds wryly that Faith is an example of "what God could do if he was paying attention" and transforms the situation into an advantage: "I can walk into a room looking like I've slept in a torture chamber with poisonous snakes, and people mostly ignore it. But when Faith looks bad, she's got a crowd around her telling her about it" (16). That is, being beautiful imposes its own burdens.

When true calamity does strike, she distances herself from it by representing the event in third-person headlines. "Drunken Dad Disgraces Daughter," she thinks when her father unexpectedly appears at Gladstone's, obviously inebriated. The humorous tone serves to signal readers that they can relax and enjoy Jenna's emotionally harrowing roller coaster ride. Her motto is "Cope or die" (49), and coping seems a sure bet.

Despite the comedy that weaves itself throughout the novel, *Rules of the Road* is more than a lightweight sitcom. In an article published nine years before *Rules of the Road* was published, Alleen Pace Nilsen contrasts humor in TV sitcoms with the humor in young adult novels to the advantage of the latter, and her analysis fits this story perfectly.[18]

- "Sitcom writers skirt serious subjects while novelists have room to develop both serious and humorous strands" (120). Bauer treats Jenna's problem with her alcoholic father seriously while using humor and hyperbole in developing the other aspects of the story. However, the serious strand lends weight to a novel that might otherwise fail to command the reader's thoughtful attention.
- "Sitcoms rely on an 'Innocent' for humor, a character who always stays the same, while book characters outgrow their innocence" (121). Jenna moves past her "innocence" about her father in particular and life in general as she learns "the rules of the road," and it is this growth that provides the novel's purposeful direction.
- "Sitcom plots are circular, with characters ending close to where they began, while in novels the characters make progress" (122). Although Jenna returns to Chicago and her mother's home, she is hardly "close" to where she began. In the last chapter, she purchases a used car with the money she has earned during her journey, a standard rite of passage in our culture. As important as the car is to Jenna, however, it serves only to signify a much more important passage as she learns to value herself and take control of her life.

Much of Jenna's development evolves from her job at Gladstone's. Her grandmother, once her best friend but now an Alzheimer's victim living in a nursing home, had told Jenna that "everyone needs something in life that they do pretty well" (*Road,* 6). For the gawky adolescent girl, this "something" is selling shoes. At work, she "doesn't feel big, awkward, and lost" (6); she knows the business, and customers seek her out. Gladstone's is known for quality shoes at fair prices, but Mrs. Gladstone is retiring, and the business will fall into the hands of her son, Eldon, who is buying up Gladstone stock to gain control of the company. Eldon is not a worthy heir. Jenna describes him as "pond scum," and he evolves into the primary villain of the novel, whose plans to merge the respected Gladstone empire with a shoddy outfit called the Shoe Warehouse may mean profit for the shareholders but augurs doom for the company's fine reputation.

When Mrs. Gladstone recognizes Jenna's knowledge of the shoe business and "unusual knack for understanding the customer's needs" (35), she offers her a six-week job as a chauffeur/assistant. Together they will visit and evaluate most of the company's outlets between Chicago and Dallas. The offer is tempting—"Trusted Teen Takes Texas by Storm" (38)—but Jenna worries about leaving her family: who will visit Grandma? will Dad come around drunk? how will Faith and Mom manage? She feels responsible for them all, even her alcoholic but affable father, whose behavior has created a painful void in her life. She has tried her best to be important to him. "I didn't call him a drunk even though he was one. I just tiptoed around his life, hoping he'd notice," she says (109). Her mother, bitter after years of dealing with the drunk, cannot comprehend why Jenna continues to care about him, a lack of understanding that evokes a passionate response from her daughter: "*He's my father! . . . I've got to know he's okay. I've got to make sure he gets some place safe! I don't hate him like you do*" (38). Like other empowered heroines, Jenna has a nurturing heart, but she also must respond to her own needs. Doubtful that she can "handle" another prolonged visit from her father, she wants to get out of town.

And she does, leaving behind her family, her best friend Opal Kincaid, and Matt Wicks, the only boy she's ever liked—"a seriously intelligent tall senior" who doesn't know she exists (31). In a conventional romance, Matt would sit up and take notice by the closing pages when Jenna returns, especially since she gets a makeover during her long journey: a new hairdo and new clothes that compliment her coloring and build. She also is given shares in Gladstone's. But this is not a conventional romance. Instead, Jenna's transformation depends more on internal self-perception than external appearances, and Matt is not part of the novel's resolution.

Jenna begins her voyage as someone so anxious to please, so anxious not to give offence, that her voice is often silenced. But as she and Mrs. Gladstone drive deeper into the South, her voice grows stronger, and she becomes sufficiently empowered to speak up even to her formidable employer. When the elderly woman, who suffers from a hip problem, refuses to seek medical help, Jenna drops her subservient demeanor and addresses Mrs. Gladstone bluntly:

> You can keep being the tough person you are and still have a bad hip and need some help. . . . Because if you don't get some help it's going to eventually affect your strength, and something tells me . . . you're going to need all the strength you can get, and I'm not just talking legs here. (83)

When Mrs. Gladstone asks what has given Jenna the right to "order [her] around, Jenna impishly replies, "I have the car keys, ma'am. No disrespect intended" (84).

Part of Jenna's growing empowerment has been inspired by Harry Bender, "the world's greatest shoe salesman and manager of Gladstone's flagship store in Dallas" (76). Like the many famous literary characters who have populated the serio-comic novels of writers such as Henry Fielding and Charles Dickens, Harry Bender's name provides a clue to his character: he is an alcoholic, albeit a recovering one, and from him, Jenna learns much about dealing with that illness, realizing that she has enabled her father's drinking. She remembers how, when she was a little girl, her father had made her answer the phone and say he wasn't there. As she revisits the scene in memory, she "dug [her] red sneakers into the blue braided rug and said *no*. Not this time, Daddy" (137).

Jenna confides in Harry how she feels about her father: "He hurts me so much when he's around and when he's gone I worry about him and never know if he's coming back. It's like I lose if he's here and lose if he's gone" (151). Harry encourages her to tell her father how she feels, even if he "makes excuses" and refuses to take responsibility. "Maybe saying it isn't as much for him as it is for you," he says (152).

Harry Bender also gives Jenna some practical, if metaphorically phrased, advice. "Never punch a man who's chewing tobacco," (95) he tells her, and "Don't drink downstream from the herd" (99). More importantly, he shares his primary rules of life:

Rule Number One: Care more about people than what you're selling.
Rule Number Two: Never miss a good opportunity to shut up. (150)

Harry's self-confidence allows Jenna to believe that he and Mrs. Gladstone will win out over the evil Eldon. Harry is a "presence of hope, even after all he'd been through, able to laugh darkness in the face," and Jenna wonders if, having known the darkness so well, "he'd figured out how to beat it" (153). Then, just as everything seems to be going so well, Harry is hit head-on by a drunk driver and dies. His death deals a crushing blow to Jenna and the future of Gladstone's, but even the scene of his funeral ends on a comic note. When the mourners arrive at the cemetery, they find that the epitaph on his tombstone says, "HERE LIES HARRY BENDER. HE GAVE IT HIS BEST SHOD" (159).

With Harry gone, the shareholders' meeting appears destined to seal the merger between Gladstone's and the Shoe Warehouse. To ensure the merger's success, Eldon fires Jenna as she is headed into the meeting, gives her a ticket on a flight back to Chicago, and puts her in a taxi bound for the airport. Part way there, Jenna orders the cab to turn around, gains entry to the meeting by identifying herself as a stockholder in Gladstone's, and follows Mrs. Gladstone's public resignation with an impassioned speech from the podium, in which she emphasizes that Gladstone's customers have returned again and again because they "trusted" the company's products. She ends by imploring Mrs. Gladstone to stay on and ensure the quality shoes for which the company is noted. In a completely romantic novel, Jenna might have ended up in an executive position at Gladstone's, but Bauer is careful to keep her narrative reasonably credible, and the shareholders vote the merger. Still, Jenna's argument has made its point. A quarter of the voters request that Mrs. Gladstone remain with the company, and the CEO of the Shoe Warehouse insists that Mrs. Gladstone join the board of directors, with (to Eldon's dismay) "complete charge of quality control" (184). Mrs. Gladstone accepts, reminding her son that "the women in my family live to a ripe, ornery old age" and that she's "going to be around for a long, long time" (184). Only a few chapters earlier, the old woman was in a wheel chair, ready to concede defeat. *Rules of the Road* portrays female empowerment of both the old and the young. The secret: courage, caring, and conviction.

Earlier, Jenna had wished that there were signs on the highway of life as clearly posted as the rules of the road, and she imagines a sample: "CAUTION: JERKS CROSSING; blinking yellow lights when you're about to do something stupid; stop signs in front of people who could hurt you" (89). But in the best tradition of the accomplishment novel, she does learn the unwritten "rules" of life, and by the time she returns home to Chicago, she is even able to cope with her father's alcoholism. She used to "keep on being a good sport, hoping [her father] would change," but now, as she tells Mrs. Gladstone, she is angry. "I've been afraid of it for so long. Afraid that if I let him know how I felt, he'd hate me, like I was supposed to be perfect and make up for the fact that he had all these problems" (167).

Powerless no longer, Jenna musters the courage to turn her father into the police for drunken driving, "the hardest thing" she has ever had to do: "Terrified Teen Has Drunk Father Arrested" (190). When she returns home, she flees into the shower, weeping as she remembers the good as well as the bad times with her father. She employs this same selective memory when she takes her ailing grandmother on a picnic, recalling aloud some happy times with her. She hasn't forgotten the difficult times, but recognizes that she must let go of them. "So much sadness. So much pain. But remembering the good things—that's what keeps anyone going" (196).

In her final meeting with her father, she tells him, "If you keep drinking, I won't see you, I won't talk to you on the phone. I need a sober father. Faith does too" (197). Although there is no happily-ever-after to this meeting—her father shrugs, then leaves without promising to reform—Jenna gains an epiphany following it: "I always wondered why I had a father who was an alcoholic. Now I knew. It made me strong. It made me different. It showed me how to say no to the darkness" (200). In the novel's last sentence, she sees herself as a "survivor"—and, indeed, she is.

Like Jenna, the other girls discussed in this chapter have also overcome odds that might crush weaker adolescents. But they have learned by going where they "have to go" and withstanding the challenges that mark their respective journeys. The independence they have gained is hard-won but worth winning. It has made them strong. Survivors all, they have learned to say "no" to the darkness.

## SUGGESTIONS FOR FURTHER READING

*Social Realism*

Bauer, Cat. *Harley: Like a Person*. New York: Winslow, 2000. Harley resists the authority of her parents, sure that they are not her "real" parents. A surprising discovery sends her on a mission to uncover her biological roots and results in near academic and social disaster, but her artistic abilities help her emerge as a stronger person who appreciates both her heritage and present circumstances.

Bauer, Joan, and Nancy Paulsen. *Hope Was Here*. New York: Putnam, 2000. Hope, abandoned by her mother as a baby, grows up cared for by Aunt Addie. She finds a true test of strength when she helps with a campaign against a corrupt politician on behalf of a man who has been a father-figure to her.

Bennett, Cherie. *Life in the Fat Lane*. New York: Delacorte, 1998. When Lara Ardeche gains weight and more weight, she tries to solve her problem by refusing to eat. After a life-threatening bout of anorexia, she accepts herself as "not perfect" but "okay."

Block, Francesca Lia. *The Hanged Man*. New York: HarperCollins, 1994. Set against the Los Angeles background common to Block's fiction, Laurel's story is a fight for emotional survival. Haunted by memories of sexual abuse, she turns to drugs and dangerous sexual relationships, but finally confronts her past to gain self-respect.

———. *Violet and Claire*. New York: HarperCollins, 2000. Violet, a wannabe filmmaker, and Claire, a fragile dreamer, are both outcasts at their high school. They find strength in each other and maintain their unconventional friendship amid the glitz of Hollywood and despite tensions over the manipulative men in their lives.

Brooks, Bruce. *Vanishing*. New York: HarperCollins, 1999. Hospitalized with severe bronchitis, Alice goes on a hunger strike as a way of escaping the home of her mother and step-father. A dying boy she meets in the hospital gives her the will to live.

Cook, Karen. *What Girls Learn*. New York: Vintage, 1997. When Tilden's mother falls in love, Tilden and her sister are forced to move north into the household of the new man, who proves himself a loving father-figure to both girls. All goes well until Tilden's mother falls victim to breast cancer.

Fox, Paula. *The Moonlight Man*. New York: Morrow, 1995. In search of her father, Jessie finds both disillusionment and strength at the end of her journey.

Grant, Cynthia D. *The White Horse*. New York: Atheneum, 1998. Raina is a desperate young girl with a dysfunctional family and drug-addicted boyfriend. Through her writing and the help of a sympathetic teacher, she emerges stronger and is able, in turn, to help her lonely teacher.

Hesse, Karen. *The Music of Dolphins*. New York: Scholastic, 1996. When Mila, who has been raised by dolphins, is rescued off the coast of Florida, she must learn human ways and adjust to people who fear her.

Johnson, Angela. *Humming Whispers*. New York: Scholastic, 1995. Afraid that she will fall victim to schizophrenia like her older sister, fourteen-year-old Sophy finds strength in her caring family and community.

————. *Heaven*. New York: Simon and Schuster, 1998. Marley leads an idyllic life in Heaven, Ohio, until she discovers that the two people she knows as Momma and Pops are not her real parents.

Lasky, Kathryn. *Memoirs of a Bookbat*. New York: Harcourt Brace, 1994. When Harper Jessup's parents become "migrants for God," she carves out a new life for herself with the help of a young friend and her caring grandmother.

Mazer, Norma Fox. *Missing Pieces*. New York: Morrow, 1995. Jessie longs to know more about her father, who deserted her mother when she was an infant. She begins a search that ends when she meets him and finds herself.

————. *When She Was Good*. New York: Scholastic, 1997. Em Thurkill learns how to wrest happiness from life after the death of an older sister whose mental instability has threatened both her own emotional well-being and physical safety.

Naylor, Phyllis Reynolds. *Ice*. New York: Atheneum, 1995. Chrissa's life is disrupted when her father disappears and she is sent to live with her grandmother. During this troubling period, Chrissa learns that time and new friends are sources of healing.

Nelson, Theresa. *Earthshine*. New York: Laurel Leaf, 1994. Slim travels with her AIDS-infected father, his companion, and her friend Isaiah, who has heard of the Miracle Man and his reputation as a healer. Although no miraculous cure awaits them, Slim learns the healing power of family and friends.

Nolan, Han. *Send Down a Miracle*. New York: Harcourt Brace, 1996. The return of an unconventional woman to her small Alabama town sparks an uproar among the conservative townspeople and effects a profound change in the thinking of fourteen-year-old Charity.

Rodowsky, Colby. *Hannah In Between*. New York: Farrar, 1994. Hannah finds strength in trying to help her alcoholic mother overcome her problem.

Rylant, Cynthia. *Missing May*. New York: Bantam Doubleday Dell, 1992. Summer and her Uncle Ob, accompanied by a friend from school, travel in search of a psychic who will contact the spirit of her beloved Aunt May, who died recently. The journey helps Summer find peace and reconciles her to the loss of May, with whom she has lived since she was six.

Stoehr, Shelley. *Weird on the Outside*. New York: Delacorte, 1995. Tracey Bascombe runs away from home and assumes an identity as Amanda, a topless dancer. After a year of inhabiting a seamy world of sex and drugs, she must decide whether to return to her father's home.

Voigt, Cynthia. *When She Hollers*. New York: Scholastic, 1996. Determined to put an end to her stepfather's sexual abuse, Tish finally finds the strength to confide her secret to a classmate's father, who is a lawyer, and begins to take control of her life.

Wolff, Virginia Euwer. *True Believer.* New York: Atheneum, 2001. In this sequel to *Make Lemonade,* LaVaughn must cope with a series of crises: her mother is dating, she is drifting away from her two best friends, who have joined a fundamentalist club ("Cross Your Legs for Jesus"), and the object of her first crush loves another. By the end, LaVaughn's strength and capacity for love see her through.

Woodson, Jacqueline. *I Hadn't Meant to Tell You This.* New York: Bantam Doubleday, 1995. Marie, a leader among her African American peers, unexpectedly makes friends with a white girl, Lena, a relationship based in part on the sad fact that both girls are motherless. When Lena reveals that she is a victim of sexual abuse, Marie must decide how she can best help her friend.

## Multicultural Novels

Farmer, Nancy. *A Girl Named Disaster.* New York: Orchard Books, 1996. Nhamo flees from her African village to escape an arranged marriage to an older, diseased stranger. During her journey, she uses her wits and courage to overcome mortal threats and finds that potential disasters can prove empowering.

Hamilton, Virginia. *Plain City.* New York: Scholastic, 1993. Buhlaire Sims, a gifted young African American girl, feels herself an outcast. She learns the importance of family and heritage as she probes for answers to the mystery of her absent father.

Kessler, Christine, and Patricia Lee Gauch. *No Condition Is Permanent.* New York: Philomel Books, 2000. When Jodie accompanies her anthropologist mother to Sierra Leone, she adapts to the difficult living circumstances slowly, but her friendship with Khadi helps her adjust. Then she learns that her friend must undergo female circumcision, and she is horrified as her western values clash with age-old African customs.

Levy, Marilyn. *Run for Your Life.* New York: Putnam and Grosset, 1996. In this novel based on a true story, Kisha escapes from the dreariness of her gritty life in the projects when she joins a track team. She wins acclaim as an athlete and wrests hope from the despair that hangs over her community.

Mori, Kyoko. *Shizuko's Daughter.* New York: Henry Holt, 1993. When her mother commits suicide and her father marries his long-time mistress, twelve-year-old Yuki calls on her sharp intellect and strong will to create a satisfying life for herself.

Senna, Danzy. *Caucasia.* Riverhead, NY: Riverhead, 1999. Birdie's white Jewish mother is an activist for social causes, and her black father is involved in the Black Power movement. After her parents divorce, Birdie remains with her mother, initially denying her black heritage to emerge as a white Jewish girl.

## Romance and Adventure

Bauer, Joan. *Backwater.* New York: G. P. Putnam's, 1999. Ivy Breedlove, who doesn't fit in with her conventional family of lawyers, sets out to find a mysterious aunt who lives a reclusive life in the Adirondacks. During her adventurous trip Ivy discovers a strength and value in herself that both surprises and empowers her.

Cooney, Caroline. *The Party's Over.* New York: Scholastic, 1991. A popular girl in high school whose boyfriend is the perfect beau, Helen feels alienated from her old friends when she chooses a job over college. Enduring loneliness and the loss of her boyfriend, Helen learns after a difficult year that she "has guts."

Keller, Beverly. *The Amazon Papers.* New York: Browndeer Press, 1996. Iris Hoving's chaotic life is complicated when her mother leaves on a trip and a friend crashes the family's car. But she manages to emerge a little older and a lot wiser.

McDaniel, Lurlene. *Until Angels Close My Eyes.* New York: Bantam, 1998. Leah's bout with cancer seems safely in the past, but then she discovers that her father is suffering a recurrence of his cancer. Her relationship with Ethan, an Amish boy she met during her hospitalization, proves both a challenge and a means by which she comes of age.

Plummer, Louise. *The Unlikely Romance of Kate Bjorkman.* New York: Delacorte, 1995. Kate uses *The Romance Writer's Phrase Book* to tell the story of her own romance, from which she emerges as the unlikely but triumphant heroine.

Waddell, Martin. *The Kidnapping of Suzie Q.* Cambridge, MA: Candlewick Press, 1994. When Suzie Quinn is kidnapped as part of a supermarket holdup, she proves herself less a victim than a victor.

# NOTES

1. *Make Lemonade* does not specify the ethnicity of its characters, nor is it revealed in the cover illustration. Although both girls speak variations of a non-standard vernacular, leading many readers to assume that both are African Americans, Wolff has said that she had Eastern Oregon poor whites in mind when she wrote this novel.

2. Virginia Euwer Wolff, *Make Lemonade* (New York: Scholastic, 1993), 9; hereafter cited in text.

3. This awareness of gender in positioning people within the social construct is limited mostly to female protagonists, with some notable exceptions such as Norma Fox Mazer's *Out of Control.*

4. In *True Believer,* the sequel to *Make Lemonade,* Jolly and LaVaughn are still friends.

5. Suzanne Fisher Staples, *Shabanu: Daughter of the Wind* (New York: Random House, 1989), 38; hereafter cited parenthetically in text.

6. Suzanne Fisher Staples, *Haveli* (New York: Random House, 1993), 226; hereafter cited parenthetically in the text.

7. Naomi Sihab Nye, *Habibi* (New York: Simon and Schuster, 1997), 5; hereafter cited parenthetically in the text.

8. Cynthia Leitich Smith, *Rain Is Not My Indian Name* (New York: Harper-Collins, 2001), 115; hereafter cited parenthetically in the text.

9. Although the word "Indian" has fallen from favor as a reference to Native Americans, Smith uses the former term often, and this discussion, following suit, uses both terms.

10. Marie G. Lee, *Saying Goodbye* (Boston: Houghton Mifflin Company, 1994), 1; hereafter cited parenthetically in the text.

11. The entire text of "Get Down, Nuke Koreatown," reads as follows:

All these years it's been something that you're missing,
You think you get away with it when it's us you be dissin',
But from the doors of your stores,
Some chinks gone be hung,
Or taken care of with a gun.

You call me brother then won't advance me a nickel,
Yellow motherfuckers to blame for they own pickle
You be chillin when you take my dough
Then you put my change down on the floor.

This time, brothers stand up like we should,
To kick chop-suey asses out of our 'hood.
So watch out for the gun we aim at your yellow throat
When we bust yellow asses all the way down to that boat.

12. Helena Maria Viramontes, *Under the Feet of Jesus* (New York: Dutton, 1995); hereafter cited parenthetically in the text.

13. Lori Aurelia Williams, *When Kambia Elaine Flew in from Neptune* (New York: Simon and Schuster, 2000); hereafter cited parenthetically in the text.

14. Nancy Garden, *The Year They Burned The Books* (New York: Farrar Straus Group, 1999); hereafter cited parenthetically in the text.

15. Ellen Wittlinger, *Hard Love* (New York: Simon and Schuster, 1999); hereafter cited parenthetically in the text.

16. Donelson and Nilsen note that romances aimed at young male readers are usually written by men and put less emphasis on courtship, more on sexuality (*Literature for Today's Young Adults*, 6th ed., 169).

17. Joan Bauer, *Rules of the Road* (New York: G. P. Putnam's Sons, 1998), 8; hereafter cited parenthetically in the text.

18. Alleen Pace Nilsen, "Why a Funny YA Novel Is Better Than a TV Sitcom," *School Library Journal* (March 1989), 120–123.

## • 5 •

# Empowered Girls
# in Literature of the Fantastic

Fantasies are more than substitutes for unpleasant reality; they
are also dress rehearsals, plans. All acts performed in the world
begin in the imagination.

Barbara Grizzutti Harrison

*In* a world where growing up is often equated for girls with the shut-
ting down of possibilities and the diminishing of expectation, where females can still expect to earn significantly less than their male counterparts, where working wives do significantly more housework and
child-rearing than their husbands, it is not hard to understand the widespread appeal of literature of the fantastic for female young adult readers.
In such a world girls can escape domestic drudgery, become knights, save
a king—and even have a rewarding sexual relationship with him. They
can free astonishingly handsome teenage boys from the curse of vampires, help kindly aliens return to their homelands, and on a daily basis
redefine what it means to be female. Though a distinction has historically
been made between science fiction and fantasy (each, for example, is assigned its own section in libraries or bookstores), it has been increasingly
common for scholars to focus on what the two have in common. Neil
Barron, for example, editor of *Anatomy of Wonder: A Critical Guide to Science Fiction,* argues that recent attempts "to distinguish sharply and completely between science fiction and fantasy instead of seeing them as in-
termingling in a complex literary tradition"[1] are misguided. Likewise,
Cathi Dunn MacRae, author of *Presenting Young Adult Fantasy Fiction,* argues that "The borders between fantastical and scientific approaches are
fuzzy, sometimes blended. . . . Thus, while there are differences between

127

the genres, their similarities are greater than these differences. Both create alternate worlds that challenge the world of the reader."[2] In this study, fiction that theorizes an alternate world (e.g. sci-fi, fantasy, horror) is categorized as literature of the fantastic, a phrase used to describe all fiction that speculates about worlds significantly different from our own but with a psychological connection to them. Each of the novels discussed in this chapter makes that connection.

Though the escapist aspects of literature of the fantastic are not to be denied, the tension and connection between the real world and the fictional one offers an even more satisfying explanation for the genre's widespread popularity. In addition to a mere escape from the known world, literature of the fantastic functions both as a critique and an alternative to that world. And though literature of the fantastic can be broken down into a variety of sub-genres—fantasy, science fiction, utopian, time travel, and horror, which can be further broken down into vampire, werewolf, mummy, etc.—each with its own history and set of conventions, all types can be read as assuming readers critical of their own world. Female readers in particular are often hungry for a world with more expansive possibilities for selfhood.

Aliens, dragons, mages, vampires and werewolves often populate literature of the fantastic. Its protagonists fight (and vanquish) these creatures, move through time, and speak to animals that nurture and challenge them. Often the female protagonists experience physical changes more startling than the onset of puberty, more traumatic than the addition of a few pounds or an outbreak of blemishes. They become werewolves, vampires, and even aliens themselves. These aspects of literature of the fantastic, whether directed toward young adult or adult audiences, have often made it seem a very distant, somewhat suspect cousin of other, ostensibly more reputable types of fiction. It has been dismissed, not infrequently, as appropriate for those who have not grown beyond their "intellectual puberty."[3] Yet the literature of the fantastic for young adults covers the same emotional territory as historical and contemporary fiction, exploring issues of voice, autonomy, and empowerment in as much depth as more realistic young adult literature. Like these other genres it attempts to mediate the tension between the needs of the self and those of the community. In fact, the tendency of immensely popular authors such as Tamora Pierce and Patricia Wrede to write series novels that take their heroines from early adolescence to young womanhood may allow for a more in-depth exploration of gender and developmental issues than is possible for a writer whose heroine's experiences must fit between the covers of one novel. Further, the apparatus of literature of the fantastic coupled with its referential nature to the experiential world create a testing ground, a safe space as it were, to explore more imaginative possibilities for the self. While often criticized for plot resolution that reinforces conventional notions of gender (Charlotte Bronte's "Reader, I married him" concludes many of these works), these novels have since the seventies enthusiastically promoted as a major theme the necessity for girls to gain control over their own lives by embracing their gifts, to engage in self-definition, and to use their own empowerment to challenge oppressive social structures.[4] A distinguishing feature of literature of the fantastic is that it has a longer history than other forms of young adult literature featuring and exploring female strength, perhaps because the authors who conceive of alien and fantastic worlds can also imagine new ways for girls to be in the world.

## Beauty and Deerskin

The tradition of empowering girls in literature of the fantastic is firmly rooted in the works of Robin McKinley, author of many novels that have at their center strong-minded girls determined to make their own way in the world. Each girl does this by battling a variety of demons, some internal, some external. In her earlier novel *Beauty*, and the more recent *Deerskin,* McKinley retells or rewrites traditional fairy and folk tales. Feminist critic Carolyn Heilbrun has argued that traditional fairy and folk tales have often been read as warnings against the rebellious female, the girl who rejects a passive role in her life's story. She advocates the need for "contrary models to catch the imagination of the young woman and girl . . . tales that will break the cycle of female commitment to passivity and fear of aggression."[5] And, in fact, some recently retold fairy tales by female authors have reversed the conventional pattern of weak heroine-strong hero. In stories such as *Just Ella* by Margaret Peterson Haddix and *Goose Chase* by Patrice Kindl, it is the young female who is strong and clever and whose resourcefulness provides a stark contrast to the story's dimwitted prince.

Certainly McKinley's retelling of Perrault's "Beauty and the Beast" and "Donkey Skin" allows her to provide the "contrary models" that Heilbrun advocates. And her expansion of short tales promotes the development of both character and conflict in ways that the much shorter originals cannot.

*Beauty*, published in 1979 and still in print and widely read today, introduces many of the themes, motifs, and patterns of development that structure the later *Deerskin*. Like many fairy tales, both begin with a conflict and a sense of loss. In *Beauty*, this initial conflict is not between the protagonist and another character, an evil stepmother for example, but is internal, stemming from the dissonance between what the title character wishes to be and what she is. This aspect of the protagonist's characterization distinguishes her from the heroines of traditional fairy tales who seem to have no internal life and places her squarely in the ranks of contemporary young adult female protagonists.

Not understanding as a five-year-old the meaning of the name Honour her parents have given her, she states her preference for the name "Beauty." The name sticks, though unlike her sisters she loses her beauty as she leaves childhood and enters adolescence, and she articulates the change in language charged with negative images:

> I don't know what happened to me. As I grew older, my hair turned mousey, neither blond nor brown, and the baby curl fell out until all that was left was a stubborn refusal to cooperate with the curling iron. My eyes turned a muddy hazel. Worse, I didn't grow; I was thin, awkward, and undersized, with big long fingered hands and huge feet. Worst of all, when I turned thirteen, my skin broke out in spots.[6]

Beauty's complaint echoes the emotions of many adolescent girls today. Peggy Orenstein argues that the transition into adolescence is, for girls, characterized by a more dramatic drop in confidence than it is for boys of the same age: "Today's girls fall into traditional patterns of low self-image, self-doubt, and self-censorship of their creative and intellectual potential. Although all children experience confusion and a faltering sense of self at adolescence, girls' self-regard drops further than boys and never catches up" (*School Girls,* 16). The phenomenon that Orenstein cites is dramatically evident in the female protagonists of speculative fiction.

Consequently, an important theme in both *Beauty* and *Deerskin* is the heroine's quest for self-confidence.

McKinley builds *Beauty* around a character who, unlike the fairy tale original, is not beautiful but is very wise to the ways of the world. She mourns her loss of beauty because she recognizes that its loss is, in fact, the loss of cultural capital that determines female value. Beauty's intellect and her love of books and reading become her defining characteristics and release her from the inevitable comparisons between herself and her sisters. By emphasizing Beauty's intellect and wit, McKinley gives her readers a new kind of fairy tale heroine, one who is smart and funny, with a self-deprecating sense of humor. Beauty tells her own story from her own perspective. That she has a voice distinguishes her dramatically from other heroines of conventional fairy tales, who are mostly noteworthy for their passivity and acceptance of their fate. She also possesses a strong sense of family solidarity. McKinley discards the competitiveness between the sisters that marks Perrault's version of the story and instead presents her readers with a widowed father and three daughters who function as a close-knit family. Still, the plot follows the old tale: Beauty accepts that she is better suited than her father to go to the Beast and, after living with him for a time, comes to see the beauty of his inner self and loves him for what she finds there. Her love transforms him back into the handsome prince he once was and transforms her as well, from an ugly duckling to a beautiful woman, one who is now a fit consort for this handsome prince.

The transformation is problematic for the reader: If an integral component of Beauty's journey to selfhood is learning to look beyond surfaces, why is it necessary for her to regain her beauty? If she can love all aspects of *his* Beastliness, appearance included, why cannot he love her as she is? And why can she not love herself? What kind of message does this send to adolescent girls immersed in a culture that privileges appearance over character? The relationship between beauty and character in this novel is confused and confusing. Is Beauty being rewarded with the gift of beauty because she has learned to overlook appearance? Or is her renewed or regained beauty simply the objective correlative of her internal transformation from a state of dissatisfaction with herself to one of acceptance? Is it nitpicking to expect McKinley to abandon so much of the fairy tale apparatus, apparatus that assumes a beautiful heroine? None of these questions are answered in this novel. Not until her 1993

*Deerskin* does McKinley fully wrestle with the relationship between the cultural preoccupation with beauty and the effect of that preoccupation on individual character.

Though *Beauty* has moments of darkness, its overall tone is light-hearted, at times even comic. This is due in part to the plucky character of Beauty, who is seldom downhearted for long, and in part to the story's well-known plot that assures the reader a happy ending. *Deerskin*, however, is another matter entirely. Based on Charles Perrault's "Don-keyskin," its subject matter, a mother's obsessively destructive preoccupation with her own beauty and a father's rape of his daughter, requires somber treatment. *Deerskin*'s content makes its classification as a YA novel problematic, a fact reflected by the fact that bookstores like Barnes and Nobles and Borders, as well as community libraries, shelve it variously under YA fiction, Fantasy and Fiction/General. Yet any quick survey of the table of contents of magazines geared towards teenage girls or of weekly TV shows with large teenage audiences shows that *Deerskin*'s subject matter, incest and its aftermath, is neither foreign nor even particularly shocking to young adult readers.

*Deerskin* begins with the protagonist's childhood vision of her parents. Their daughter Lissar sees them as romantic figures of fairy tales: each astonishingly beautiful, totally devoted to one another, and surrounded by splendor. But there is something off-putting about this vision. We learn that Lissar finds them "too splendid to be real,"[7] and McKinley quickly validates the child's perception. Under the glorious exterior is a couple so obsessed with one another that they seem barely aware of their daughter's existence. The parents' disregard for the daughter is conveyed to their retainers who quickly come to share it. When it is time to educate Lissar, no attempt is made to tailor her education to either her needs or talents. Rather, because she is viewed only as a smaller, less attractive version of her mother, she is given the same education her mother received: "Even her dancing-master, her riding instructor, and her mistress of deportment seemed to think of teaching her only in terms of the queen's gifts and graces, and so the princess, who was only a child, thought little of her own talents, because by that standard she could not be said to succeed" (8).

The Queen's defining characteristic is her beauty. She is "the most beautiful woman in seven kingdoms" (3), and it is this attribute that determines female worth in her kingdom. Lissar's gifts for friendship, her talent with plants, and later with dogs, cannot compete with her mother's beauty, a fact of which she is well aware. The daughter's troubles begin in earnest when her mother becomes ill. The nature of the Queen's illness is revealing: it is self-willed, induced because the Queen cannot live with the thought of her beauty ever diminishing. She cannot, in short, accept that she will age: "Her illness, the strange invisible illness with no name, had robbed her of the tiniest fraction of her beauty. . . . And when she guessed she might no longer be the most beautiful woman in seven kingdoms she lost her will to live" (10). The Queen cannot live without her beauty because she has nothing else. She seldom speaks, and the implication is that she has no need to: her appearance is all that she needs, and, it turns out, all that she has. Before she dies, she makes her grief-stricken husband promise to never remarry until he finds a woman as beautiful as she. To ensure he never forgets her beauty, she has her portrait painted. The portrait, ironically, "is more beautiful than the Queen ever was" (17), and it hangs after her death in the King's throne room, a incessant reminder of his loss.

Not until Lissar reaches adolescence does her father find a potential new wife, a woman as beautiful as the first. That woman is his daughter, "for Lissar, upon close inspection physically resembled her mother a great deal" (48). At this point, the novel's critique of our culture's obsession with female pulchritude provides a contrast to the subtext of *Beauty*. The heroine of that story regains her beauty as a reward for or as an emblem of an inner beauty. In *Deerskin,* the heroine's beauty is a curse that brings about disaster: at the ball held to commemorate her seventeenth birthday her father turns his attention to her. Prior to this, insulated by his grief for his dead wife, "he seemed willing to let her avoid him, and live out her young girlhood with few adult restraints and admonitions" (44). On this night, however, he fastens his gaze on her and "courted the young princess as assiduously as a young lover might; rarely and reluctantly did he release her into another man's arms" (56).

Though she has not the language to articulate her fears, Lissar instinctively recoils "from his nearness" (52). She intuitively recognizes that her father's reaction to her puts her at a peril she cannot even name: "She looked briefly into his face and saw there the look she had spent the last two years eluding; the look she found treacherous but with no word for the treachery" (53). Even after the ball has ended, when Lissar has scrubbed herself over and over to try to eliminate her father's presence, she is haunted by a nameless fear of him: "She felt trapped, squeezed; she was imagining things. She didn't even know what the things she was imagining were. But when she picked up the hairbrush again, her hand trembled" (65). Again, this development contrasts with the father-daughter relationship in *Beauty*, a relationship that calls upon the daughter to shield her father from danger. Here the father *is* the danger.

Soon after this Lissar's fears are given both form and name: her father announces to his court that he will marry her because "she is my daughter and I can do with her as I please" (57). The reactions of the court as well as Lissar to the King's announcement are telling. Both are horrified by the prospect of a marriage which will be "the death of the country. The country must rot, go to ruin and decay under such a coupling" (73). Yet the court, looking for a villain, bypasses the King and assigns the blame for this plan to the daughter: "What had she done to him, this witch daughter that he should desire to devastate his country and his people this way?" (73)

Lissar faints at her father's announcement, causing her devoted dog to come to her. When her father orders her dog killed, Lissar finds her voice and resists him: "'No, Ash is my best friend! You will not take her away from me!' The court was startled again in this morning full of shocks by the strength of the princess's voice, that little weak creature who could barely stand on her feet, saying such words, and about a dog" (71). While Lissar's resistance to her father suggests strength, she is not strong enough to protect herself from the coming ordeal. Though she locks her bedroom door against her father, he breaks in and savagely rapes her three times, once for each day she has kept her door locked against him. Lissar's rape, which leaves her near death, closes the first part of *Deerskin*. The second and third parts of the book chronicle stages of her recovery from her father's violation: her efforts to try to heal herself in solitude, then to find a place for herself in a community, and, finally, her use of her pain to help other victims.

The three parts of *Deerskin* correspond to the pattern that Northrop Frye argues structures all romance narratives: the first, a preliminary episode that involves testing of the hero; the second, a conflict; and the third, a triumph over adversity.[8] Adversity for the heroes of Frye's narrative generally comes in the form of an external challenge. While the events of *Deerskin* follow much of Frye's pattern, at each stage the heroine is additionally confronted by an intense self-doubt that must be over-come before she is able to proceed.

Barely alive, Lissar leaves her father's palace, driven simply by an impulse to "get away" (94). She retreats to a mountain wilderness where for an unspecified period she drifts in and out of consciousness. Only her ability to recognize edible and healing plants (a very un-princess like skill she has acquired from an old woman she befriended as a child) sustains her during this time. Eventually Lissar finds sanctu-ary for herself and her dog in an abandoned hut. Here she reclaims her self and tries to overcome the self-hatred that is the product of her fa-ther's rape. Though she cannot remember either the assault or, indeed, any part of her past life, she knows she is alienated from her body. The mere contact of her breast with her arm, for example, makes her "retch with great force. There was little in her stomach to lose but she felt as if her body were turning inside to get away from itself" (106). Lissar forces herself to reclaim her body as a way of reclaiming the self that has been violated and fragmented by her father. Forcing herself to touch her breast, she says: "Go on. This is my body. I reclaim my own body for myself: for my use, for my understanding, for my kindness and care" (106).

Lissar's alienation from her body exceeds the "adolescent angst" that Joan Brumberg, author of *The Body Project*, maintains "every [adolescent] girl suffers about her body."[9] Rather, Lissar's emotions are the product of the sexual abuse that separates her from an essential part of herself. Be-fore she can claim a place in the external world, she must first reclaim that part of herself that her father has made seem foreign, even hateful. Shortly after this point Lissar miscarries her father's child. The pain of the miscarriage drives her out of doors where, delirious, she is pursued by demonic images of her parents. Finally, she falls into a deep sleep during which she is visited by a strange woman, identified later as the Moon-woman, guardian of the weak and lost. Sitting next to Lissar, addressing her as "My poor daughter" (116) the Moonwoman tells Lissar to "rest you now with a quiet mind and heart, for this short story within this life's journey has an ending you may call happy . . ." (118).

Lissar's vision of the Moonwoman, whom she refers to simply as the Lady, does not completely cure her, or restore her memory, but it does start to heal her internal wounds. At the same time it establishes a model of intervention that will ultimately govern Lissar's own relationship with others. Lissar is calmed for the first time since the rape, and McKinley makes clear that the calm is the consequence of someone else's concern:

> What remained was a sense of the Lady, of her voice, the touch of her fingers, the calm of knowing the Lady had intervened on Lissar's behalf. The peacefulness was a part of the intervention: Lissar knew she was grateful, beyond grateful, for having been plucked from her old fate and set down again facing some new direction, leading to some new fate: but the memory of why she needed the intervention was an empty battered trunk or box or cupboard. (119)

Though McKinley is working within the parameters of a fairy tale, she is also dealing with the hard psychological truth that neither healing nor the transformation from victimhood to empowerment happen quickly or easily. Lissar is literally transformed after her experience with the Lady: her hair turns white and her eyes black. She no longer looks like the girl who was raped, but she bears that girl's scars. She leaves the mountain cabin that provided shelter (after cleaning and stocking it for the next person who might need it), wearing a dress made of white deerskin that has miraculously appeared (and just as miraculously is always clean) and that accounts for her new name, Deerskin. Pulled by an internal magnet, she goes to the nearest kingdom. This is the kingdom of one of the kings who had briefly courted her mother before he "thought better of his third cousin twice removed and went home and married her . . . . And she such a plain girl, with heavy jaw and thick legs" (5). The irony of this passage, of course, is that the girl who was defined and initially dismissed because of her physical inferiority has become a strong-minded queen infinitely more capable of active engagement with the world than Lissar's beautiful mother ever was.

If the kingdom of her parents is the kingdom of fairy tale romance, then the kingdom Deerskin is drawn to is that of mundane reality. It is a place where a plain king and equally plain queen love one another, their children, and their subjects, a place where its inhabitants seldom stand on ceremony. It is a kingdom where the crown prince, who falls in love with Lissar, has sterling character as well as a plain face and a pot belly. None of these features alter during the course of the novel. Deerskin's relationship with Prince Ossin forces her to confront the trauma of her past. In doing so, she takes on a new role as protector of the weak. Hired by the prince to care for a new litter of puppies, she and the prince are quickly drawn together by their shared love of dogs; a solid friendship develops but is shaken when the prince declares his love and his desire to marry Deerskin. Overwhelmed by her sense of her unworthiness and powerless to control it, she flees the city and with her dogs becomes an inhabitant of the countryside. Because of her striking white hair and black eyes, peasants who see her take her for the legendary Moonwoman, the figure who had visited her on the mountainside. Like the Moonwoman, Deerskin helps those in need. Yet her ability and willingness to help others does not free her from the shame and guilt that are the result of her father's actions.[10]

As winter approaches, Deerskin once again retreats to the mountain cabin that first sheltered her, and here she wrestles with her overwhelming sense of unworthiness that has made it impossible to accept Prince Ossin's offer of marriage. Finally, though, she is able to acknowledge her father's guilt: "Why should the prince not be married? It [his proposal] was nothing to her because she had made it nothing. No, it was not she who had made it nothing, but her father" (283). Lissar's newfound willingness to hold her father responsible for his actions signifies an important emotional shift. Prior to this, she, like her father's court and like many rape victims, has held herself responsible at least on some level for her abuse. Just as earlier she needed to come to terms with her body before she could seek a place for herself in the world, so must she now place guilt where it properly belongs before she can form an intimate relationship with another. But even her newly discovered awareness of her father's wrongdoing cannot motivate her to return to the prince. She does that only when she learns that the prince's younger sister, Camilla, is to be married to her father. It is her determination to save the princess that initiates her own empowerment and frees her from the twin burdens of guilt and shame: "What she knew was that she had to get to the throne room before Camilla's vows were uttered; somehow, that Camilla should merely be bodily rescued was not enough. Those vows would be a strain on her spirit, and a restraint on her freely offering her pledge to some other, worthier husband: that Camilla should have that clean chance of that other husband seemed of overwhelming importance to Lissar" (292–3).

Lissar's decision to save Camilla literally transforms her. When she strides into the throne room, she is described as "so tall her head seemed to brush the lintel of the door, blazing like white fire" (294). Lissar screams her pain and anger and in doing so reclaims her self once and for all:

> I carried your child—my own father's child—five months for that night's work; and I almost died again when the poor thing was born of me. I had forgotten how to take care of myself. I had forgotten almost everything but a madness I could not name; I had often thought I would choose to die rather than to risk remembering what drove me to madness. For I believed the shame was mine. For you were the king and your will was law and I was but a girl, or rather a woman, forced into my womanhood. (298)

Lissar broadens her indictment of her father to include her dead mother as well: "In a hard, new voice she said 'I was no child, for you and my mother gave me no childhood; and my maidenhood you tore from me, that I might never become a woman; and a woman I have not become, for I have been too afraid'" (298). Lissar cries out in a "hard, new voice," signifying a crucial moment in her progress toward empowerment and membership in a nurturing community. As noted earlier, in her studies of the psychology of adolescent girls Carol Gilligan has documented the relationship between girls finding their own voices and a strong sense of self. Finding her voice and using it allows Deerskin to save not only Camilla but also herself. And in doing so, she continues to practice the protective intervention the Moonwoman modeled for her earlier in the novel. Finally, she cements her place in the community as hero of the weak and unprotected. In almost all of the novels discussed in this chapter a similar moment occurs, in which the heroine raises her voice and in doing so asserts her self worth. This event is always a watershed moment in the girls' journey toward selfhood. Typically, it occurs when the protagonist's battles with an external enemy lead her to confronting her internal demons as well, and it is often precipitated by anger at those who doubt her.

By all rights, and the logic that governs fairy tales, Lissar's exposure of her father's sins and her rescue of Camilla should grant her the happy ending the Moonwoman promised her. But while the ending of Lissar's story is a happier one than might be imagined, it is not the unreservedly happy ending of *Beauty*. Though vindicated, Lissar still bears the scars of her trauma. For the third time she flees a king's palace and heads for the woods with her pack of protective dogs. But this time Prince Ossin follows her and once again declares his love. This time she reciprocates but adds: "I am . . . not whole. I am no wife for you, Ossin . . . I don't mean . . . only that I have no maidenhood to offer a husband on a wedding night. I am hurt . . . in ways you cannot see, and that I cannot explain, even to myself, but only know that they are there and a part of me, as much as my hands and eyes and breath are a part of me" (306). Finally, Lissar agrees to marry Ossin but her consent carries not the promise of happily ever after but only that "she would try to stay there, for as long as the length of their lives; that she would put her strength now and hereafter toward staying and not fleeing. 'But I do not know how strong I am,' she said. 'I cannot promise'" (308).

In spite of dramatic differences in tone and subject matter, *Beauty* and *Deerskin* share aspects of character and theme that have dominated literature of the fantastic throughout the '80s and '90s. These novels tend to have a female protagonist who at the beginning of her journey toward empowerment is defined by self-doubt, who feels uncomfortable with the place her society has assigned her. Often she has passions and skills not generally viewed as feminine. Over the course of the novel she achieves a sense of self—strong enough to accept her gifts and to use them to help others. The tension between the self and the world pervades these novels and is obviously connected to themes of identity. Yet more often than not the authors of these novels make clear, as Sklar maintains, "one must seek the answer to one's identity through action in the world."[11] The action that Sklar refers to takes the form of helping others: Beauty transforms the Beast, Deerskin overcomes the damage inflicted by her father's rape to rescue the young girl he intends to marry.

The female heroine is a fairly new development in literature of the fantastic. The best known quest stories all have male protagonists, and some critics have charged that the female protagonists who more recently have appeared in the genre are, to borrow a phrase from Lissa Paul, "heroes in drag."[12] Anna E. Altmann discusses this matter in some depth in an analysis of McKinley's *The Hero and the Crown,* arguing that McKinley is not just "welding brass tits on the armor" but created a distinctively female character.[13] Her argument applies to *Deerskin* as well, for she maintains that quest stories are tales "of winning selfhood and of claiming a world. . . . The quest is not a masculine exercise of force that involves putting on armor. Rather it is a process of stripping off the armor of the identity we have constructed for ourselves out of how we look, how we act, from whom we were born, and how we are valued" (150). Lissar's quest is distinctly female, for she begins as a marginal figure, not a knight in training, and, unlike the traditional male hero, she goes not with the blessing of the court but as an outcast who must chart her own course to victory.

It is noteworthy that the protagonists in McKinley's novels as well as those by other popular writers of literature of the fantastic like Tamora Pierce and Patricia Wrede emphasize their character's sense of solidarity with other girls. Though none of these authors completely disregard female competitiveness, using it occasionally to advance plot, each offers abundant examples of female solidarity that not only provide support to individual characters but suggest new models of community, ones more egalitarian, more nurturing of difference.

With the exception of the sub-genre of horror, which frequently has a contemporary, suburban setting—perhaps because the mundane setting increases the story's ability to horrify and titillate by making the boy at the next desk in advanced algebra a vampire or werewolf—fantasy and science fiction, the two main forms of literature of the fantastic, are usually set in either an unspecified past or future. Either setting allows for a world populated by beings or technology not found in a contemporary setting. Yet while the world of the novel is significantly different from the world of the reader, it frequently is plagued by the same anxieties about the same conflicts as the world the reader inhabits.

## Blood and Chocolate

In his novel *Howard's End* E.M. Forster suggests that the great challenge for all human beings is to connect with the "other," that which is different from ourselves. This idea is an important component in literature of the fantastic where girls struggle to connect not only with those parts of themselves that their culture does not validate but with beings that are dramatically alien to themselves. In either case, authors base the need to connect on an awareness of the interdependence of all life, an idea that has a long history in both utopian and feminist literature. The willingness or unwillingness to connect with elements that are seemingly alien, either internal or external, often determines whether a girl is able to achieve a positive sense of self and become an agent of empowerment for others. If she is able to do this, then she often moves from a state of isolation to active, engaged membership in a community. Annette Curtis Klause has written three novels—*The Silver Kiss* (1990), *Alien Secrets* (1993) and *Blood and Chocolate* (1998)—that are noteworthy for the extent to which they embody this pattern while exploring the notion of the alien in three different sub-genres of literature of the fantastic: the vampire, the space travel/alien and the werewolf. As in the previously discussed novels, all have in common a protagonist who at the start of the novel feels herself isolated, an outcast. Puck in *Alien Secrets* has been expelled from her school on Earth and is sent home to her parents on another planet. During her journey she befriends an alien, helps him recover a sacred totem, solves a murder and, as a result of all this, reevaluates her own abilities. In *The Silver Kiss* Zoe is estranged from her mother and father because her mother is dying of cancer, a factor none of them can control. Zoe's encounter with the young, beautiful, and tragic vampire Simon starts her on a process of reconciliation with her family and provides her with the knowledge necessary to free Simon from the curse of being one of the living dead. Both of these girls clarify their sense of self through their encounters with creatures different from themselves. Vivian, the heroine of *Blood and Chocolate*, has a more complicated challenge: in learning to accept the alien other, she learns to accept herself as an alien—as the werewolf she is.

Vivian is in the superficial aspects of her life very much a typical seventeen-year-old girl: she fights with her mother over what she wears and whom she dates. A relative newcomer to her high school, she feels "isolated and friendless."[14] These typically adolescent issues are made murkier by the fact that she, her mother Esme, and all of their close associates are werewolves, loup-garou. Vivian, for example, fights with her widowed mother because Esme is battling another woman in their pack over a man. Esme, in turn, tries to prevent Vivian from dating the human boy on whom she has a crush.

Vivian's crush on Aiden has many components, all of which are part of the adolescent desire to belong to the group of one's choice. She longs to be accepted by other "normal" teenagers and to move out of the social circle circumscribed by her pack. She wants to differentiate herself from her mother. Finally, she wants to escape the fate of being the mate of some other werewolf that the pack has mandated for her, resisting the rigid gender definition the pack maintains. But her desire to escape her fate is matched by an equally strong desire to give into it: "It's hard not be a wolf," she thought. She missed the mountain where humans were far apart and the pack was close, and she hardly ever had to pretend" (13). For three quarters of *Blood and Chocolate*, pretending is what Vivian does: she pretends to be wholly human as she sets about ensnaring Aiden; she pretends to herself that "they would like me if they took the time to know me. . . . They just don't know me" (13).

Just as Alanna in *The Lioness Quartet* is warned of the consequences of not accepting all aspects of herself, Vivian learns just what those consequences are when her pursuit of the human boy puts not only his life but the existence of her whole pack at risk. Ultimately, Vivian accepts her wolfishness and accepts her fate as Gabriel's mate, something she has resisted throughout the novel. Disappointing as this may be to readers who harbor the hope that Vivian might not only get to keep her human boyfriend but also maintain her membership in the pack, the ending does, nevertheless, suggest an important aspect of empowerment: self-acceptance. Vivian is not human, and her attempts to pretend otherwise have, by the end of *Blood and Chocolate*, left her literally suspended between two states. She has her human body and face as well as claws and fangs. And though an older female member of the pack tells her, "It's up to you now" (253), Vivian remains "like a rusty lock stuck in between—no matter how hard she forced, the key would move neither forward or back" (253). Vivian's paralysis, which leaves her neither wolf nor human, stems from her awareness that her desire to be what she is not has had negative consequences for both her pack and the humans she has been drawn to: "I tried to be what I wasn't and now I can't even be what I should. I'm a freak. . . . And because of her an innocent boy was dead" (254). Isolating herself in her room, wondering how long the pack can accept one who has brought so much chaos to them, Vivian cannot forgive her wrongdoings until Gabriel, the pack's leader, reminds her of what he loves about her, her caring for others: "You cared so much for your people, it broke your heart to see the pack in ruins. You cared so much for your mother, you risked your life for hers. You cared enough to save someone who wished you dead" (264). Gabriel's assertion of her worth completes Vivian's transformation. She accepts him as her mate, accepts a life "bound by duty," but does so with her "blood singing in her veins" (264).

## Parable of the Sower

As Vivian's story demonstrates, self-acceptance is often an integral aspect of the protagonist's empowerment, and nowhere is this portrayed more dramatically than in Octavia Butler's *Parable of the Sower*. This novel is written as the journal of Lauren Olamina, an African-American girl living in the twenty-first century in California in an environment of social chaos and violence. She does not fit the conventional notion of innocent girlhood so frequently depicted in young adult literature: sexually active, she keeps herself supplied with condoms. The chaos of *Parable of the Sower* stems from sources both social and environmental. Across the country the infrastructure has broken down, the environment has been destroyed, the government is a sham, and violence has become a way of life. Lauren lives with her father, stepmother, and brothers in a walled community, one of many established by middle-class families trying to protect themselves from the violence outside its walls. In Lauren's world water is a luxury, and to leave the protection of her walls is to risk death. During the course of the novel one of her brothers is violently killed, her father disappears on his way home from work and is assumed dead, and the walls surrounding her community are breached by drug addicts who burn the community's homes and kill Lauren's remaining family.

The novel, beginning on Lauren's fifteenth birthday and her father's fifty-fifth, covers a three-year period. Though young, Lauren is well aware that the world she lives in is a terrible place and bound only to get worse. Yet her initial concern is not just with the very real external threats to her life but with an issue that divides her from her father: religious faith. Lauren's father, a college professor, college dean, and Baptist minister, is sustained by his strong Christian faith, a faith she no longer shares. But like so many of the girls discussed in this chapter, she cannot initially voice her disagreement and assert her beliefs. Her religious differences are part of a larger, typical adolescent struggle to establish her own identity when components of it are at odds with her parents' beliefs: "I had my recurring dream last night. I guess I should have expected it. It comes to me when I struggle—when I twist on my own personal hook. . . . It comes when I try to be my father's daughter."[15] Lauren, who characterizes herself as a "coward," is unable to share her religious doubts and disagreements with her father during his life. Ironically, only after he is assumed to have been murdered and a funeral is planned for him does she find her voice to speak his eulogy. Despite her doubts about his father, she is able to do this because of her deep empathy for those around her who have lost him as a minister and her desire to help them in whatever way she is able:

> When I stood up, it wasn't just to say a couple of words. I meant to give
> them something they could take home—something that might make

them feel that enough had been said for today. . . . I talked about perseverance. I preached a sermon about perseverance if an unordained kid could be said to preach a sermon. (119)

In contrast to many of the girls discussed previously, Lauren does not suffer from a lack of confidence nor is she ignorant of the harshness of her world. Still, like many young adult protagonists, she has to move from a state of relative innocence to one of informed experience. In her case this entails learning just how hard it will be to convince others to share her vision of community. Lauren is determined to survive, and she has faith in her ability to create something good out of the terrible world where she lives, but others do not easily accept her convictions. When she urges her friend, Joanne, to prepare for the inevitable attack on their walls by studying how to survive, Joanne dismisses her, saying, "We're 15. What can we do?" (48). Lauren responds, "I mean to learn everything I can while I can. . . . None of us knows very much but we can all learn more. Then we can teach each other. . . . Nothing is going to save us. If we don't save ourselves we're dead" (51).

When the walls of Lauren's neighborhood are finally breached and her family destroyed, she is cast out of what has been her society's version of Eden. Supplied only with the emergency backpack she has prepared for such an event, she decides to make her way north. The journey she proposes to undertake recalls those of runaway slaves intent on escaping lives of enforced servitude. Along the way she encounters others who have actually been enslaved by corporations who, promising them physical security, trap them in a system reminiscent of the company stores of mining towns in the 1930s.

During her travels Lauren slowly recreates the family she has lost. She begins by convincing two of her surviving neighbors, a white eighteen-year-old boy and a young black widow, to join her. Because they all fear others' reaction to black women traveling with a white male, Lauren cuts her hair and disguises herself as a man. This male disguise, a frequent motif in young adult fantasies about empowered girls, serves both to acknowledge her female vulnerability as well as to reject the traditional gender roles of which she has been critical. Lauren carries with her two notebooks, one a journal in which she records the chaos around her and her reaction to it and the other a workbook for her poetry. This poetry, verses of which begin each chapter of the novel, is her attempt to formulate an ethical response to the world she exists in and demonstrates the need for expression as an element of empowerment. Lauren calls this notebook, "Earthseed: The Books of the Living."

Joan Gordon has suggested that *Parable of the Sower* can be read as a primer of post-modern ethics, and the astuteness of her observation is apparent with even the most casual of readings.[16] In her poems Lauren argues that change is the only constant in life, that change is, indeed, God, and that humans can shape God. More specifically she suggests ways to connect with others at a time when all humanity seems lost and humans are no more than predatory beasts. Her poems range from the one line "Kindness eases Change" (149) to the longer, admonitory pieces:

> Embrace diversity
> Unite
> Or be divided
> Robbed,
> Ruled,
> Killed,
> By those who see you as prey.
> Embrace diversity
> Or be destroyed. (176)

Lauren's Earthseed philosophy is, in part, the product of her deliberate attempt to find ways to survive. But it also springs from her status as a sufferer of hyperempathy syndrome (9), caused by her dead mother's drug abuse. Victims of this syndrome are called "sharers" because they literally share the sufferings of others. Not surprisingly, more women suffer from this than men, and Lauren, perhaps disingenuously, explains this inequitable distribution of pain with the statement that "sharing would be harder on a man" (291), implying that neither sharing nor empathy come naturally or easily to men. Her affliction enables her to provide genuine comfort to those in distress, such as her father's grieving congregation, but takes its toll on her.

In her struggle to survive Lauren is forced to commit acts of violence. She kills the men who try to kill her. But each time she does so, she literally experiences that person's dying and then briefly dies herself. Each time this happens, she revives (one might even say she is resurrected), but her recovery is itself painful, for Lauren must learn to manage the pain of literally caring too much for others. Within this context her poems can be read as attempts to address and understand her own pain as well as blueprints for establishing community, and as such, they emphasize the primacy of language in constructing a strong sense of self.

By the time the novel ends, Lauren has gathered twelve others to her cause. The temptation to refer to them as disciples is great, and it is clear we are to see Lauren as a non-Christian Christ figure. Thus, they consist of children, Hispanics, former prostitutes, former slaves, and other African-Americans. They come to her at first because she convinces them there is safety in numbers and only later accept her Earthseed philosophy. When one of the group, Bankole, a fifty-six-year-old African American doctor who becomes Lauren's lover, reveals that he owns three hundred acres in an isolated rural area, Lauren convinces him to give it to the group for a permanent sanctuary. She makes clear to him that unless he shares her efforts to forge a community, she cannot be with him. Refusal to accept the religion she lives by is a refusal to accept her, and she tells him he must "take me the way I am" (258). When he does, he and the others start to plan a future of intentional community. They do this with hope but not with blind optimism. In fact, Bankole says outright, "I don't think we have a hope in hell of succeeding here" (295). Rather than dismissing his or others' fears, Lauren offers only what she realistically can: the hope that their group, at least, "doesn't have to sink any lower" (294).

Reading contemporary young adult literature of the fantastic, one seldom encounters the happily-ever-after of the fairy and folk tales that are the ancestors of this genre. But what we do encounter is perhaps more inspiring: stories in which girls struggle with both internal and external foes and out of these struggles wrest something positive. And while the external apparatus of these stories—the wizards, the aliens, the magical shifts in time and place—distinguish these stories from realistic fiction, they tap into the same psychological tensions that most adolescent girls experience: the need to achieve independence, to come to grips with one's gifts, to reconcile one's expectations with those of a larger culture, and to be a contributing member of that culture. Ultimately, these works stimulate reader's imaginations to consider the ways in which they can "rebuild with new lumber, new ways of doing, acting and being."[17]

## SUGGESTIONS FOR FURTHER READING

Billingsley, Fanny. *The Folk Keeper*. New York: Atheneum Books/Simon and Schuster, 1999. Corinna disguises herself as a boy to assume the role of a folk keeper. She learns what powers she has over the folk and herself.

Calder, David. *The Dragonslayer's Apprentice*. New York: Scholastic Inc., 1997. As a dragonslayer's apprentice, Jackie displays wit, courage, and strength. Her persistence is rewarded when she becomes the first female dragonslayer.

Crispin, A.C. *Starbridge*. Berkley, CA: Berkley, 1991. Earth establishes its first contact with an alien race. Initially, the interchange is friendly, but when it erupts into unexplainable violence, interstellar war looms. Two people—Mahree Burroughs, a female with the ability to forge friendships and acquire new languages, and Dhurrkk, a male Simiu with limitless curiosity—avert disaster by creating bonds of understanding with the alien culture.

Hopkinson, Nalo. *Brown Girl in the Ring*. New York: Warner Books, 1998. Ti-Jeanne, a Caribbean-Canadian girl of color, resides in the burnt-out center of Toronto, in a post-apocalyptic time. An unwed mother, she must learn to love the child she did not want to have and to use the healing arts her grandmother has tried to teach her before she can establish her place in the community and defeat Rudy, the evil, predatory drug lord.

Klause, Annette Curtis. *Alien Secrets*. New York: Laurel-Leaf Books, 1993. Mischievous Puck becomes expelled from her boarding school on Earth only to embark on more adventures as she travels back to Shoon, her home planet. Her detective work solves a mysterious murder as well as allowing her to explore her potential and talents.

——. *The Silver Kiss*. New York: Laurel-Leaf Books, 1990. Zoe is a girl in an extraordinary situation. Not only must she struggle to accept her mother's impending death, she puts forth heroic efforts to saver her friend Simon, a young and beautiful vampire.

Lackey, Mercedes. *Arrows of the Queen*. New York: Daw Books, 1996. Talia is a young runaway who rises above her outcast position through her empathetic powers. After she rescues one of the legendary Companions, she earns the title of herald at the royal court. She then discovers a plot to seize the throne and uses her extraordinary powers to save the Queen.

McCaffrey, Anne. *Nimasha's Ship*. New York: Ballantine, 1993. Lady Nimasha Boynton-Randymense, a brilliant and beautiful spaceship designer, must rely on the strength and intelligence of her daughter Cuiva when a test flight goes awry.

Napoli, Donna. *The Magic Circle*. New York: Dutton, 1993. More the story of an empowered woman than an empowered girl, this retelling of the Hansel and Gretel folk tale explores the psychology of the witch, portraying her as a caring mother who, trapped by greed, sacrifices her own life to save Hansel and his sister.

Nix, Garth. *Sabriel.* New York: HarperCollins, 1997. Sabriel has supernatural powers and must call upon them to liberate her necromancer father from the spirits of the dead and help rescue the Old Kingdom from the destructive forces of the evil undead. She overcomes exhaustion and violence to assert her powers and fulfill her destiny.

——. *Lireal: Daughter of Clayr.* New York: HarperCollins, 2001. This sequel to *Sabriel,* opening many years after the close of its predecessor, returns readers to the Old Kingdom and introduces them to young Lireal. She despairs of ever gaining the gift of sight that will mark her as an adult, but with the help of Sameth, teenage son of Sabriel, she fights to stop the evil forces that threaten her kingdom.

Perry, Steve. *The Female War* (Aliens, No. 3). New York: Bantam, 1993. When Lieutenant Ellen Ripley awakes from her long space travels, she cannot remember certain parts of her life. Only when she aligns herself with two veterans in the war against aliens does she begin her fight for victory and uncover the mystery behind her long sleep.

Pierce, Tamora. *Circle of Magic: Sandry's Book.* New York: Scholastic, 1997. Sandry, Briar, Daja, and Tris are outsiders with strange magical powers. All must first confirm their own unique identity before uniting to sustain and save one another.

——. *Wild Magic.* New York: Random House, 1992. First book of The Immortals series, this novel explores the life of a young girl, Daine, whose magic skill is an ability to speak to animals. Daine's skills prove both treacherous and rewarding.

Pullman, Philip. *The Dark Materials* (trilogy):

*The Golden Compass.* New York: Knopf, 1997. In the first of Phillip Pullman's *Dark Materials* trilogy, the reader meets twelve-year-old Lyra Belacqua. She is a precocious girl growing up at Oxford University, but her Oxford is hardly the one familiar to most readers. Everyone there has a personal daemon, an animal that manifests the essence of the owner's soul, and science and theology—conventional subjects of a university curriculum—are allied with a strange kind of magic. It is difficult for Lyra to identify the evil forces that masquerade as kindly adults, but she eventually triumphs over them after she learns that they are stealing children and using them as the subject of deadly experiments to discover the nature of Dust—the very stuff of the universe.

*The Subtle Knife.* New York: Knopf, 1997. Lyra continues her quest to find the origins of Dust. She joins forces with Will Parry, who is searching for his long-lost father. In their journey they are drawn closer to the Subtle Knife, an ancient tool of magic that cuts windows between worlds.

*The Amber Spyglass.* New York: Knopf, 2001. In this last volume of the trilogy, Lyra finds herself at the center of what is to be the final battle between good—as found in people's ability to think and plan for themselves (their free will)—and evil, as represented, ironically, by the Church. Her choices will affect not just her world but the myriad worlds that overlap each other.

Tomlinson, Theresa. *The Forestwife*. New York: Orchard Books, 1995. In this retelling of a classic legend, Maid Marian meets Robin Hood and his band of outlaws. She joins forces with them to resist tyranny and find romance.

Wrede, Patricia C. *Dealing with Dragons*. New York: Scholastic Inc., 1990. The witty Princess Crimorine not only outwits a prince or two, she also lives with a dragon.

———. *Searching for Dragons*. New York: Scholastic Inc., 1990. Princess Cimorine must rescue a kidnapped dragon using her novice magic skills and help from an eclectic cast of characters.

———. *Calling on Dragons*. New York: Scholastic Inc., 1993. Cimorene, now Queen of the enchanted forest, must recapture the King's sword in order to save the dying forest.

## NOTES

1. Neil Barron, ed. *Anatomy of Wonder: A Critical Guide to Science Fiction* (New Providence, NJ: R.R. Bowker, 1995), 4.

2. Cathi Dunn MacRae, *Presenting Young Adult Fantasy Fiction* (New York: Twayne, 1998), 3.

3. Allen, Virginia, and Terri Paul, "Science and Fiction: Ways of Theorizing about Women," in *Erotic Universe: Sexuality and Fantastic Literature,* Donald Palumbo, ed. (New York: Greenwood Press, 1986), 180.

4. Though many of the novels, especially those traditionally labeled fantasy, end with marriage, the conditions under which those marriages occur are significant. Marriage occurs only after the protagonist has achieved the goals she has set for herself and is always to a male who shares her goals and endorses her sense of self. Often the male partner, though gifted, is significantly less so than the female hero and requires her strong sense of self to bolster his own weaker one. See Patricia Wrede's *Dealing with Dragons* and Fanny Billingsly's *The Folk Keeper*.

5. Carolyn Heilbrun, *Reinventing Womanhood* (New York: W. W. Norton, 1979), 147.

6. Robin McKinley, *Beauty* (New York: Pocket Books, 1979), 4; hereafter cited parenthetically in text.

7. Robin McKinley, *Deerskin* (New York: Ace Books, 1993), 3; hereafter cited parenthetically in text.

8. Northrop Frye, *Anatomy of Criticism* (Princeton, NJ: Princeton UP, 1957). See also Richard Patterson, "LeGuin's Earthsea Trilogy: The Psychology of Fantasy, " in *Children and Fantasy* (New York: Greenwood Press, 1979). Patterson, drawing heavily on Frye, argues that the structure of the fairy tale, from which fiction of the fantastic frequently draws, parallels the three-part structure of romance narratives.

9. Joan Jacobs Brumberg, *The Body Project: An Intimate History of American Girls* (New York: First Vintage Books, 1998), xvii.

10.  McCarthy argues that a girl's sense of power or powerlessness fluctuates and is contextual. This is the case for Deerskin. (Margaret McCarthy, "Transforming Visions: A French Toast to American Girlhood in Luc Berron's *The Professional,*" in *Millennium Girls: Today's Girls around the World,* Sherri A. Inness, ed. (Lanham, MD: Rowman & Littlefield, 1998), 196.

11.  Robert Sklar, "Tolkien and Hesse: Top of the Pops," in *Nation* 204: 598–601 (May 8, 1967), 600.

12.  Lissa Paul, "Enigma Variation: What Feminist Theory Knows About Children's Literature," *SIGNAL* 54 (1987), 199.

13.  Anna E. Altmann, "Welding Brass Tits on the Armor: An Examination of the Quest Metaphor in Robin McKinley's *The Hero and the Crown,*" *Children's Literature in Education* 23.3 (1992), 144.

14.  Annette Curtis Klause, *Blood and Chocolate* (New York: Warner Books, 1998), 12; hereafter cited parenthetically in text.

15.  Octavia Butler, *Parable of the Sower* (New York: Warner Books, 1994), 1; hereafter cited parenthetically in text as *Parable.*

16.  Joan Gordon, ed., *Science Fiction Research Quarterly;* telephone interview, August 2000.

17.  Donna Rogers, student essay. Quoted with permission.

# Empowered Girls in Memoir

No sooner did I realize that I was likely to grow up to be a
woman than I wanted to know what the possibilities were for
women. I myself was ambitious. I wanted to be a cowgirl. I was
seeking something no terms existed for—a role model. I
sensed it would be hard to find biographies or autobiographies
of cowgirls, but the story of almost any woman who had
achieved something . . . would have served.

Phyllis Rose, *Women's Lives*

*Bi*ographer Rose's girlhood desire to use the stories of other women's
empowerment to shape her own ambitions and desires still resonates
with females today. The popularity of TV shows like *Oprah*, where guests
regularly entertain and inspire a primarily female audience with stories
of overcoming hardships, is evidence of this. The brisk sale of autobiographies and memoirs suggests, too, that the impulse to look toward the
lives of others for guidance in shaping one's own is consistently powerful, fed, as Joyce Carol Oates maintains, by a "desperate wish that some
truth of the spirit be presented to us."[1] Correspondingly, authors of autobiographical works are often driven to write by their desire to provide
readers with guidance as well as hope and encouragement. Adeline Yen
Mah, author of *Chinese Cinderella: The True Story of an Unwanted Daughter*, writes with the hope that "other unwanted children . . . may be encouraged"[2] by her story. Mah further emphasizes the importance of stories such as hers as a form of bibliotherapy, the use of books to help
readers gain insight into their own lives by identifying with characters
and situations in literature: "In one way or another, every one of us has
been shaped by the stories we have read and absorbed in the past" (n.p.).

And while academics have historically viewed autobiographical, or life writing, as the poor cousin of other genres, Martine Watson Brownley maintains that since the publication in 1980 of James Olney's *Autobiography: Essays Theoretical and Critical*, the genre has gained in stature. The relatively recent academic endorsement that the genre has received, coupled with popular culture's embracing of life stories, may account for the increased publication and popularity of all forms of autobiographical writing, including those directed toward an audience of young adult readers.

Rose points to the 1951 publication of Anne Frank's diary in English as the start of the "golden age of women's autobiographical writing."[3] She argues that if Holden Caulfield was the "quintessential male literary adolescent of the fifties, Anne Frank . . . [was] the representative female adolescent" and further suggests that the appeal of Frank's diary is twofold. Anne stands first "for all Jews who were murdered in the Holocaust" (13) and, second, "for adolescent girls trying to assert their individuality in the complicated context of family life" (13). Anne Frank's *Diary* has never gone out of print, and her voice, by turns brave, petulant, sarcastic, and determined, has influenced hundreds of memoirs written by women looking back on their adolescent years and recording their struggles toward selfhood in the face of obstacles both external and internal. Like Anne Frank, they record journeys toward self shaped by circumstances they did not create, but which they must, on some level, overcome if they are to move on with their lives. It should be noted, however, that most of these works are more accurately labeled memoirs rather than autobiographies because they focus on a relatively narrow span of time as opposed to a whole life. Authors may, as Maya Angelou has, publish successive volumes that take the author beyond childhood to adulthood, but young adult readers are more likely to be drawn to those texts that offer a chronological, if not a historical, parallel to their own experience. Another appealing aspect of these works for young adult readers is that authors write from a position of empowerment, and so their works and lives can be read as road maps to that desired state.

All writing provides an author with the opportunity to revisit sites of intense emotion and to shape or reshape them in ways that address emotional and psychological needs. But autobiographical writers must do this within a framework of historical events that generate multiple commentaries and responses. Thus, their works unfold in two ways: they invite the reader to experience historical events that have affected many, while encouraging the reader to share their unique experiences with that event. Suzette A. Henke, in *Shattered Subject: Trauma and Testimony in Women's Life Writing*, notes that "the twentieth century may well be remembered as a century of historical trauma. . . . We daily confront the unthinkable in news and television reports, in bizarre public trials, and in relentless statistics exposing rape, murder, torture in . . . an increasingly violent society."[4] At a time when it is neither possible, nor necessarily desirable, to shield children from the violence that is everywhere around them, memoirs serve a particularly helpful function for young readers: they suggest it is possible to make order from chaos and offer concrete examples of how to do so. Writer bell hooks argues that "telling one's personal story offers a meaningful example, a way for folks to identify and connect."[5]

## IN MY OWN HANDS: MEMOIRS OF A HOLOCAUST RESCUER

A memoir such as Irene Gut Opdyke's *In My Hands: Memoirs of a Holocaust Rescuer* continues Anne Frank's story of the effect of the Holocaust on individual girls' lives, but does so from perspectives different from Frank's. Unlike Frank, who moves us by her courage in the face of destruction the reader knows is certain, Opyke writes as a survivor, a Catholic whose Polish homeland is occupied by the Nazis. She had the audacity and courage to hide Jews in the basement of the home of her Nazi employer, a high SS official, until she could bring them to safety, and her bravery empowered not only herself, but also those around her. Opdyke's story functions as an example of what can be endured and accomplished under excruciatingly oppressive conditions.

She dedicates her book to the "young people who can accomplish the impossible and can achieve greatness,"[6] and her story tells of a growing desire to help those less fortunate than she and of an enduring belief that though she is "only a girl" (16), she can make a difference. Opdyke grows up in a home where her father and mother are "kind to everyone, even the Gypsies who camped in the woods outside town and made people suspicious with their strange customs and language" (15). As a young girl, Irene "was always caught up in heroic struggles" (14). She saw herself "saving lives, sacrificing herself for others" (14), becoming convinced that she was destined to have "righteous adventures" (14).

When she reaches adolescence, Opdyke's desire to have adventures dovetails with her desire to serve. She first becomes a Red Cross volunteer and then a candy striper. She considers entering the convent, moved not by a religious vocation so much as the nuns' "devotion to service" (15). But her desire to serve others is interrupted when the Germans invade Poland and she is forced to use all her abilities simply to save herself. Separated from her family, she joins a group of refugees fleeing the city where she has been studying nursing. Motivated by a desire to drive the Germans out of their country, the refugees form a leadership committee. Although both males and females resist the Germans, only men are on the leadership committee. Opdyke acerbically notes that "they never asked my opinion" (30).

Over the next months she has adventures, though they are not of the sort she would call "righteous." She flees the Germans and is caught by the Russians who beat and rape her. She is forced to work in a Russian hospital where a Russian doctor attacks her. Finally, she flees the Russians and is reunited with her family in German-occupied Poland, where her transformation from a victim into a "rescuer" begins. Assigned to work in a hotel that has been taken over to house Nazi officers, she gains her early political education, and in the process her moral vision becomes increasingly complex. Though reared by her parents to believe there should be "no distinctions between people" (17), she has been, like many teenagers, someone for whom "politics are too abstract" (13). Caught up in her own struggle for survival, she is ignorant of the Nazi solution for the "Jewish problem" until she sees one of the enclosed ghettos outside the kitchen where she works. Sickened by what she has observed, Irene castigates herself for forgetting "the Jews, driven from their homes, crowded into the ghetto. I was sure they were worse off than even the rest of us Poles. . . . Now I berated myself for the good food I had eaten" (104). She cannot reconcile the kindness of her Nazi superiors to her with the treatment of the Jews. Though she is surrounded by loudspeakers that blare, "Whoever helps a Jew shall be punished by death" (105), she begins to help. Her first step is to sneak boxes of food out of the kitchen, slipping them under the fences that surround the ghetto. She does this daily, retrieving the empty boxes every morning and returning them full every evening, never knowing who has received her gifts. At night, unable to sleep, she thinks back to her childhood and recalls "friends who were Jewish but who were not different from us"

(110). As she contemplates their fate, she connects it to her own: "if our childhood friends could be considered enemies, what was to keep us from the same fate? Weren't we all the same? Hitler would finish the Jews, ghetto by ghetto, and then turn his full attentions to the rest of us Poles" (110). Her determination to help the Jews intensifies, even when a Jewish friend says, "You're only a young girl. What can you do?" (121). Even though Irene asks herself the same question, her efforts increase in both frequency and audacity. As winter approaches, she asks her German supervisor for extra blankets for herself. When he gives her many more than one person would need, she realizes that he is well aware that she is diverting the blankets to the Jewish kitchen workers. His silent complicity confuses her because it makes "hating the Germans a complex matter, when it should have been such a straightforward one" (134).

When she learns of the Nazis' plans to further "thin" (142) the Jewish population, she realizes that more drastic action is required than simply smuggling food and blankets. Importantly, she understands that this is a crossroads in the development of an acceptable sense of self: "I did not ask myself, Should I do this? But, How will I do this? Every step of my childhood had brought me to this crossroads; I must take the right path, or I would no longer be myself. You must understand that I did not become a resistance fighter, a smuggler of Jews . . . all at once. One's first steps are always small" (143). Opdyke's representation of herself as someone who develops slowly into a heroic figure is a necessary corrective to the many mainstream cultural narratives that suggest that individuals become strong and heroic in a moment rather than over time and that they do so on their own. Irene makes clear that her personal journey was gradual and painful and that the strength necessary to be heroic, at least in part, was the consequence of the examples of her parents, especially her mother. Equally helpful to young female readers is her repeated assertion that the desire to be strong and to use one's strength to help others can become an integral part of individual identity. Irene first smuggles Jews from the ghetto to the surrounding forests. Then a Nazi colonel who commands the town where she lives decides to move from his hotel to a private home, and she is ordered to become his housekeeper. Visiting the house for the first time, she immediately realizes its potential as a hiding place for Jews. For several months she hides Jews in the basement of her employer's house, feeding them well from Nazi stores. Eventually, the Major discovers what she has been doing when he returns early from work one day. His shock leaves him speechless, but he agrees to remain silent if Irene will become his mistress. She agrees to do so. But when her shame drives her to the confessional and her priest tells her she must stop sleeping with the Major even if it means the death of the Jews, she refuses. She "bursts" out of the church still convinced that she is doing the right thing: "God had saved my life so many times that I had to believe there was a reason. . . . I knew what that reason was: It was to save my friends' lives. The price I had to pay for that was nothing by comparison. I had not received consolation from the priest, but I had God's blessing. I was never more sure of anything" (217–18).

Irene's efforts to save Jews gradually extend beyond those who have been her personal friends. Her efforts finally end when the Russian army invades Poland. The German retreat gives Irene the opportunity to escape the Major and make her way toward her native city. But though her individual efforts end, they have permanently shaped what she wants from her life, that is, to be a fighter: "I would continue to fight. That was my life. That was the life I wanted to lead, struggling against the enemies of Poland" (230). Irene's story ends when the war does. Afterwards, like Ruth, she emigrates to the United States where she marries. She maintains contact with the Jewish friends she rescued and with the Nazi Major who turned a blind eye to her use of his home as an Underground Railroad of sorts. Ironically, in the last years of his life when he is shunned by his family for his relationship with Irene, he is taken in by the Jews who hid in his home. The likelihood that this would have occurred without her examples of bravery is slight, indeed, and suggests that the bravery that leads to her empowerment has had a ripple effect.

## *WARRIORS DON'T CRY*

Opdyke looks backward at her girlhood to show how she was shaped by the events of World War II. Although she hardly chose the chaos and trauma of war, she emerged from it convinced of the importance of asserting her voice to ensure that such events did not recur. Melba Pattillo Beals' *Warriors Don't Cry* tells a similar story in terms of physical sufferings, but different in one significant respect. As one of eight black students who tried to integrate Central High School in Little Rock

Arkansas in 1957, she chose to put herself in a situation that incurred physical and emotional abuse. Her story is one of a fifteen-year-old girl learning, over the course of a year, how to draw on internal resources in order to endure what she believes must be endured, achieve her own ambitions, and promote a better life for all African-Americans.

Melba Pattillo Beals grows up with her mother and younger brother in a household headed by her maternal grandmother. These two strong women give young Melba mixed messages about the possibilities for her own life. Her grandmother believes that Melba's recovery from a serious infection as an infant signifies she has a special destiny "to carry this banner for our people."[7] The banner she refers to is one of integration and requires much more than simply carrying a flag. Her mother, a college graduate and high school teacher, stresses the value of getting the best education possible, and it is assumed that both Melba and her brother will attend college. Both her mother and grandmother applaud the Supreme Court's decision in Brown vs. Board of Education, though at the same time they are well aware that white anger over the decision puts them in danger. As she matures, Melba realizes that growing up in a segregated society is like "stealing a teaspoonful of your self-esteem each day" (6). By the time she is three, she is afraid of white people, her fear stemming from her observations of adults of her own race who frequently whisper, "The white folks won't like us to do that" or, "We don't want to anger the white folks" (7). Yet her family also applauds Rosa Parks' courage. Shaped by her mother's and grandmother's fears and expectations, Melba decides to apply to be one of the first black teenagers to integrate Central High. She does not inform her family of this decision, and when they learn of it over the national news, their initial reaction is one of horror. They "grill" her, asking if she realized her decision "might endanger [her] family" (32). Despite their horror, they ultimately consent to her attending Central and maintain their support in the face of anonymous phone callers who shout, "Niggers don't belong in our schools. You all are made for hanging" (39). Melba's own motives for wanting to attend are both mature and yet very much those of a typical fifteen-year-old. Central is the best high school in her state and she believes that if she attends it she will "get other opportunities" (29). Her notion of what these "other opportunities" might be, however, is at this stage in her life similar to those of many adolescent girls. She is, for example, "heartbroken" when segregation prevents her from going to hear

Elvis Presley at a "whites only auditorium" and cries, "Why? Why can't I go everywhere whites go?" (29)

Her first day at Central sets the tone for her entire year at this school: National Guardsmen, under orders from the Governor of Arkansas, prevent her and seven other teenagers from entering the high school. When the teenagers and their parents try to enter the school, crowds of angry and abusive white adults verbally threaten them. The students finally enter after a period of days when President Eisenhower orders the 101st Airborne Division to Little Rock to escort the students into the school and to serve as their body-guards while they attend classes. In spite of the soldiers' protection, Melba and the other teenagers are abused both verbally and physically by white students for the entire year. Melba is kicked, tripped, slapped, punched, and spat upon on a daily basis. She even has firecrackers thrown at her, ink thrown on her clothes, and acid thrown in her face. Teachers turn away when these things happen, and when the black students complain to administrators, they are reminded that they chose to come to Central and are warned not to cause trouble. Friends from her old high school abandon Melba, fearful that her decision will endanger them.

When Melba becomes discouraged, cries, and suggests returning to her old high school, her grandmother calls her up short: "You make this your last cry. . . . You're a warrior on the battlefield. . . . The women of this family don't break down in the face of trouble. We act with courage, and with God's help, we ship trouble right on out" (57). Her grandmother advises her to follow the Biblical injunction to "WATCH, FIGHT, and PRAY" (3), and over the course of the year she does all three at various points. She watches the white students closely for any signs that they may be warming toward her. She fights back physically when overwhelmed with anger. And she prays regularly for the strength to continue at Central. Like other empowered heroines, both fictional and actual, she also uses writing as a way of imposing some order on what she is experiencing. Her journal allows her a safe place to assert her voice, something she rarely feels able to do during the school day or even at home where she is expected to defer silently to the adults around her. She records her hopes, fears, and anxieties, telling herself that the journal will give "God himself a chance to see what is going on" (245). Selections from this journal are interspersed throughout her memoir. The entries record the physical abuse she endures and track the mental resources she develops for dealing with it. In addition to her journal, she is also able to express herself to the many reporters who have flocked to Little Rock to record the process of integration. As she watches the reporters and realizes the power they have to shape public opinion, she develops the desire to become one herself.

Melba's capacity to cope with the ongoing abuse is strengthened by one of the young white soldiers assigned to be her bodyguard and by the teachings of Ghandi. Though these two men represent diametrically opposed systems of dealing with violence, both teach the value of inner strength and focus. Danny, the soldier, teaches her to focus her energies when physically threatened. When Melba learns that Eisenhower is reducing the forces at her school, she is at first terrified. She then reflects on what Danny has taught her, and "the warrior growing inside me squared my shoulders and put my mind on alert to do whatever was necessary to survive. I tried hard to remember everything Danny had taught me. I discovered I wasn't frightened in the old way anymore" (182). From the teachings of Ghandi, recommended to her by her grandmother, she learns to turn a situation to her advantage by not giving her tormenters the response they expect. When a white student tells her, "Study hard now, nigger bitch, but you gotta leave this place sometime and then we got you," Melba responds with, "'Thanks for the compliment' . . . a mask of fake cheer on my face" (260). Melba's seeming nonchalance flummoxes the white boy, who "seemed astonished as he slowly started to back away. . . . I felt safer, even comfortable, as something inside me settled to its center. I had a powerful feeling of being in charge. I was no longer allowing hecklers' behavior to frighten me into acting a certain way. For that moment I was the one making the decisions about how I would behave" (260). Melba's newfound sense of control affects her behavior at home as well as at school. Suddenly, she starts to assert herself even when her wishes contradict those of her grandmother. She begins with small things, such as her desire to wear nylon stockings and heels and choose her own Easter outfit, finding that even assertions in relatively small matters affect her positively: "I felt power surging up in me once again, so I had to speak for myself" (268).

Though she finishes out the year at Central High, Melba is uncertain of the value of her experiences. Her grandmother tells her, "Later, you'll be grateful for the courage it built inside you and the blessing it will bring" (303). But Melba is left wondering just how long it will take for "that feeling of gratitude to come to [her]" (303). The value of what she endured remains problematic to Melba until she is an adult able to make some order of the contradictory nature of both her experiences and her reactions to them. Tallying up the cost of that year she says: "It cost us our innocence and a precious year of our teenage lives" (305). But as an adult, watching videotapes of herself entering Central protected by the 101st soldiers and later visiting Central where she is greeted by the student body president, a young African-American man, she is "moved by the enormity of that experience. I believe that was the moment when the whole nation took a giant step forward" (309). Irene Opdyke and Melba Pattillo Beals both gain a stronger sense of self and purpose by coping with events external to them. These forces, which in each case are ones of violence and hatred, force them to clarify who they are and what they will be. Each girl begins her story with a sense of personal worth fostered by their families. In attempting to preserve what they value and regain their sense of self-worth, each of these girls moves from a sense of passivity to one of relative assertiveness. An additional by-product of their doing so is a much greater sense of connection to the larger world.

## STICK FIGURE:
## A DIARY OF MY FORMER SELF

In the preceding memoirs the authors' battles for survival are with clearly defined external forces, anti-Semitism and racism. Opdyke and Beals both derive their sense of selfhood and empowerment from their ability to resist the dominant power structure and to define themselves in opposition to it. Lori Gottlieb, in *Stick Figure: A Diary of My Former Self*, describes a battle in which the enemies are less well defined and, indeed, often masquerade as desired friends. Her memoir, culled from diaries she kept as an eleven-year-old, describes, first, in excruciating detail the social forces that make girls susceptible to eating disorders and, then, the internal resources that must be cultivated to ensure recovery. *Stick Figure* as a narrative can be labeled an autopathography, defined by G. Thomas Courser, in *Recovering Bodies*, as an "autobiographical narrative of illness or disability."[8] Courser maintains that the importance of this relatively new form of life writing is that it treats "the body's form and function . . . as fundamental constituents of identity" (12). That adolescent girls do, to varying degrees, base their sense of self-worth on the extent to which their bodies meet culturally mandated standards of attractiveness is evidenced by the popularity of teen magazines, all of which share the subtext that the female body is innately flawed and in need of endless products and procedures to reduce, cleanse and enhance it. The extraordinarily high number of adolescent girls who suffer from eating disorders shows girls' susceptibility to these narratives.

At the beginning of her book, Lori Gottlieb is a strongly opinionated eleven-year-old, interested in math, chess, and sports. She is also aware that she is considered a unique child and that "unique" is code for being a complete "weirdo." Lori's academic interests alienate her from her girlfriends, whose conversations revolve around "clothes and boys"[9] and who, unlike Lori, have learned the rule that "as you get older you have to keep your real feelings inside, like a secret" (18). A self-described "blabbermouth," Lori is a source of anxiety, especially to her mother who "hates me being unique" (18) and whose sense of her own and her daughter's worth is dependent totally on appearance. She bemoans that Lori, "a gorgeous child" (19), is now going through that "awkward stage girls go through" (19). Confronted at a school open house with her daughter's many academic accomplishments, her only response is, "why can't you look like your friends?" (118).

Lori's increasing sense that she is a problem to be solved, rather than an individual to be loved, casts her own sense of self into doubt. When her father asks her after a quarrel, "Who do you think you are, young lady?" (20), her response reveals her awareness of the cultural imperative to silence herself as well as her sense of loss and confusion: "If I was allowed to say what I feel, I'd probably say 'I have no idea anymore'" (20).

On a family vacation to Washington, D.C., Lori determines that losing weight is the way to become an acceptable female. Though she only weighs sixty-nine pounds, she compares herself to a cousin who is four years older and notes that "my butt looked big compared to Kate's" (59). She feels "ugly" standing next to Kate, who is "so much taller and thinner, like a real woman" (57). As the trip progresses, Lori appropriates Kate as a model of how to transform herself into a socially approved model of femininity. Described by her own mother as a girl who "used to be a loudmouth" (56), Kate now "talks so quiet, like she's whispering secrets to everyone" (56). Previously viewed as "too spirited" by her father, Kate is now said to have "matured" (56). Two important components of Kate's maturation process, at least to the adults around her, are the abandonment of her earlier interest in becoming a doctor like her father and the adoption of her mother's eating habits.

Lori notices that Kate, Kate's mother, her own mother, and, indeed, all the adult women around her eat very little: "Kate and her mother took tiny helpings of everything, just like Mom does" (57). When Kate's mother passes on the dessert that is her "favorite cake in the world" because she wants to "maintain my girlish figure," Lori learns another "rule" for females: "If you're a woman, you're suppose to look like a girl with a 'girlish figure.' But if you're a girl, you're supposed to act like a woman by not being 'spirited.' Except I eat and talk like guys do. No wonder everyone thinks I'm a weirdo" (58). Lori stops eating and refuses to resume doing so despite her parent's orders to the contrary. From this point on her life follows a pattern that Naomi Wolf has argued is common to the anorexic: "The anorexic may begin her journey defiant, but from the point of view of a male-dominated society, she ends up the perfect woman. She is weak, sexless, and voiceless, and can only with difficulty focus on the world beyond her plate."[10] By the time she is hospitalized, Lori weighs less than sixty pounds, is prone to bouts of dizziness, and seldom expresses herself to anyone other than her diary. The girl who at the beginning of the book worries that the "sun's gonna burn us all to death because ladies use too much hair spray" (15) now spends all of her free time reading diet books, counting calories, and wondering "what are girls to wish for other than to be thin?" (135).

Though she is hospitalized, Lori's recovery is neither quick nor easy. What hinders her is the extent to which she has internalized the cultural ideals that women can never be too thin and that they have no reason to exist other than to be thin. When she first begins to lose weight, other girls notice and flock to her for dieting advice, "like I was a movie star" (87). When she sees a poster of a starving child, Lori's responds, "I wish I was that beautiful" (87). Sadly, adult women around her reinforce this ideal. Lori carries with her the image of her mother who denies hunger, eats little at meals, and yet sneaks downstairs in the middle of the night to stuff pastries into her mouth. While Lori is in the hospital, her mother, who is deeply embarrassed by her daughter's illness, warns that unless she does something about "[her] figure, [she'll] never find someone . . . to marry" (149). Even the nutritionist who has been assigned to work with Lori skips breakfast and exercises through lunch. Little wonder then that

Lori wishes "I was a woman already so I could diet and people think it's normal" (79).

Early in the book, when she is frustrated by her ignorance of the unspoken rules her peers and parents seem instinctively to know, Lori speculates that "maybe you have to be invisible to survive" (49). Certainly, starving herself is one way of ensuring invisibility. But eventually, Lori opts for more drastic measures and decides to kill herself. Exhausted, she "cannot wait to be dead" (190). Ironically, she is by this time tired of her own obsession with weight but is at a loss to imagine an existence for females that doesn't involve constant dieting: "I'd also rather be dead all the time than worry about being skinny all the time. But if you don't worry about being thin, everyone thinks you're a complete weirdo" (193).

Lori's suicide attempt is discovered and thwarted by one of her nurses, Elizabeth. Elizabeth becomes her savior in more ways than one. Most important, she provides an example and dissenting voice to those Lori has grown up hearing. A woman with healthy eating habits and a corresponding healthy self-image, Elizabeth has interests beyond shopping and dieting and tells Gottlieb that she is "much more interesting than people who worry about their weight all their lives" (195). After hearing this, Lori finally finds something to wish for, that "being thin didn't matter so much to everyone, even me" (195). She then begins to eat again and vows not to listen to people "who say you have to diet your whole life" (196). Gottlieb's decision to commit herself to recovery is significant on several levels. In nurturing her own body, she is reclaiming it from the cultural imperative, voiced by her mother, that females "can never be too thin." The process of reclamation is especially painful for her on a personal level. Unlike Opdyke and Beals, who are close to their mothers and value their guidance, Gottlieb's recovery is largely dependent on a rejection of her mother's values and a resigned acceptance that she will never be the daughter her mother wishes her to be.

## ALMOST A WOMAN

A mother's power to shape her daughter's sense of self has been widely documented. In the books discussed in this chapter, there is a clear distinction between mothers who support their daughters' journey toward empowerment, either directly (Beals) or indirectly (Opdyke, who is inspired by the memory of her own mother), and those who either directly or indirectly hinder it. Lori Gottlieb's mother's commitment to a repressive concept of femininity not only wounds her daughter but impedes Lori's recovery from that wound. Gottlieb's mother's narcissism seemingly blinds her to the damage she does and, in fact, allows her to convince herself that she is helping Lori become normal.

Esmeralda Santiago's memoir, *Almost a Woman*, traces her coming of age as a Puerto Rican transplanted to the United States. Like Gottlieb, she moves toward empowerment by negotiating an identity that meets the expectations of a mother who hopes her daughter will be "smarter about life than she had been," while achieving her own desire to "move from the margin to the center."[11] The movement she desires, from being on the margins of life to its center, requires sorting what is good from what is bad in her home life and determining which aspects she will keep. Unlike Gottlieb, who occupies a position of social privilege, Santiago must resolve issues of class and ethnicity, sources both of strength and of barriers to be overcome, which complicates her journey.

Santiago's mother, Mami, leaves Puerto Rico and the father of her children when Esmeralda is thirteen, driven by the need to find better medical care for one of her sons. Already the mother of seven children, she gives birth in the next eight years to four more children by two different men. Though unable to speak English, Mami finds work in a variety of factories that pay barely enough to feed her growing family. During lay-offs and pregnancies, she relies on welfare to support her brood, using Esmeralda's growing English to help her navigate the welfare bureaucracy. When money is still short, she moves her children and her mother (and often her mother's boyfriend) from one tenement to another. In the twenty-one years Esmeralda lives with her mother, their family moves twenty times. Like Melba Beals, Santiago grows up in a matriarchal family. But unlike Beal's mother and grandmother who live the values they promote, Esmeralda's mother and grandmother's lives are beset with contradictions: "My sisters and I were advised to learn from their [mother's and grandmother's] mistakes. . . . It was a path with no precedent in our family . . . each adult was a model of impulsiveness and contradiction. . . . Mami and Tata both spouted rules they didn't live by and were prime examples of the aphorism, 'Do as I say not as I do'" (209).

The contradictions that characterize the lives of the adult women closest to Esmeralda involve ethnicity, sexuality, and aspiration. To achieve a strong sense of self and the empowerment that goes with that selfhood, Esmeralda must resolve these contradictions in a way that allows her both a hold on the love and loyalty she associates with being part of a large, closely knit family and the independence she needs to achieve her own aspirations.

As soon as she arrives in New York, Esmeralda is confronted with issues of ethnic identity: Is she Puerto Rican? Hispanic? What's the difference between the two? Place of birth? First language? Her attempts to answer these questions are stymied by her mother's fears that the world outside their family, outside their apartment, contains nothing but threats that she cannot name but that are "algo" [ominous]. Though Mami ostensibly comes to the United States hoping for a better life for her children, she is adamant that "although we live in the United States, we were to remain 100% Puerto Rican" (25). Esmeralda notes that when Mami speaks of relatives who have become Americanized, "it sounded like a terrible thing, to be avoided at all costs" (12). When her children become increasingly fluent in English, she becomes distanced from them. Esmeralda sees that as Mami watches her children learn English, her expression changes from "pride, to envy, to worry" (19). As Esmeralda learns more English, she feels overwhelmed by the new words in her head, but her solution to this is to "learn English well enough never again to be caught between languages" (21).

Much of Mami's negative associations with being Americanized have to do with female sexuality. Though she has never married any of the men who have fathered her eleven children, she tells her daughters, "Don't think because we are here you can act like the fast American girls" (29), girls who are presumably freer with their sexual favors than Puerto Rican girls. But it is not American girls who teach Esmeralda her most potent lessons about female sexuality, but rather Mami herself. Seeing her mother pregnant yet again by a man who has made no commitment to her, seeing that Mami is not immune "to the seductive power of a man with a sweet tongue and a soft touch" (135), Esmeralda vows to get an education and carve out a different life for herself: "All I had to do was look around me to know what happened to a girl who let a man take the place of an education" (89), and she vows to sign up for "the pill as soon as there was any possibility I'd need it" (157). Her attitudes about her sexuality reflect her ambivalence about both being Puerto Rican and being poor. Angered by the negative stereotypes of Puerto Ricans who surround her, she wishes she could return to Puerto Rico (39) and escape the "ghetto." Knowing this is not a possibility and determined to resist the characterizations of female Puerto Ricans as a "hot tamale right out of West Side Story"(172), she dresses conservatively, does not drink or smoke, and creates a secret life where "I wasn't Puerto Rican. I wasn't American. I wasn't anything. I spoke every language in the world, so I was never confused about what people said and could be understood by everyone. My skin was not a particular color, so I didn't stand out as black, white, brown" (84). Through education Esmeralda achieves a better understanding, if not a resolution, of the conflicts and contradictions that surround and shape her life. She is encouraged by a junior high teacher to audition for New York's Performing High School and wins a place there. Mami, proud of her daughter's acceptance into such a prestigious school, nevertheless characterizes it as a school for "blanquitos." And while Esmeralda realizes that "if I looked at Performing Arts strictly along racial lines, Mami was right, it was a school where almost all the students and teachers were white. . . . [But] the hierarchies set up along racial lines that I had come to accept in junior high school weren't as marked. At Performing Arts, status was determined by talent" (69). But even talent, she comes to realize, is secondary to material advantage. Perhaps the most important aspect of her education, gleaned from her years at Performing Arts, is an enhanced understanding of the importance of class in American culture. She articulates this awareness by delineating the differences between being "advantaged" and "disadvantaged":

> It meant trips to Europe during vacations, extra classes on weekends with dance Masters or voice coaches, plastic surgery to reduce large noses or refine broad ones. It meant tennis lessons and swim meets, choir practice, clubs, academic tutoring. It meant money for lunch at the deli across the street. . . . Being disadvantaged meant I found my dance tights and leotard in a bin in the guidance office. It meant washing them and setting them to dry on the barely warm radiators of our apartment . . . it meant a pass so I could get a free bowl of soup and half a sandwich for lunch. . . . (69–70)

Though she has grown up poor and understands very well the hand-to-mouth existence her mother leads, it is only when she is confronted on a daily basis with wealth that Esmeralda understands how her own life has been shaped by poverty. Throughout his memoir *Hunger of Memory,* Richard Rodriguez argues that while education for minority students may have the effect of making it easier for them to move within mainstream or dominant culture, it also alienates them from the home and family that have been their traditional sources of support.[12] This proves the case for Esmeralda. Her increased sense of the importance of class in determining opportunity, coupled with the new experiences she has at Performing Arts, make her feel that "[t]he more time I spent away from home, the more it felt as if I were a visitor in my family" (217). When her best friend tells her that "to become a woman . . . I must rebel against my mother" (283), she agrees, increasingly aware that her success in life, even her survival, is dependent on breaking away from her mother's life of unplanned pregnancies, low paying jobs, and reliance on welfare. When an actor friend, also Puerto Rican, takes her to task for her "pathetically undeveloped" (286) social conscience and lack of obligation to "our people," she responds that she feels no obligation in the abstract but, "felt, in fact, weighed down by duty to my people in the concrete: Mami, Tata, my ten sisters and brothers" (286). Indeed, breaking away from her family is made difficult, even painful, by her genuine love for them as well as her awareness that her mother expects her to model high expectations for her younger siblings: "For as long as I could remember, I'd been told that I was to set an example for my siblings. It was a tremendous burden, especially as the family grew, but I took the charge seriously, determined to show my brothers and sisters that we need not surrender to low expectations" (287).

*Almost a Woman* takes Esmeralda from the age of thirteen to twenty-one. In the years following her graduation from Performing Arts, she makes slow and gradual attempts to increase the distance between herself and her mother. Though Mami insists "that the only way she'd let me go was on the arm of a man, preferably a legal husband" (283), Esmeralda increasingly expands her freedom by lying about how her time is spent. She contributes to the family's finances, but takes jobs that fit her needs rather than those her mother finds appropriate. She continues to take acting and dance lessons and lands a role that allows her to tour with a children's theater company. She stays out later at night and at the age of twenty begins her first sexual relationship. This relationship with a Turkish film director, at thirty-seven as old as her mother, allows Esmeralda to leave her Mami's home and begin her life as an independent adult. She does so, sneaking away and leaving a letter in Mami's mailbox explaining what she has done. Though her method of departure hardly embodies the courage of an Irene Opdyke or a Melba Beals, it still represents a movement toward empowerment, something that becomes clear in Esmeralda's retrospective characterization of it.

Describing the man for whom she leaves her mother's home, Esmeralda represents him in an unflattering light and her choice as a poor one born out of psychological need. She characterizes her lover, Ulvi, as someone who wanted to "be Pygmalion, and I became the stone upon which he sculpted Galatea . . . to be with him, I had to discard who I was and evolve into the woman he wanted to be with" (305). To the reader's implicit question of why she aligns herself with such a man she responds, "He took care of me in a way no one else did . . . I felt safe and protected. . . . Unlike the other adults in my life, he didn't say one thing and do another" (306). This last sentence makes clear that a large part of Ulvi's appeal for Esmeralda was his ability to merge his beliefs with his practice and to lead a life that seemed consistent and focused, unlike that of her own family. Though the first chapter of her memoir suggests the relationship did not endure, it nevertheless seems to have been a necessary step toward enlarging her world. It is important, too, to place her departure within the context of her family structure. The act of leaving home, though done covertly, overtly rejects a way of life she no longer views as feasible. Ironically, she leaves in the only way her mother could view as feasible, on the arm of a man. The final pages of *Almost a Woman* are ambiguous and can be read as a recognition of the problematic nature of her decision:

> Over the years of watching Mami . . . my aunts and cousins as they loved, lost, loved again, I'd learned that love was something you got over. If Ulvi left, there would be another man, but there would never be another Mami. . . . I stood up, put my dishes in the sink, and burrowed into the room I shared . . . covers pulled over my head to block out the noise, the confusion, the drama of my family's life, I knew, just as Ulvi knew when he asked, that I had already made my choice. (311)

In this passage she clearly rejects her mother's way of life while acknowledging her mother's enduring love. Like Irene Opdyke, who argues that heroism is approached and achieved slowly, Esmeralda Santiago demonstrates that empowerment is often achieved in a series of small stops that follow a two-steps-forward, one-step-backwards pattern. In the seven years covered in her memoir she begins the process of constructing an identity that will accommodate different cultural expectations and loyalties. She pushes herself to learn English, inspiring her younger siblings to do the same. She gains entrance to a prestigious high school, the first in her junior high school to achieve this distinction. She graduates from that high school, the first member of her family ever to do so. She takes control of her sexuality and learns that being female and Puerto Rican does not doom one to a life of unplanned pregnancies and grinding poverty. Though ultimately she graduates from Harvard and receives an MFA from Sarah Lawrence College, Santiago, like Melba Beals, also demonstrates that for minorities the status of "other" both redefines and impedes empowerment.

## CHINESE CINDERELLA: THE TRUE STORY OF AN UNWANTED DAUGHTER

Like Lori Gottlieb, Adeline Yen Mah, author of *Chinese Cinderella: The True Story of An Unwanted Daughter*, is damaged by a mother, in her case a stepmother who sees her not just as a problem to be solved but a child to discard. To this end she employs all the tools of the wicked stepmothers of fairy tale and folklore—beatings, isolation, and exile. She is aided in her endeavors by her husband, Adeline's father (a man so little interested in his daughter that he cannot remember either her Chinese name or her birthday), and by a culture that allows unwanted daughters to be abandoned or sold.

Adeline's problems begin at birth. Her mother dies shortly thereafter, and her four older siblings "blamed me for causing mama's death and never forgave me" (*Chinese Cinderella*, 4). A year later her father marries a seventeen-year-old girl and orders his children to call her Niang, or mother. Niang quickly has two children of her own and makes no effort either to hide her preference for them or to treat the two sets of children equally. The entire family, stepchildren included, seems to accept that Niang's biological children are "better looking and smarter than her stepchildren—simply superior in every way" (10). Disliked already by her siblings for the "bad luck" (3) she represents, Adeline becomes the particular focus of her stepmother's hostility when, at the age of six, she tries to stop her stepmother from beating her two-year-old stepsister. Watching as her stepmother "deliberately and viciously . . . set about beating her child " (34) in front of a room full of adults, Adeline cannot understand why the adults do nothing other than avert their eyes. Though she is frightened and knows she should remain silent, Adeline finally blurts out, "Don't beat her anymore. She is only a baby" (34). Adeline's words have the desired effect; her stepmother does stop the beating. But her audacity at speaking out has enduring consequences: "Fuming with rage, Niang slowly extended her right arm and pointed her index finger at me. . . . Then I heard her words loaded with malice. . . . 'Get out. . . . I shall never forgive you! Never! Never! Never! You'd better watch out from now on! You will pay for your arrogance!'" (35).

Niang makes good on her words. Adeline functions as the family scapegoat for the next seven years, enduring a variety of indignities and abuses until she graduates several years early from high school, wins an international playwriting contest, and is allowed to attend college in England. The least of these abuses is being ignored. Though her family is very wealthy, no one, for example, arranges to take her to her first day of school after her family has moved to Shanghai. Finally, a servant, moved by the child's tears, agrees to take her to school on his bike. At the end of that first day, no one arrives to pick her up and she is left, at the age of six, to try to make her way home alone. When a strange woman sees Adeline, obviously lost, she asks, "What's your mother doing that she would leave you waiting here all by yourself? Doesn't she know it's dangerous for a little girl your age to be hanging around on streets like this?" (29). Adeline only hangs her head and is silent. Her mother obviously does know that it is dangerous and just as obviously doesn't care.

A few years later, angry because her stepdaughter's school friends have appeared at their home uninvited to celebrate Adeline's election as head girl of her school's top grade, her parents exile her to a convent school and orphanage in Tianjin. They do this in 1948, when Tianjin is in imminent danger of being invaded by Mao's army. A mother of one of Adeline's new classmates, horrified by this move, asks: "What are your parents thinking? Everyone is fleeing Tianjin for Shanghai or Hong Kong. And here you come from the opposite direction . . . don't they read the newspapers?" (129). Later Adeline escapes from Tianjin only by chance when Niang's sister accidentally learns that Adeline is in Tianjin and assumes that Niang would want the child to accompany her when she flees the city. The convent school in Tianjin is the first of a series of convent schools to which Adeline is exiled. In each she is sustained by the kindness of the nuns. Her parents, however, never visit, never write, and forbid the nuns to allow her letters from anyone else. They do not inform her when they move from Shanghai to Hong Kong in flight from the Communists.

Adeline copes with her abusive environment in two ways, her methods similar to those of other girls struggling to become empowered. Rejected by those adults who might be expected to care for her, she finds others who fill a nurturing role. With their support she cultivates her mind so that she will have the internal resources to shape and control her own life. Though Adeline is ignored by most of her family, her grandfather, YeYe, and her aunt, Baba, love her. In return, she, of all of her siblings, remains loyal to YeYe and Baba, though her parents punish her for doing so. Even when Baba warns her not to "make waves," Adeline actively but silently defies her parents for the sake of Baba and YeYe. Doing so increases her physical sufferings, yet she refuses to desist, recognizing that both aunt and grandfather, too, suffer from Niang's tyranny. Though YeYe and Baba are significantly older than Niang, both are made dependent on her by Adeline's father's unwillingness to oppose his wife. Adeline's ability to form sympathetic and empathetic bonds with others strengthens her and makes her better able to endure the abuse heaped on her.

Second, she is sustained by the approval of teachers and classmates who recognize her intellectual abilities and her strength of character. During her second week of kindergarten, only four years old, she wins her first award, and henceforward her academic life becomes a series of prizes and accolades. School provides her with a sense of belonging: "My classmates made me feel as if I 'belonged.' Unlike my siblings, nobody looked down on me" (13). But though she does well in school and has the constant love of two family members, the disparity between how she is treated by her teachers and classmates, who respect her, and her family, who despise her, creates a crisis of identity. Labeled the "scholar" by her classmates but told by her stepmother and father that she is "bad blood . . . [and] deserves to be sent away" (103), Adeline cannot help but wonder, "Which is the true me?" (119) Her siblings use her achievements as justification for further abuse ("Take that! Medal winner, Teacher's pet!") while her aunt and grandfather reinforce and celebrate her efforts.

Her aunt keeps Adeline's report cards in a locked strongbox and brings them out when Adeline is in need of support and encouragement. On one occasion, a discouraged Adeline asks, "What good does it do? Being top of my class and skipping grades and all that. . . . Not that it'll get me anywhere" (181). Her grandfather replies, "Don't talk like that . . . I've tried to tell you over and over that far from being garbage you are precious and special. . . . But you can vanquish your demons only when you yourself are convinced of your own worth" (181). Hearing this, Adeline vows "When I get back to school I'll try even harder" (182).

Ultimately, it is Adeline's intellectual and creative abilities that allow her to escape her family. She learns of an international playwriting contest for "English speaking children anywhere in the world" (183). Inspired by her grandfather's faith in her and by the teacher who tells her, "Believe you can do anything you set your mind to" (182), Adeline enters and wins. Significantly, her winning entry creates an African girl separated from her family, a girl Adeline infuses with her own qualities and dreams: "I had her triumph over her adversaries through her own efforts" (184). Only by chance, her father learns of her triumph from a business acquaintance who reads about it in a newspaper and informs him. Though he is "radiant . . . for once proud of me" (192), the happiness Adeline might be expected to feel at his joy is undermined by his puzzlement about how she could have won: "Tell me, how did you do it? How come you?" (192). Finally, though, he admits she has potential and agrees to send her to college in England with her brother.

The memoirs discussed in this chapter are by authors of different religions, ethnicities, races, and social classes. Yet they have much in common. Each records the girlhood of a young female whose sense of self and of her place in the world is shaped by social forces she has had no part in creating and over which she has limited control. Anti-Semitism, war, racism, lookism, sexism, and family structure all present obstacles that the authors must surmount in order to survive, and, yes, thrive. All do, and though their individual experiences differ, they all draw on similar resources to overcome the circumstances of their lives.

Each girl finds strength from the examples of other adults, often women who have acted bravely in their own lives. Separated from her mother, Irene Opdyke carries with her examples of her mother's strength and courage. Melba Patillo Beals comes home from school every day to the unconditional love and support of her mother and grandmother. Lori

Gottlieb finds in the example of a middle-aged nurse hope for a life not dominated by the wish to be thin. Esmeralda Santiago finds teachers and female co-workers who encourage her. Even when her mother, overwhelmed by the material circumstances of her own life, is unable to provide the support Esmeralda wishes for, she assures her daughter of her "intelligence." Adeline Yen Mah takes comfort in the unconditional support of her aunt Baba. Each girl also believes that she is capable of more than her culture would allow her and uses her own suffering, first, to connect with and, then, to enhance the lives of others. Though she lost sight of her dream for awhile, Lori aspired to a career in science. She is now in medical school. Irene Opdyke hoped for a life of heroism and achieved one, rescuing many Jews. And Melba Patillo Beals' year of suffering in Little Rock did, indeed, open opportunities for improved education for other African-Americans and led her to a career in journalism. Esmeralda Santiago clung as an adolescent to the belief that by breaking away from the life that had been modeled for her both by family and cultural stereotypes, she would be able to help "my" people. She has written three other books that explore the intersections of gender, ethnicity and culture, all directed to young adult readers. Adeline Yen Mah went to Oxford, became a physician and wrote, in addition to *Chinese Cinderella*, the New York Times bestseller *Falling Leaves*.

For several of these women, writing about their girlhood experiences helps them understand and survive those years. Melba Beals' journal is a place for her to pour out her anger and fears. It also becomes the foundation for her future career and her memoir. Surrounded by reporters during her year at Central High, she realizes that the writing that gives her pleasure and relief also has the potential to support her as an adult. She decides to become a journalist and does so. The diary Lori Gottlieb keeps during her eleventh year also serves multiple functions. Though she is initially contemptuous of the diary because her mother chose it for her, it becomes a refuge as she becomes increasingly aware of how odd adults find her. When she finds the diary as an adult, it provides a history of her disorder and a way of using her own illness to help girls similarly afflicted. Though Esmeralda Santiago aspires as a teenager to being an actress, it is writing that ultimately captures her interest and gives shape to her dreams. The play Adeline Yen Mah writes frees her from a home and parents who have done all they can to cancel out her existence. Eventually each of the authors discussed in this chapter uses

writing as a way of transforming their personal conflicts and traumas
into constructs that will enhance the understanding, and lives of others.
James Pennebaker, author of *Opening Up*, believes that simply writing
about trauma facilitates the recovery from it: "Writing about the
thoughts and feelings associated with traumas . . . forces individuals to
bring together the many facets of overwhelmingly complicated events.
Once people can distill complex experiences into more understandable
packages, they can begin to move beyond the trauma."[13]

But if writing out of trauma helps an author recover from her experience, might it not be equally true that the reader encountering that
trauma, even second hand, is somehow strengthened and appropriates
some of the author's strength? Katherine Paterson has said that books
"allow us to enter imaginatively into someone else's life. And when we
do that, we learn to sympathize with other people."[14] The special gift,
then, of memoirs of girlhood is that they allow today's girls to experience vicariously events and circumstances that few of us would wish for
them to experience directly, to sympathize with the struggles and sufferings of others, and to use those struggles as examples to empower
their own lives.

## SUGGESTIONS FOR
## ADDITIONAL READING

Britton-Jackson, Livia. *I Have Lived a Thousand Years: Growing Up in the Holocaust.* New
York: Simon and Schuster, 1997. The author was living in Hungary in 1944 when
the Nazis invaded. Although her experiences were terrifying, she and her mother
help each other to survive the horrors, and this memoir focuses on her experiences
after the war.

Dominick, Andie. *Needles.* New York: Scribner, 1998. The author narrates the story
of her struggle with diabetes, with which she was diagnosed when only nine. At
first she rebels, refusing to administer her shots and undergoing an abortion when
she is only seventeen. When her older sister dies of the same disease and reckless
lifestyle, Andie reexamines her life-threatening behavior.

Filipovic, Zlata. *Zlata's Diary: A Child's Life in Sarajevo.* New York: Scholastic, 1994.
The horrors of the war in Sarajevo are recent enough that many readers will be
familiar with them, but Zlata's diary provides a personal record of the effects of that
war on her family and friends.

Grealy, Lucy. *Autobiography of a Face.* New York: Harper Perennial, 1995. After bone cancer disfigures her face, Grealy struggles to endure her peers' taunts and be loved for herself.

Higa, Tomiko. *The Girl With the White Flag.* Tokyo: Kodansha International, 1995. When she is only seven, the author is separated from her siblings during World War II and wanders alone, terrified, through the streets of war-torn Okinawa.

Jiang, Ji-Li, and Hwang, David Henry. *Red Scarf Girl: A Memoir of the Cultural Revolution.* New York: HarperCollins, 1997. The Chinese Cultural Revolution destroys Ji-Li's peaceful life, and she and her family, who had enjoyed prosperity in the years before Chairman Mao seized power, must destroy family treasures to demonstrate that they no longer cling to the "Four Olds"—old ideas, old culture, old customs, and old habits.

Lobel, Anita. *No Pretty Pictures: A Child of War.* New York: Greenwillow, 1999. The award-winning illustrator tells of her childhood in Poland following the Nazi occupation and her experiences as, first, a concentration camp prisoner and then a displaced person living in Sweden.

Novac, Ana. *The Beautiful Days of My Youth: My Six Months in Auschwitz and Plaszow.* Translated from the French by George L. Newman. New York: Henry Holt, 1997. Based on the author's diary during her internment in the title's two concentration camps, this memoir records the horrors of her time there.

Thornton, Yvonne S., and Jo Coudert. *The Ditchdigger's Daughters: A Black Family's Astonishing Success Story.* New York: Penguin Putnam, 1996. Thornton, now a physician, tells how her father, a poor African American man, raised five daughters during the 1950s to succeed in a racist world.

Turner, Ann. *Learning to Swim.* New York: Scholastic, 2000. Turner recounts the horror of childhood sexual abuse in this poetic memoir. Using her writing as therapy, she describes her initial efforts at healing.

Uchida, Yoshiko. *The Invisible Thread.* New York: Simon and Shuster, 1991. Uchida narrates her sorrow when she and her Japanese American family are held in an internment camp following the bombing of Pearl Harbor.

## NOTES

1. Joyce Carol Oates, "Believing What We Read and Vice Versa" *New York Times* (February 26, 1998), Op Ed section, 39.

2. Adeline Yen Mah, *Chinese Cinderella: The True Story of an Unwanted Daughter* (New York: Dell Laurel Leaf, 1999), 4; hereafter cited parenthetically in text.

3. Phyllis Rose, *Women's Lives* (New York: W. W. Norton, 1993), 13; hereafter cited parenthetically in text.

4. Suzette A. Henke, *Shattered Subject: Trauma and Testimony in Women's Life Writing* (New York: St. Martin's Press, 2000), xii–xiii.

5. bell hooks, "Keeping Close to Home: Class and Education," in *Breaking Boundaries,* Carrol Comfort, ed. (Upper Saddle River, NJ: Prentice Hall, 2000), 222.

6. Irene Gut Opdyke, as told to Jennifer Armstrong, *In My Hands: Memoirs of a Holoaust Rescuer* (New York: Random House, 1996) 3; hereafter cited parenthetically in text.

7. Melba Pattillo Beals, *Warriors Don't Cry* (New York: Washington Square Books, 1994), 4; hereafter cited parenthetically in text.

8. G. Thomas Courser, "Illness, Disability, and Life Writing," in *Recovering Bodies* (Madison, WI: University of Wisconsin Press, 1997), 14; hereafter cited parenthetically in text.

9. Lori Gottlieb, *Stick Figure: A Diary of My Former Self* (New York: Simon and Shuster, 2000), 18; hereafter cited parenthetically in text.

10. Naomi Wolf, *The Beauty Myth: How Images of Beauty Are Used Against Women* (New York: Doubleday, 1992), 197.

11. Esmeralda Santiago, *Almost a Woman* (New York: Vintage Books, 1999), 111; hereafter cited parenthetically in text.

12. Richard Rodriguez, *Hunger of Memory: The Education of Richard Rodriguez* (New York: Bantam, 1983).

13. James Pennebaker, *Opening Up: The Healing Power of Confiding in Others* (New York: Avon, 1992), 193.

14. Katherine Paterson, as quoted in *Quotations on Education,* Rosalie Maggio, ed. (Paramus, NJ: Prentice Hall, 1997), 175.

# · 7 ·

# Conclusion

In schoolbooks, the Dick and Jane syndrome reinforced our
emerging attitudes. The arithmetic books posed an appropriate conundrum: "Ann has three pies. . . . Dick has three rock-
ets . . ." We read the nuances between the lines: Ann keeps her
eye on the oven; Dan sets his sights on the moon.

Letty Cottin Pogrebin

*I*t is the rare girl today who bakes pies. Rather, girls are as likely to
study astrophysics and to be astronauts as their male counterparts. Since
the second wave of feminism began in the early sixties, they have had
greater opportunities to dream dreams that historically have been the
properties of males. It is not uncommon today, for example, that the entering freshman classes at universities or colleges will have a higher percentage of female students than males. Almost as many females as males
enter medical, law, and professional schools. This world of greater opportunity for females is reflected in young adult literature, which, increasingly, features assertive young female protagonists determined to
carve their own niche in the world.

Unlike Jo March, who abandons her aspirations to write for the
socially sanctioned roles of wife and mother, female protagonists in
young adult literature aim for the stars and, sometimes, literally land on
them. Yet while young adult literature reflects the world of increased
possibility available to girls, works like Mary Pipher's *Reviving Ophelia*
suggest that real girls still struggle psychologically to take advantage of
those opportunities. To a greater degree than their male counterparts,
girls often suffer a lessening of self-esteem at the onset of puberty, and

a consequence of this diminished sense of self is a lack of faith in their ability to claim what should be theirs.

Pipher describes female adolescence as a minefield to be carefully navigated if girls are to emerge into adulthood with an intact sense of self and in possession of the goals and ambitions adolescent boys often see as their entitlement. To a much greater extent than males, girls grow up surrounded by various mainstream media that direct their energies toward perfecting their supposedly innately faulty bodies to meet standards of beauty determined mainly by males and intended to gain their laudatory attention. Even a cursory survey of the table of contents of magazines like *Seventeen*, *Mademoiselle*, and *Glamour* shows a high percentage of articles that stress developing the personal attributes and social skills that will increase girls' attractiveness to males. *Cosmo Girl* regularly suggests that acquiring sexual skills is as important—if not more so—as doing well in school, and even the more progressive *Jane* places a heavy emphasis on how to maintain relationships with the opposite sex. Part of the difficult psychological work facing girls, then, is reconciling the conflicting messages they receive about the lives available to them. As a consequence, girls today, more than ever, need texts that acknowledge these mixed messages about being female while providing models of resistance to the still powerful cultural imperative that suggests that girls simply "be" and boys "do." The great value of recent young adult literature with strong female protagonists is that, unlike its predecessors, it meets this need.

The authors discussed here, whatever genre in which they write, acknowledge on some level that their readers are the recipient of mixed messages about "being a girl" and, most important, that these conflicts must be resolved before girls are empowered to take charge of their own lives. They portray diverse young women who struggle with issues of gender in ways very different from their literary ancestors. Despite differences in genre, each of their protagonists must determine if her own sense of what it means to be female can be reconciled with the models her culture offers. When it cannot, she is then faced with resolving the conflict, with constructing an identity that allows her an active place in the world. She has much in common with her real-life counterparts, who are constructing their own codes of female behavior, and any quick glance at the articles of Web-based 'zines[1] intended for girls reveals an in-your-face determination to resist societal dictates that girls find too confining or constraining. Sherrie Inness argues in *Millennium Girls* that today's young women are "are reinvisioning what girlhood actually means in numerous contexts . . . girls today are not passive consumers of mass culture around them but actively interact with popular culture in such a way as to reimagine and reshape cultural norms of what constitutes acceptable girlhood."[2] The girls of today's world often resist the behavioral codes of previous centuries. The texts discussed here show their fictional counterparts doing this as well. In novels as varied as *Make Lemonade* and *Alanna,* the reader encounters girls taking culturally gendered scripts and subjecting them to significant revisions. Though this process of revision always involves both internal and external struggles, these struggles take a much different form and result in much different outcomes than those depicted in earlier young adult literature.

Compare, for example, the patterns of conflict of two protagonists discussed in the first chapter. Although separated by almost a century, Jo March and Angie Morrow both struggle as adolescent girls. Though different in specifics, the general movement of their respective stories is remarkably similar. The challenge for each is to accept the gendered role society has mandated for her, to learn the rules that inevitably accompanied being a girl. In each of the novels, the protagonist has to learn and accept the rules of girlhood her society has set in place. Neither has the option of successfully challenging either the roles or the rules. The acceptance of these rules, though it leads to an ostensibly happy ending, is also accompanied by the acceptance of a diminished place in the world and a closing off of options. Jo gives up writing the Gothic tales that allow her to earn an independent income and, at least imaginatively, to roam the world unconfined by limitations of time or place; instead, she settles for the homey domestic tales that her parents and future husband find appealing and instructive. In shifting from one type of fiction to another, she moves from a literature that suggests emotional complexity and contradiction to one that is emotionally transparent and that reinforces existing gendered roles. Similarly, though Angie Morrow ends her summer by breaking up with her boyfriend and heading off for college, there is no indication that her emotional life either in or after college will be radically different from the one she has lived during her seventeenth summer. She has had one boyfriend, has gained from her relationship with him an understanding of how girls should behave with boys, and will apply that understanding to future boyfriends. Along the way she may well get her college degree, but she will neither question nor challenge the rules she has learned.

The pattern that characterizes Jo and Angie's experience as girls—discover first what society expects of you and then learn to enact the behavior—was the dominant pattern of young adult literature for girls until recently. Although female protagonists still struggle with their cultures' expectations, seldom does their struggle conclude with the protagonist passively or totally accepting a script she has had no part in writing. Rather, she becomes an active participant in constructing her life's story and, in doing so, models ways of resisting cultural expectations that limit or damage her sense of self. Because the characters in these most recent novels seldom see their lives as a closed book, to be read once and interpreted narrowly, their stories seldom end with all loose ends tied up. The "Reader, I married him" ending that characterizes so much nineteenth century literature for females, or the "Reader, I got a date to the prom" equivalent that has characterized so much literature of the earlier twentieth century has been replaced with endings that imply possibilities to be considered and questions still to be answered.

Chris Crutcher, popular author of young adult fiction, maintains that adolescence is "the time in which we first ask ourselves important questions."[3] If we accept his statement, it is not at all surprising that almost every novel or memoir discussed in this study begins with a girl wrestling with an "important question." These questions may be more overt in some genres than others. Historical fiction and literature of the fantastic are likely to begin with protagonists who have specific questions of identity. Literature set in the contemporary world is more likely to present a protagonist vaguely dissatisfied with the status quo but unsure of even the source of her dissatisfaction. Nonetheless, the need to resolve either her questions or unrest starts each girl on a journey of self-discovery that ultimately leads to empowerment. That journey may be more internal than external, but it is a journey nevertheless. More often than not, the questions with which she begins connect with issues of identity and her place in the world. Though factors such as race, class, ethnicity, and religion necessarily affect the shape of both her questions and her answers, each girl begins her journey unsure of how to reconcile her dreams and aspirations with the expectations of the world around her. Initially, her questions tend to isolate her, but as her journey progresses, she begins either to find sympathetic communities or to create them for herself.

Stories of empowered girls have nudged adolescent literature in new directions. In 1981, Anne Macleod charged that "a consistent feature of adolescent literature is its . . . nearly total preoccupation with personality. The typical adolescent novel is wrapped tightly around the individual and the personal."[4] The stories of the empowered girls discussed in this study oppose that description. The vision these girls acquire of what is possible extends beyond themselves, and their awareness of the larger world makes them strong. As they go beyond themselves, they find themselves. Doing so, they do not hesitate to circumvent and subvert oppressive social structures. Not all the girls in contemporary young adult fiction, of course, are empowered nor does empowerment lead automatically to formulaic happy endings. Many young female protagonists are still worried about their hair and the guy who will (or will not) have them. But the spunky, fiery, empowered girls who were too often absent in earlier fiction are appearing now with heartening regularity.

In *The Little House in the Big Woods*, Laura asks Ma: "Did little girls have to be as good as all that?" and Ma replies, " It was harder for little girls because they had to behave like little ladies all the time, not only on Sundays. Little girls could never slide downhill like boys. Little girls had to sit in the house and stitch on samplers."[5]

The restricted, almost claustrophobic world that Ma describes for Laura has little meaning for girls today. Whether fictional or real, few of them would even know what a sampler is. The girls of today's young adult fiction live in a world that offers them increased opportunities while demanding that they make complex choices. They skim down hills with the same gusto as their male counterparts, and though the ride may be bumpy, they come to its end ready to climb the hill and slide down again.

## NOTES

1. Virtual magazines for adolescent readers.

2. Sherri Inness, ed. *Millennium Girls: Today's Girls Around the World* (Lanham, MD: Rowman & Littlefield, 1998), 196.

3. Chris Crutcher, as quoted in *Responding to Young Adult Literature,* Virginia Monseau, ed. (Porstmouth, NH: Boynton/Cook, 1996), ix.

4. Anne Mcleod, "Robert Cormier and the Adolescent Novel," *Children's Literature in Education* 12.7 (Summer 1971), 74.

5. Laura Ingalls Wilder, *The Little House in the Big Woods* (1953) (New York: Harper Trophy, 1971), 96.

# Selected Bibliography

*Note:* This selected bibliography contains only the titles of young adult literature discussed in the book. Asterisks indicate works that are discussed at length.

Armstrong, Jennifer. *The Dreams of Mairhe Mehan*. New York: Knopf, 1996.

———. *Mary Mehan Awake*. New York: Knopf, 1997.

Avi. *The True Confessions of Charlotte Doyle*. New York: Orchard Books, 1990.

———. *The Secret School*. New York: Harcourt Brace, 2001.

Bauer, Cat. *Harley: Like a Person*. New York: Winslow, 2000.

Bauer, Joan. *Backwater*. New York: Putnam, 1999.

*———. *Rules of the Road*. New York: Putnam Sons, 1998.

Bauer, Joan, and Nancy Paulsen. *Hope Was Here*. New York: Putnam, 2000.

*Beals, Melba Pattillo. *Warriors Don't Cry*. New York: Washington Square Book, 1994.

Bennett, Cherie. *Life in the Fat Lane*. New York: Delacorte, 1998.

Billingley, Fanny. *The Folk Keeper*. New York: Simon and Schuster, 1999.

Britton-Jackson, Livid. *I Have Lived a Thousand Years: Growing Up in the Holocaust*. New York: Simon and Schuster, 1997.

Block, Francesca Lia. *The Hanged Man*. New York: HarperCollins, 1998.

———. *Violet and Claire*. New York: HarperCollins, 2000.

Brooks, Bruce. *Vanishing*. New York: HarperCollins, 1999.

*Butler, Octavia. *Parable of the Sower*. New York: Seven Stories Press, 1994.

Calder, David. *The Dragonslayer's Apprentice*. New York: Scholastic, 1997.

Cook, Karen. *What Girls Learn*. New York: Vintage, 1997.

Cooney, Caroline. *The Party's Over*. New York: Scholastic, 1991.

*Cushman, Karen. *The Midwife's Apprentice*. New York: Clarion, 1995.

———. *Catherine Called Birdie*. New York: Clarion, 1995.

———. *The Ballad of Lucy Whipple*. New York: Houghton Mifflin, 1996.

*Daley, Maureen. *Seventeenth Summer* (1942). New York: Scholastic, 1952.

Dominick, Andi. *Needles*. New York: Scribner, 1998.

Dowell, Frances O'Roark. *Dovey Coe*. New York: Atheneum, 2000.

Farmer, Nancy. *A Girl Called Disaster*. New York: Puffin Books, 1996.

Filipovic, Zlata. *A Child's Life in Sarajevo*. New York: Scholastic, 1994.

Fox, Paula. *The Moonlight Man*. New York: Morrow, 1995.

Garden, Nancy. *Dove and Sword*. New York: Scholastic, 1995.

★————. *The Year They Burned the Books*. New York: Farrar, Straus, and Giroux, 1999.

★Gottlieb, Lori. *Stick Figure: A Diary of My Former Self*. New York: Simon and Schuster, 2000.

Grant, Cynthia D. *The White Horse*. New York: Atheneum, 1998.

Grealy, Lucy. *Autobiography of a Face*. New York: HarperPerennial Library, 1995.

Hamilton, Virginia. *Plain City*. New York: Scholastic, 1993.

Hesse, Karen. *Letters from Rifka*. New York: Henry Holt, 1992.

————. *The Music of Dolphins*. New York: Scholastic, 1996.

★————. *Out of the Dust*. New York: Scholastic, 1997.

Higa, Tomiko. *The Girl with the White Flag*. Tokyo: Kodansha International, 1994.

Ho, Minfong. *Rice without Rain*. New York: Lothrop, Lee & Shepard, 1990.

Holland, Isabelle. *Behind the Lines*. New York, Scholastic, 1994.

Hopkinson, Nalo. *Brown Girl in the Ring*. New York: Warner Books, 1998.

Jiang, Ji-li, and David Henry Hwang. *Red-Scarf Girl: A Memoir of the Cultural Revolution*. New York: HarperCollins, 1997.

Johnson, Angela. *Humming Whispers*. New York: Scholastic, 1995.

————. *Heaven*. New York: Simon and Schuster, 1998.

Karr, Kathleen. *Oh, Those Harper Girls*. New York: Farrar, Straus, and Giroux, 1992.

Keller, Beverly. *The Amazon Papers*. New York: Browndeer Press, 1996.

Kessler, Christina, and Patricia Lee Gauch (ed.). *No Condition Is Permanent*. New York: Philomel, 2000.

Klause, Annette Curtis. *Alien Secrets*. New York: Yearling Books, 1995.

★————. *Blood and Chocolate*. New York: Bantam Books, 1997.

————. *The Silver Kiss*. New York: Laurel Leaf Books, 1990.

Lackey, Mercedes. *Arrows of the Queen*. New York: Daw Books, 1996.

★Lasky, Kathryn. *Beyond the Divide*. New York: Macmillan, 1983.

————. *Memoirs of a Bookbat*. New York: Harcourt Brace, 1994.

★————. *True North*. New York: Blue Sky Press, 1996.

★Lee, Marie G. *Saying Goodbye*. Boston: Houghton Mifflin, 1994.

Levy, Marilyn. *Run for Your Life*. New York: Putnam and Grosset, 1996.

Lobel, Anita. *No Pretty Pictures: A Child of War*. New York: Greenwillow Press, 1999.

★Mah, Adeline Yen. *Chinese Cinderella: The True Story of an Unwanted Daughter*. New York: Delacorte, 1999.

Matas, Carol. *After the War*. New York: Simon and Schuster, 1996.

Matcheck, Diane. *The Sacrifice*. New York: Farrar Straus Giroux, 1998.

Mazer, Norma Fox. *Missing Pieces*. New York: Morrow, 1995.

————. *When She Was Good*. New York: Scholastic, 1997.

McCaffrey, Anne. *Natasha's Ship*. New York: Ballantine, 1993.

McDaniel, Lurlene. *Until Angels Close My Eyes.* New York: Laurel Leaf, 1998.

*McKinley, Robin. *Beauty.* New York: HarperCollins, 1979.

*———. *Deerskin.* New York: Ace Books , 1993.

———. *The Hero and the Crown.* New York: Greenwillow, 1985.

Meyer, Carolyn. *White Lilacs.* New York: Harcourt Brace, 1993.

Mori, Kyoko. *Shizuko's Daughter.* New York: Henry Holt, 1993.

Naylor, Phyllis. *Ice.* New York: Atheneum, 1995.

Nelson, Theresa. *Earthshine.* New York: Orchard Books, 1994.

Nix, Garth. *Sabriel.* New York: HarperCollins, 1997.

Nolan, Han. *Send Down a Miracle.* New York: Harcourt Brace, 1996.

Novac, Ana. *The Beautiful Days of My Youth: My Six Months in Auschwitz and Plaszow.* New York: Holt, 1997.

*Nye, Naomi Sihab. *Habibi.* New York: Simon and Schuster, 1997.

*Opydyke, Irene Gut. *In My Hands: Memoirs of a Holocaust Rescuer.* New York: Random House, 1999.

Osborne, Mary Pope. *Adaline Falling Star.* New York: Scholastic, 2000.

Paterson, Katherine. *Lyddie.* New York: Dutton/Lodestar, 1992.

Perry, Steve. *The Female War.* New York: Bantam Spectra, 1993.

*Pierce, Tamora. *The Lioness Quartet.* New York: Random House, 1983-88.

———. *Wild Magic.* New York: Random House, 1989.

Plummer, Louise. *The Unlikely Romance of Kate Bjorkman.* New York: Delacorte, 1995.

Porter, Tracey. *Treasures in the Dust.* New York: HarperCollins, 1999.

Pullman, Philip. *The Golden Compass.* New York: Knopf, 1997.

———. *The Subtle Knife.* New York: Knopf, 1997.

———. *The Amber Spyglass.* New York: Knopf, 2001.

Rinaldi, Ann. *In My Father's House.* New York: Scholastic, 1993.

———. *Wolf by the Ears.* New York: Scholastic, 1991.

Rodowsky, Colby. *Hannah in Between.* New York: Farrar, 1994.

Rylant, Cynthia. *Missing May.* New York: Bantam Doubleday Dell, 1992.

*Santiago, Esmeralda. *Almost a Woman.* New York: Perseus Press, 1998.

Schwartz, Virginia Frances. *Send One Angel Down.* New York: Holiday House, 2000.

Senna, Danzy. *Caucasia.* Riverhead, NY: Riverhead Press, 1999.

Sinclair, April. *Coffee Will Make You Black.* New York: Hyperion, 1995.

*Smith, Cynthia Leitich. *Rain Is Not My Indian Name.* New York: HarperCollins, 2001.

*Staples, Suzanne Fisher. *Haveli.* New York: Random House, 1993.

———. *Shabanu: Daughter of the Wind.* New York: Knopf, 1989.

Stoehr, Shelley. *Weird on the Outside.* New York: Delacorte, 1995.

Thornton, Yvonne S., and Jo Coudert. *Ditchdigger's Daughters: A Black Family's Astonishing Success Story.* New York: Penguin Putnam, 1996.

Turner, Ann. *Learning to Swim.* New York: Scholastic, 2000.

Uchida, Yoshiko. *The Invisible Thread.* New York: Simon and Shuster, 1991.

*Viramontes, Maria Helena. *Under the Feet of Jesus*. New York: Dutton, 1997.

Voigt, Cynthia. *When She Hollers*. New York: Scholastic, 1996.

Waddell, Martin. *The Kidnapping of Suzie Q*. Cambridge, MA: Candlewick Press, 1994.

White, Ellen Emerson. *The Road Home*. New York: Scholastic, 1995.

*Williams, Lori Aurelia. *When Kambia Elaine Flew in from Neptune*. New York: Simon and Schuster, 2000.

*Wittlinger, Ellen. *Hard Love*. New York: Simon and Schuster, 1999.

*Wolff, Virginia Euwer. *Make Lemonade*. New York: Simon and Schuster, 1993.

———. *True Believer*. New York: Atheneum, 2001.

Woodson, Jacqueline. *I Hadn't Meant to Tell You This*. New York: Bantam Doubleday, 1995.

Wrede, Patricia. *Dealing with Dragons*. New York: Scholastic, 1990.

Yolen, Jane. *Briar Rose*. New York: Tom Doherty Associates, 1992.

# Index

accomplishment stories, 113–114
adolescence: in early American
  fiction, 7; self in, 9; separation
  versus connection in, 34–35
adventure novels, 113–120; further
  reading in, 124
Afrika (in *True North*), 71–76
Alanna (in *The Lioness Quartet*),
  43–49
Alcott, Louisa May, *Little Women*,
  10–15
Alger, Horatio, 14–15
*Almost a Woman* (Santiago), 163–169
Altmann, Anna E., 139
Alyce/Beetle (in *The Midwife's
  Apprentice*), 58–66
American fiction, 6–8
Angie Morrow (in *Seventeenth
  Summer*), 10, 15–22, 179–180
anorexia, in *Stick Figure*, 160–163
appearance, 1, 178; in *Beauty*,
  130–131; in *Deerskin*, 132–133; in
  *The Leaving*, 38; in *The Midwife's
  Apprentice*, 60, 64; in *Rules of the
  Road*, 115; in *Seventeenth Summer*,
  19
Armstrong, Jennifer, 77
Ashcroft, Leslie, 27
aunts, in *Chinese Cinderella*, 171–172

Austen, Jane, 4
autonomy, 26–27
autopathography, 160
Avi, 56, 76–77

Barron, Neil, 127
Bauer, Cat, 121
Bauer, Joan, 121, 124; *Rules of the
  Road*, 114–120
Beals, Melba Pattillo, *Warriors Don't
  Cry*, 156–160
*Beauty* (McKinley), 129–132,
  139–140
Beetle/Alyce (in *The Midwife's
  Apprentice*), 58–66
Bennett, Cherie, 121
*Beyond the Divide* (Lasky), 27–37
bibliotherapy, 151
Billie Jo (in *Out of the Dust*), 66–71
Billingsley, Fanny, 147
Block, Francesca Lia, 121
Blume, Judy, 9
Boreen, Jean, 55–56
Britton-Jackson, Livia, 174
Brooks, Bruce, 121
Brown, Lyn Mikel, 32
Brownley, Martine Watson, 152
Brumberg, Joan, 135
Burney, Fanny, 3–5

Butler, Octavia, *Parable of the Sower,*
    142–146

Calder, David, 147
Campbell, Patricia J., 7, 53
Canby, Henry Seidel, 76
Carroll, Virginia Shaefer, 21–22
*Chinese Cinderella: The True Story of an
    Unwanted Daughter* (Mah), 151,
    169–173
*Clarissa* (Richardson), 3
college: in *Almost a Woman,* 169; in
    *Chinese Cinderella,* 170, 172; in
    *Saying Goodbye,* 100–101; in
    *Warriors Don't Cry,* 157
community: in *Beyond the Divide,* 28,
    35–36; in *Deerskin,* 138; and
    empowerment, 49; in *Habibi,* 94;
    in *The Leaving,* 42; in *The Lioness
    Quartet,* 46; in *Out of the Dust,* 67;
    in *The Parable of the Sower,* 146; in
    *Rain Is Not My Indian Name,* 98;
    in *Saying Goodbye,* 101–102; in
    *True North,* 75–76
connection: in *Parable of the Sower,*
    145; versus separation, in
    adolescence, 34–35
contemporary fiction, 81–125; further
    reading in, 121–124
Cook, Karen, 121
Cooney, Caroline, 124
Coudert, Jo, 175
Courser, G. Thomas, 160
credibility, 56–57
Crispin, A. C., 147
Crutcher, Chris, 180
Cushman, Karen, 53, 56, 77; *The
    Midwife's Apprentice,* 58–61

Daly, Maureen, *Seventeenth Summer,*
    10, 15–22
de Beauvoir, Simone, 87

deceit: in *Haveli,* 89; in *The Midwife's
    Apprentice,* 61; in *Out of the Dust,*
    67
*Deerskin* (McKinley), 129, 132–140
Demarest, Jack, 9
diaries. *See* self-expression
difference, 87; in *Blood and Chocolate,*
    141–142; in *Stick Figure,* 161
Dominick, Andie, 174
Donelson, Kenneth L., 8, 113
Douglas, Ann, 35
Dowell, Frances O'Roark, 77
Duncan, Lois, 9

eating disorders, in *Stick Figure,*
    160–163
Ellen (in *Saying Goodbye*), 100–103
empowered girls: in contemporary
    fiction, 81–125; current status of,
    177–181; defining, 26–49; in
    fantastic literature, 127–150; in
    historical fiction, 53–80; in
    memoir, 151–176
empowerment: in *Almost a Woman,*
    168–169; culture and, 86–87;
    definition of, 27; in *Habibi,* 96; in
    *Make Lemonade,* 83; in *The
    Midwife's Apprentice,* 62; in *Rules of
    the Road,* 118
English sentimental novels, 3–6
Estrella (in *Under the Feet of Jesus*),
    103–106
*Evelina* (Burney), 3–5

Fair Maiden, 6
fairy tales, 2–3, 129
fantastic literature, 127–150; further
    reading in, 147–149
Farmer, Nancy, 123
fathers: in *Beyond the Divide,* 28–30;
    in *Chinese Cinderella,* 172; in
    *Deerskin,* 132–134, 137–138; in

*Habibi,* 92, 95–96; in *The Leaving,*
38–40; in *Little Women,* 11–12; in
*Out of the Dust,* 68–70; in *The
Parable of the Sower,* 143; in *Rules of
the Road,* 114–118, 120; in
*Seventeenth Summer,* 17; in *When
Kambia Elaine Flew in from
Neptune,* 107
Feiwel, Jean, 71
Fiedler, Leslie, 6–7
fighting: in *The Lioness Quartet,* 44; in
*Warriors Don't Cry,* 158
Filipovic, Zlata, 174
folk tales, 2–3
forgiveness, in *Out of the Dust,* 68–70
Forster, E. M., 140
Fox, Mem, 2
Fox, Paula, 121
Frank, Anne, 152
Frye, Northrop, 134

Garden, Nancy, 77; *The Year They
Burned the Books,* 109–111
Garfield, Leon, 53
Gauch, Patricia Lee, 123
gender roles: in *Beyond the Divide,*
30; in *Habibi,* 92; in *Little Women,*
11–13; in *The Midwife's
Apprentice,* 61; in *True North,*
73–74
"Get Down, Nuke Korea Town,"
102, 125n11
Gilbert, Sandra, 5–6, 13
Gilligan, Carol, 32, 34–35, 138
Good Good Girl, 6
Gordon, Joan, 145
Gottlieb, Lori, *Stick Figure: A Diary of
My Former Self,* 160–163
grandfathers: in *Chinese Cinderella,*
171–172; in *True North,* 73–75
grandmothers: in *Habibi,* 94; in
*Rules of the Road,* 120; in *Warriors*

*Don't Cry,* 157–159; in *When
Kambia Elaine Flew in from
Neptune,* 107
Grant, Cynthia D., 121
Grealy, Lucy, 175
Gubar, Susan, 5–6, 13
Guy, Rosa, 9

*Habibi* (Nye), 91–97
Haddix, Margaret Peterson, 129
Hall, Lynn, *The Leaving,* 37–43
Hamilton, Virginia, 123
Hammerstein, Oscar, 1
*Hard Love* (Wittlinger), 111–113
Harrison, Barbara Grizzutti, 127
Haugaard, Erik Christian, 54
*Haveli* (Staples), 87–97
Heilbrun, Carolyn, 129
Henke, Suzette A., 153
Hesse, Karen, 78, 121; *Out of the Dust,*
66–71
Higa, Tomiko, 175
Hinton, S. E., 9, 54
historical fiction, 27–37, 53–80;
further reading in, 77–79
Ho, Minfong, 78
Holbrook, Sara, 25
Holland, Isabelle, 78
Hollingdale, Peter, 10
hooks, bell, 153
Hopkinson, Nalo, 147
horror genre, 140
humor: in *Beauty,* 131–132; in *Make
Lemonade,* 84–85; in *Rules of the
Road,* 115–116; in sitcoms versus
YA novels, 116
Hwang, David Henry, 175

incest, in *Deerskin,* 132–134, 138
*In My Hands: Memoirs of a Holocaust
Rescuer* (Opdyke), 153–156
Inness, Sherrie, 178–179

Jamie Crawford (in *The Year They Burned the Books*), 110–111
Jenna Boller (in *Rules of the Road*), 114–120
Jiang, Ji-Li, 175
Johnson, Angela, 122
Jolly (in *Make Lemonade*), 82–86
Jo March (in *Little Women*), 10–15, 179–180
journals. *See* self-expression
juvenile fiction, early, 8–22

Karr, Kathleen, 78
Keller, Beverly, 124
Kessler, Christine, 123
Kindl, Patrice, 129
Klause, Annette Curtis, 147; *Blood and Chocolate*, 140–142
Kortenhaus, Carole, 9

Lackey, Mercedes, 147
Lasky, Kathryn, 122; *Beyond the Divide*, 27–37; *True North*, 71–76
Lauren Olamina (in *Parable of the Sower*), 142–146
LaVaughn (in *Make Lemonade*), 82–86
*The Leaving* (Hall), 37–43
Lee, Marie G., *Saying Goodbye*, 100–103
lesbianism: in *Hard Love*, 111–113; in *The Year They Burned the Books*, 109–111
Levy, Marilyn, 123
*The Lioness Quartet* (Pierce), 43–49
literacy: in *Haveli*, 90–91; in *The Midwife's Apprentice*, 63; in *Ragged Dick*, 15; in *True North*, 72
*Little Women* (Alcott), 10–15
Liyana (in *Habibi*), 91–97
Lobel, Anita, 175
loyalty, in *When Kambia Elaine Flew in from Neptune*, 108–109

Lucy (in *True North*), 71–76
Lystad, Mary, 6

Macleod, Anne Scott, 56, 180–181
MacRae, Cathi Dunn, 127–128
Mah, Adeline Yen, *Chinese Cinderella: The True Story of an Unwanted Daughter*, 151, 169–173
*Make Lemonade* (Wolff), 82–86
Mallon, Thomas, 54
Marisol (in *Hard Love*), 111–113
marriage, 5–6; in fantastic literature, 129, 149n4; in *Haveli*, 89; in *The Leaving*, 39, 42; in *The Lioness Quartet*, 48–49; in *Little Women*, 12–13; in *Seventeenth Summer*, 20–21; in *Shabanu*, 88; in *True North*, 73–75
Matas, Carol, 78
Matcheck, Diane, 78
maturing: in *The Lioness Quartet*, 46; in *In My Hands*, 155; in *Out of the Dust*, 71; in *Saying Goodbye*, 101; in *Seventeenth Summer*, 21
Mazer, Norma Fox, 122
McCaffrey, Anne, 147
McDaniel, Lurlene, 124
McKinley, Robin: *Beauty*, 129–132, 139–140; *Deerskin*, 129, 132–140
memoir, 151–176; further reading in, 174–175
menstruation: in *The Lioness Quartet*, 46; in *Make Lemonade*, 85
Meribah (in *Beyond the Divide*), 27–37
Meyer, Carolyn, 78
*The Midwife's Apprentice* (Cushman), 58–66
Mines, Jeanette, 9, 26
Mori, Kyoko, 123
mothers, 163–164; in *Almost a Woman*, 164–169; in *Beyond the Divide*, 36–37; in *Chinese*

*Cinderella,* 169–170; in *Deerskin,* 132–133, 138; in *Habibi,* 95; in *The Leaving,* 38–39, 41; in *Make Lemonade,* 83–84; in *Out of the Dust,* 67; in *Seventeenth Summer,* 17; in *Stick Figure,* 161–162; in *Warriors Don't Cry,* 157; in *When Kambia Elaine Flew in from Neptune,* 106–107
multicultural literature, 72, 80n16, 86–109; further reading in, 123

Napoli, Donna, 147
Naylor, Phyllis Reynolds, 122
Nelson, Theresa, 122
Nilsen, Alleen Pace, 113, 116, 125
Nix, Garth, 148
Nolan, Han, 122
Norman, Marsha, 37
Novac, Ana, 175
nurture: in *Beyond the Divide,* 33–35; in *Blood and Chocolate,* 142; in *Deerskin,* 135–137; in *The Lioness Quartet,* 44; in *Make Lemonade,* 82–83; in *The Midwife's Apprentice,* 59, 62; in *In My Hands,* 154; in *The Parable of the Sower,* 145–146;in *Under the Feet of Jesus,* 105
Nye, Naomi Shihab, *Habibi,* 91–97

Oates, Joyce Carol, 151
O'Faolain, Sean, 13
Olney, James, 152
Opdyke, Irene Gut, *In My Hands: Memoirs of a Holocaust Rescuer,* 153–156
Orenstein, Peggy, 22, 45, 47, 130
Osborne, Mary Pope, 78
*Out of the Dust* (Hesse), 66–71

*Pamela* (Richardson), 3
*Parable of the Sower* (Butler), 142–146

Paterson, Katherine, 55, 78, 174
Patterson, Richard, 149n8
Paul, Lissa, 13, 61, 139
Paulsen, Nancy, 121
Peck, Richard, 9
Pennebaker, James, 174
Perrault, Charles, 130, 132
Perry, Steve, 148
Persecuted Maiden, 6
perseverance, in *The Midwife's Apprentice,* 63
Pierce, Tamora, 140, 148; *The Lioness Quartet,* 43–49
Pipher, Mary, 22, 177–178
Plummer, Louise, 124
Pogrebin, Letty Cottin, 177
Porter, Tracey, 78
power, 55; in *Hard Love,* 111–113; in *Make Lemonade,* 84; in *The Midwife's Apprentice, 58,* 61; in *Warriors Don't Cry,* 159
Probst, Robert, 9
Pullman, Philip, 148

*Ragged Dick* (Alger), 14–15
*Rain Is Not My Indian Name* (Smith), 97–100
rape: in *Beyond the Divide,* 29, 31; in *Clarissa,* 3; in *Deerskin,* 134–135; in *True North,* 72
Richardson, Samuel, 3
Rinaldi, Ann, 78–79
Ritchie, Mary Kay, 9
Rodowsky, Colby, 122
Rodriguez, Richard, 167
Roethke, Theodore, 81
romance novels, 113–120; further reading in, 124
Rose, Ellen Cronan, 2
Rose, Phyllis, 151–152
Ross, Catherine Sheldrick, 25
Roxanne (in *The Leaving*), 37–43

*Rules of the Road* (Bauer), 114–120
Rylant, Cynthia, 122

Santiago, Esmeralda, *Almost a Woman*,
   163–169
*Saying Goodbye* (Lee), 100–103
Schlee, Ann, 55
Schwartz, Virginia Frances, 79
self: in adolescence, 9; in fantastic
   literature, 139; in *The Lioness
   Quartet*, 49; in *The Midwife's
   Apprentice*, 60; in *In My Hands*,
   155; in *Warriors Don't Cry*, 160; in
   *The Year They Burned the Books*,
   110
self-acceptance: in *Blood and
   Chocolate*, 142; in *The Lioness
   Quartet*, 49
self-esteem, 47, 130–131
self-expression, 173–174; in *Beyond
   the Divide*, 30–31; in *Evelina*, 4–5;
   in *Haveli*, 90; in *Little Women*,
   12–14; in *Make Lemonade*, 82; in
   *The Midwife's Apprentice*, 59, 62–64;
   in *The Parable of the Sower*,
   144–145; in *Rain Is Not My Indian
   Name*, 97–100; in *True North*, 74;
   in *Warriors Don't Cry*, 158–159.
   *See also* voice
self-image, in *Stick Figure*, 163
Senna, Danzy, 123
separation: in adventure novels, 114;
   versus connection, in adolescence,
   34–35
*Seventeenth Summer* (Daly), 10, 15–22
sexuality, 7–9; in *Almost a Woman*,
   164–168; in *Deerskin*, 132–134; in
   *Hard Love*, 111–113; in *The Lioness
   Quartet*, 45, 48; in *Make Lemonade*,
   84; in *In My Hands*, 156; in
   *Seventeenth Summer*, 18, 20–21; in

*When Kambia Elaine Flew in from
   Neptune*, 106, 108; in *The Year They
   Burned the Books*, 109–111
*Shabanu* (Staples), 87–97
Shayla (in *When Kambia Elaine Flew
   in from Neptune*), 106–109
Sinclair, April, 79
sitcoms, humor in, 116
Sklar, Robert, 139
Smith, Cynthia Leitich, *Rain Is Not
   My Indian Name*, 97–100
social realism, 81–82; further reading
   in, 121–123
Spacks, Patricia Meyer, 15
speculative fiction. *See* fantastic
   literature
Staples, Suzanne Fisher, 87–97, 124
*Stick Figure: A Diary of My Former Self*
   (Gottlieb), 160–163
Stoehr, Shelley, 122

"tend and befriend" response, 34–35
Thornton, Yvonne S., 175
Tomlinson, Theresa, 149
trickster stories, 61
Trites, Roberta Seelinger, 28, 32, 56
*True North* (Lasky), 71–76
Turner, Ann, 175

Uchida, Yoshiko, 175
*Under the Feet of Jesus* (Viramontes),
   103–106

VanderStaay, Steven, 26
Viramontes, Helena Maria, *Under the
   Feet of Jesus*, 103–106
Vivian (in *Blood and Chocolate*),
   141–142
voice: in *Beyond the Divide*, 31–33;
   in *Deerskin*, 134, 138; definition
   of, 32; in *Diary of Anne Frank*,

152; in *Habibi*, 93–96; in *The Leaving*, 43; in *Make Lemonade*, 86; in *The Midwife's Apprentice*, 59; in *The Parable of the Sower*, 143–144; in *Rules of the Road*, 118–120; in *Saying Goodbye*, 102–103;in *Under the Feet of Jesus*, 105–106; in *When Kambia Elaine Flew in from Neptune*, 106, 108–109; in *The Year They Burned the Books*, 110–111. See also self-expression

Voigt, Cynthia, 122

Waddell, Martin, 124
Walsh, Jill Paton, 54
*Warriors Don't Cry* (Beals), 156–160
*When Kambia Elaine Flew in from Neptune* (Williams), 106–109
White, Ellen Emerson, 79
Wilder, Laura Ingalls, 181

Williams, Lori Aurelia, *When Kambia Elaine flew in From Neptune*, 106–109
Wittlinger, Ellen, *Hard Love*, 111–113
Wolf, Naomi, 162
Wolff, Virginia Euwer, 123; *Make Lemonade*, 82–86
Woodson, Jacqueline, 123
work: in *The Leaving*, 40–42; in *The Midwife's Apprentice*, 61–65; in *Rules of the Road*, 115–117;in *Under the Feet of Jesus*, 104
Wrede, Patricia, 45, 140, 149
writing. See self-expression

*The Year They Burned the Books* (Garden), 109–111
Yolen, Jane, 79

Zindel, Paul, 54
'zines, 111–112, 178–179

# About the Authors

Joanne Brown is an associate professor of English at Drake University in Des Moines, Iowa, where she teaches courses in writing fiction, American drama, and adolescent literature. She earned a bachelor's degree in theater from Northwestern University and master's and doctoral degrees in English from Drake University. She has published short fiction, personal essays, and articles on young adult literature (*The ALAN Review, SIGNAL, The New Advocate*). She is also the author of *Presenting Kathryn Lasky* in Twayne's United States Authors series on writers for young adults. She and her husband, Milton, live in Des Moines. They have three children and five grandchildren.

Nancy St. Clair received her bachelor's degree from Cornell College in Mt. Vernon, Iowa, and her doctoral degree in British literature from the University of Iowa in Iowa City. She is an associate professor of English at Simpson College in Indianola, Iowa, where she serves as chair of the English Department and director of the Cornerstone and Senior Colloquium programs. She has published articles on women's studies and young adult fiction. In her spare time (limited, she admits), she enjoys gardening. She and her husband, Steve, live in Des Moines with their two daughters.